Flavors *of* Health
C O O K B O O K

Your Guide to Eating For Health™

Dr. Ed Bauman and Chef Lizette Marx

Bauman College Press

Editorial:	Edward Bauman	Design:	Michelle Gelfand
	Lizette Marx		Carol White
Copy Editors:	Mindy Toomay	Photography:	Christine Bauman
	Marilyn Sullivan		
	Cassandra Clark		
	Jimmy Wilson		

Notice of Rights

Notice of Liability

Second Edition 2012
Printed in the U.S.A.
ISBN 978-0-9857229-0-6

16 15 14 13 12   6 5 4 3 2 1

BAUMAN COLLEGE
P.O. Box 940
Penngrove, CA 94951

EMAIL: info@baumancollege.org
WEB: baumancollege.org
PHONE: 800-987-7530
FAX: 707-795-3375

BAUMAN COLLEGE
HOLISTIC NUTRITION
AND CULINARY ARTS

Cataloging-in-Publication data for this book
is available from the Library of Congress.

Contents

Culinary Alchemy
The Intuition of Taste

When we no longer have good cooking in the world, we will have no literature, nor high and sharp intelligence, nor friendly gatherings, nor social harmony.

MARIE-ANTOINE CARÊME

No one who cooks, cooks alone. Even at her most solitary, a cook in the kitchen is surrounded by generations of cooks past, the advice and menus of cooks present, the wisdom of cookbook writers.

LAURIE COLWIN, *HOME COOKING: A WRITER IN THE KITCHEN*

During the first few weeks of the culinary program at Bauman College, we teach the students a *Foundations of Cooking* class. We cover all the basics: moist and dry heat methods, time and temperature, proper kitchen equipment and gear, and – my favorite part – cooking with the senses and the elements of taste. The practical rules of cooking and the tools of the trade are certainly important, but when we understand the dynamics of flavor and how ingredients harmonize and contrast with each other, cooking becomes a creative art.

Some chefs consider cooking to be a craft and say it takes many years to transform simple culinary skill into art. While there may be some truth to this, I have known plenty of individuals (think of your grandmother's lasagna or dad's black bean chili, for instance) who have virtually no formal culinary training but can cook better food than any gourmet chef in town. These people cook from their souls and have a natural intuition in the kitchen. They are like dancers with naturally born rhythm.

So, my students wonder, how do you know what flavors work best in cooking a particular dish? I tell them to learn and memorize the cooking techniques and to practice, practice, practice. Once you can execute recipes well, begin experimenting and play with different ingredient combinations. Over time you will become more intuitive in your cooking, as you learn the theory of taste and how to be completely present while tasting the dish throughout the entire process, until the flavors have reached their full potential. This practice is often called mindful cooking, and it requires engaging all of your senses to bring out the best in your food.

My own interest in cooking began when I was a young girl. My mother had a catalogue of recipe cards from *Better Homes and Gardens*. The cards were organized in a large, white plastic box with a clear plastic cover. I remember studying those cards like they held some secret to the cooking universe. Each one had a beautiful color picture on the front and the recipe on the back. The cards were categorized under appetizing headings like County Fair Favorites, Sunday Dinners, and French Bistro. Such recipe titles as Chocolate Bombé, Steak au Poivre, and Kentucky Bourbon Sweet Potato Pie tantalized my 10-year-old imagination.

No, this was certainly not an *Eating For Health*™ menu, but you have to start somewhere. So I studied each card, gazed at the photograph of the dish until I thought I understood how it would taste, read the preparation instructions until they were nearly memorized, and then filed it back into its appropriate section. I dreamt of the day my mother would allow me to prepare not one recipe but an entire meal. When my mother finally set me loose, I surrendered to the magic of my favorite room in the house. I have never looked back. I have found solace and sanctuary in all the kitchens in my life. And creating food for others has been my comfort, my joy, and my expression of love. Cooking is home for my soul.

When it comes to developing flavor, I have always relied on my instincts more than the skills I have learned from books and cooking classes. So when students ask me what makes one dish just okay and another incredible, I tell them they must first know what flavors, textures, and combinations they love.

Many people season their food while they cook or just before they eat without fully understanding why certain flavors work well together and others do not. When students ask me if a dish they are preparing tastes good, I usually throw the question right back at them: "Does it taste good to you? Do you like it?"

From there, we will analyze specific flavor components, such as the levels of salt, sour, bitter, and sweet notes in the dish. We then consider other qualities: the mouth feel of the food, temperature, texture, and aroma. All of these sensations have a profound effect on flavor and determine how enjoyable a dish will be.

Understanding the Palate

Chefs are trained to master the basic principles of flavor so they know how to make their food taste delicious. With the vast variety of food combinations available, this task may seem daunting to the inexperienced cook, but when considering basic flavors there really are only a handful that our taste buds can detect.

The idea of categorizing taste may have started with Aristotle when he identified two basic tastes: bitter and sweet. He soon realized foods brought forth other flavors and identified sour, salty, puckery, succulent, harsh, and pungent. Today, scientists describe six basic tastes that the tongue will react to: sweet, salty, sour, bitter, umami, and fat. In addition to these five tastes, there are other qualities that create a significant sensation on the palate: astringent, pungent, texture, and temperature.

Flavor Qualities

Sweet – This taste is produced primarily by the presence of sugars in the food and stimulates the pleasure centers of the brain, creating a feeling of comfort and contentment. When cane sugar was first developed into a crystallized form, it was very expensive and therefore used only sparingly, like salt. Many cooks go for the pinch of salt to bring out the flavors in their food. A pinch of sweet from cane sugar, honey, molasses, and the like can also coax more flavor from a dish. Sweet can bring roundness to savory dishes and can tone down bitterness, sourness, and saltiness. It can also make the natural flavors of other ingredients bloom more brightly, such as mint, chocolate, and lemon.

Salty – As nature's flavor enhancer, salt is often the key to making savory food delicious and even brings a certain spark to sweets. Salt itself is an essential element in the diet of all living things, including humans, animals, and many plants. Salt retains water and activates both salivation and digestion.

Sour – The ultimate palate tickler is the taste of sour. The tart flavor of lemon or vinegar will help brighten a dull dish, stimulate the appetite, prepare the body for digestion, and sharpen the mind. Sour can also introduce a "special something" in foods that other seasonings cannot coax out.

Bitter – Of all the flavors, bitter is considered the most healing despite being the most challenging for the palate. Whereas sweetness satiates and brings comfort, bitterness stimulates high alert. In nature, a bitter taste acts as a warning against potentially poisonous plants and herbs, so it is instinctively off-putting to humans. If used in small amounts, however, bitterness can balance a cloying sweetness or cut through too much richness. Examples of bitter flavors are: greens like radicchio, arugula, mustard, and dandelion; fresh turmeric; and bitter melon, a common ingredient in Chinese cooking.

Savory or "Umami" – In 1907, a Japanese chemist named Ki Kunae Ikeda coined the term "umami" to describe "delicious and tasty" foods. He extracted the essence of umami from kombu seaweed after noticing that it had a remarkable ability to enhance and balance the flavors in soup. Umami describes an intensely savory quality that satisfies the palate, often described as "meaty." Umami comes from glutamates that are naturally present in many common foods, including blue cheese, Parmesan cheese, fermented soy foods, meats, mushrooms, anchovies, olives, fish sauce, and soy sauce.

Astringent – This taste makes the mouth feel rough or dry, creating a need for a little moisture. Astringent flavors include unripe banana or persimmon, cranberries, pomegranate, turmeric, and herbs such as parsley, basil, and cilantro. Foods containing tannins such as wine, tea, and coffee also have astringent compounds.

Fat – If salt is nature's flavor enhancer, fat is the vehicle that can bring all tastes together into one unified, well-rounded finish. Fat was not considered an official "taste" until 2010, when a group of Australian scientists tested 30 people's ability to taste a range of fatty acids in a plain solution. The verdict: fat is the sixth taste humans can detect. And what a taste it is. Fat transforms tasty into dreamy. Think of all the examples: a knob of butter added to a pan sauce at the end of cooking boosts flavor and gives an appetizing glossiness to the final sauce; a drizzle of olive oil or truffle oil on just about anything from soups to mashed potatoes sends eyes rolling in pleasure after the first taste; and then there is dessert. Why, for instance, is fat-rich ice cream so much more delicious than non-fat? Fat is a satisfying, delicious, and unforgettable flavor.

Pungent – Similar to salt and sour, pungent flavors often improve the overall taste of foods by sparking up duller or heavier flavors. The pungent taste has a purifying and awakening effect on food. To understand this, think of lemons, which have both a brightening (awakening) and cleansing (purifying) quality. Pungent flavors are often intense – very salty, sour, spicy, or all three. Some examples include: onion, radish, chili, ginger, lemon, garlic, asafoetida, cayenne pepper, black pepper, and mustard.

Texture and Temperature – The crisp crunch of a cold apple, a warm bowl of miso soup, or a silky, smooth chocolate ganache drizzled over fresh strawberries; each have a distinctive taste and a specific texture and temperature that influence mouth feel and overall flavor. The importance of knowing the correct temperature and texture of foods being served should not be underestimated.

Understanding the different taste profiles and qualities described can help you learn to balance the flavors of the meals you prepare. If you find yourself getting lost, remember the one golden rule about cooking: Always taste your food. Can you detect notes of sweetness, saltiness, and other flavors you want to coax out of the dish you are making? Another aspect of tasting is mouth feel – crunchy, smooth, chunky, and even fattiness offer up flavor sensations. Then, breathe in the aromas of your food and consider whether they are pleasing. This process may seem tedious but usually it takes only a moment to consider all of these qualities. When you are ready, season if necessary, according to the outcome you wish to achieve, and then taste, smell, and feel again.

Layer your flavors gradually; build them, enhance them, and know when to stop. That last step – stopping before the flavor of a dish is ruined by over-seasoning – is probably the hardest one to master. Keep cooking, tasting, smelling, and using all of your senses and you will gradually gain this skill.

Above all, trust in your instincts. Whether I am cooking professionally or taking my chef's hat off to cook at home for my family, I rely on my intuition and my senses. Even a simple pot of beans can produce the most extraordinary flavors if you know the guiding principles of flavor.

When my grandmother taught me to make beans, she seemed to work entirely by feel, without measuring anything. She used her senses, and has thankfully passed this wisdom on to me. Consider her method for cooking the perfect pot of beans and let these ideas inform other dishes you prepare.

Frijoles Sabroso

1. Cover a cup or two of small red kidney beans with pure, filtered water and 1 tablespoon of whey or lemon juice. Cover and soak overnight.

2. The next morning, drain the beans thoroughly and cover again with pure water to a depth of about 1 to 2 inches above the level of the beans. Cook on high until water begins to boil.

3. Reduce the heat and add a 3-inch piece of kombu or epazote herb, a bay leaf, 1 small onion, quartered, and a few cloves of smashed garlic. Cover and simmer on low for 1 hour.

4. When beans are just beginning to get tender but still hold their shape, add some olive oil (1 to 2 tablespoons or so). Set the lid ajar so the beans are partially covered and cook for another hour over low heat. The broth will begin to look thick, but the beans should still hold their shape.

5. At this point, begin adding sea salt a pinch at a time, stirring and tasting after each addition until the bean broth tastes delicious. Check the texture of the beans. They should be fork-tender, like a baked potato. When the beans are done, remove them from the heat.

6. Serving suggestion: Heat a large, high-walled sauté or chef's pan over medium heat and add about 2 tablespoons of olive oil and a pat of butter. Cut 1 yellow or white onion into thin slices and add to the pan. Sauté until soft and translucent. Add a couple of ladles full of beans and enough bean broth to just cover the beans. Cook until the broth is reduced by half. Serve this and watch the eyes of your table mates roll.

Eating 4 Health

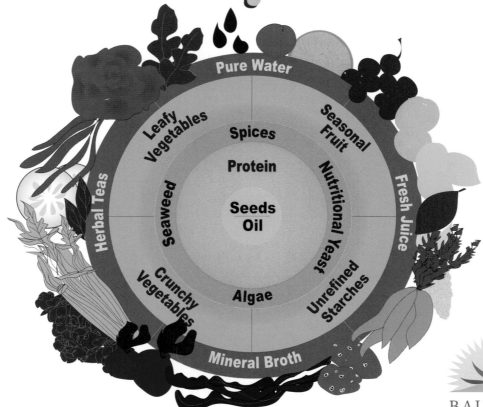

Pure Water

Leafy Vegetables · Seasonal Fruit

Herbal Teas · Fresh Juice

Spices · Protein · Seeds Oil

Seaweed · Nutritional Yeast

Crunchy Vegetables · Algae · Unrefined Starches

Mineral Broth

A Rejuvenating Food System
© by Edward Bauman, Ph.D.

BAUMAN COLLEGE
HOLISTIC NUTRITION
AND CULINARY ARTS

Organic, Seasonal, Nutrient-rich, and Individualized

	Seeds and Oil	Protein	Leafy Vegetables	Crunchy Vegetables	Unrefined Starches	Seasonal Fruit	Booster Foods
Daily Servings	2-3	2-4	1-3	1-3	2-4	2-4	2-4
Serving Sizes	1 Tbs. oil 2 Tbs. seeds	3 oz. animal 6 oz. vegetable	1 cup	1/2 cup	1/2 cup whole grains, 1 medium root vegetable	1/2 cup or 1 medium piece	1 teaspoon to 1 tablespoon
Examples	flax, sesame, sunflower, almonds	poultry, fish, eggs, milk, beans	salad mix, spinach, kale	broccoli, string beans, cukes, onions, celery	grains, bread, yams, winter squash, corn, millet, rice	berries, apple, grape, citrus	nutritional yeast, algae, spices, seaweed

Introduction by Dr. Ed Bauman

Nutritional Cooking
The New S.O.U.L. Food

Eating For Health™ (E4H) is a comprehensive approach to educating people about how to eat and enjoy a diverse, plant-based diet that provides a full range of the nutrients known to promote health and support recovery from illness and injury. It integrates the very best of both ancient and modern nutritional approaches to form a flexible mandala of wholeness, based on the earth's generous support of life on our planet in the form of healthy foods, water, air, and kind hearts. E4H is a way of being in right relationship with food and other beings, a path to creating harmony within ourselves, our families, our communities, and with the earth. I created the E4H model 20 years ago as the basis for the Nutrition Consultant and Natural Chef Training Programs at Bauman College. I have used it in a wide variety of educational and clinical settings, and it has proven to be a useful tool for countless people as they move toward a more optimal nutrition program.

E4H principles are based on the premise that our cellular health is determined by the foods we eat. Damaged foods damage our cells. Fresh, healthy foods send the right messages to our cells' DNA, encouraging healthy gene expression as well as efficient growth and repair – a process we call healing. The tragedy of losing one's health can be traced, in large part, to a history of poor-quality food, insufficient nutrients, and exposure to dietary and environmental toxins.

The healthiest diet comes from S.O.U.L. foods (Seasonal, Organic, Unprocessed, and Local) that are suited to a person's individual taste, temperament, needs, access to ingredients, and metabolic tendency. One of the great strengths of the *Eating For Health*™ system is that it can be vegan or omnivorous, raw or cooked, and it can, and naturally will, evolve over time with changing circumstances.

For example, some of us digest meat better than we do beans. For others, it is the opposite. Despite our differences though, some dietary strategies make sense for everyone. A healthy, balanced individual will be able to comfortably digest and live well on a largely plant-based diet that contains animal foods in moderate portions as complements to a variety of fruits, vegetables, nuts, seeds, grains, and legumes.

For optimal health, disease prevention, and quick healing from illness or injury, it is best to eat about 6 servings a day of fresh or fermented vegetables and 3 servings a day of fresh or dried fruits or juice. We have our work cut out for us to get to this level. It means snacking on fruits, veggies, nuts, and seeds, rather than chips, cookies, candy, and crackers.

Another universal key to vibrant health is for the vast majority of foods we consume to be from whole and natural sources, rather than out of boxes or packages. This is where E4H can help, by teaching you how to make delicious and life-enhancing foods from scratch.

At Bauman College, we place a high value on people going to their local markets and selecting the foods themselves, even getting to know their local growers and vendors, when possible. In this stress-filled world, where hurry and worry limit our opportunities for relationship and pleasure, it is an important step outside the box to learn where your food comes from.

In teaching and sharing the E4H approach, we encourage friends and families to cook together, and to collaborate in planning meals that include foods each individual can help prepare and then enjoy eating. We embrace diversity of food choices and personal diet systems.

With this *Flavors of Health Cookbook*, we look forward to introducing you to many new foods that can form the foundation of your own *Eating For Health™* meals. In my work as a nutrition consultant for the past 35 years, I have noticed that the modern overload of diet and nutrition information, along with the fast pace of life and age-related health issues, has overwhelmed a lot of people. Many do not know where to begin or whom to trust. If that sounds like you, then take a deep breath, relax your shoulders, and feel supported, as this book was created for you.

Our objective is to help you down-shift from the fast lane if you are zooming around, or up-shift from being out of commission due to low energy or a disease condition. This begins with learning how to set up a simple and functional kitchen where you can easily create delicious and healthy meals. Knowing what to stock in your pantry and how to use these ingredients to cook consciously for yourself and your loved ones will bring you greater self-awareness, self-esteem, self-love, and self-healing.

Our recipes are designed as basic templates on which you can improvise with ease when you do not have certain ingredients on hand, or when inspiration calls you to get creative.

When I was growing up, *The Joy of Cooking* was everyone's food bible. When I started a natural food restaurant 37 years ago, we consulted *The Joy of Cooking* for basic recipes and then adapted them using unprocessed foods. Out of those tasty trials came some of the recipes in this volume, which naturally have evolved over time.

I invite you to treat this book as your very own culinary lab, where you can experiment as you please based on the recipes, remedies, and information provided.

Before you dive in, here are some user-friendly reminders and recommendations:

- Slow down and allow yourself to find joy in the cooking experience.
- Good cooking is an art form. Each of us can be artists, but to do so we need instruction, practice, and feedback.
- Decide on days and times when you can allow some relaxed time in the morning, afternoon, or evening to prepare, eat, and enjoy a home-cooked meal.
- Use our suggestions to get your E4H pantry well stocked; this saves time and provides a lot of inspiration.
- Cooking alone is great, if you are in the mood. Cooking with others is also great, as you can collaborate and share the workload.
- Start by following recipes and then improvise as you gain confidence.
- Open your senses to new foods, new tastes, and new cultural influences, while not abandoning what you love to eat and what you enjoy making.
- Pay a bit more to get the best ingredients; they will make your dishes shine.
- Eat in peace and only to 90 percent fullness. This practice ensures you will have plenty of light, clear energy for all variety of creative expression.

I hope you enjoy every step of discovering the *Flavors of Health Cookbook*.

If you give a man a fish, he will make a meal.
If you teach him to fish, he will have a living.
If you are thinking a year ahead, sow seed.
If you are thinking ten years ahead, plant a tree.
If you are thinking one hundred years ahead, educate the people.
By sowing seed once, you will harvest once.
By planting a tree, you will harvest tenfold.
By educating the people, you will harvest one hundred fold.

LAO T'ZU, 640 BC

Flavor Foundations
The Homemade Pantry

Chapter 1

Flavor Foundations
The Homemade Pantry

The first step in preparing to make great meals is to set up a pantry containing a wide array of whole grains, legumes, seeds, nuts, herbs, spices, high quality oils, vinegar, salts, and peppers; some chef helpers such as organic packaged and peeled tomatoes; booster foods such as nutritional yeast, sea vegetables, bee pollen, herbal and green teas; and a health-boosting food supplement such as Bauman Nutrition's Vital Scoop™.

Establishing this supply of ingredients makes it much easier to prepare scrumptious meals and energy-boosting snacks. I suggest you implement your own pantry raid to inventory what you have on hand, right now. Feel good about tossing out old, stale, and questionable pantry staples and replacing them with higher quality, fresher ones. Most conventional canned and dried foods contain food additives, preservatives, and artificial colors, which are not health promoting.

Purchase some clear, amber, or cobalt blue glass bottles of different sizes, from small for spices to quart or even half-gallon for storing your dried grains and legumes. Using an opaque colored glass adds protection from the sunlight, which contributes to rancidity over time. If you have only clear glass bottles, you can line them with brown paper to shade your food, or store them in a dark cupboard.

In the Homemade Pantry section to follow, we share wonderful recipes and formulas for spice mixes, stocks, and mineral broths. The dry spice mixes are terrific for sparking up the flavors of soups, sauces, salads, main dishes, beverages, and desserts. They can help make a simple meal more flavorful and nutritious. You can add them according to your own taste and tolerance, "doctoring up" your meals with health as well as flavor enhancing condiments.

Homemade broths and stocks provide you with a base liquid for soups, sauces, and stews that are far tastier and healthier than bouillon cubes or pre-made cartons of vegetable, chicken, or squash broth. I remember my mom using Campbell's® French Onion or Cream of Mushroom soup as a base for cooking her favorite meats, poultry, and seafood. She would also add Accent® from a big red shaker, which I now know is pure MSG.

Today, we can do better than that. Very high-quality ingredients are available from which we can make our own potent flavor enhancers. Your homemade dried spice mixes will keep for months in a cool, closed, dark container. Stocks and broths keep for 5 to 7 days in the refrigerator, or can be frozen until needed.

Enjoy trying out these foundational formulas. If you want or need to substitute an ingredient, that is quite all right. See yourself as a culinary artist, with the foods as your main subjects and herbs and spices as minor but essential brush strokes.

Ed

Contents

Sweet Spice of Life

YIELDS A LITTLE OVER 2/3 CUP

This classic *Eating For Health*™ spice adds wonderful aroma and zest to smoothies, fruit, yogurt, and desserts.

Ingredients

2 tablespoons freshly grated
   orange peel
4 tablespoons ground cinnamon
1 tablespoon ground cardamom

3 tablespoons ground ginger
2 teaspoons ground nutmeg
2 teaspoons ground allspice

Method

1. Grate orange peel, spread out onto a sheet pan and allow to dry overnight in a warm oven. If a dehydrator is available, spread orange peel on parchment paper and put on dehydrator rack. Dehydrate on low overnight.

2. Stir dried orange peel and remaining ingredients together until well combined and store in an airtight container.

Savory Spice of Life

YIELDS A LITTLE UNDER 1/2 CUP

Another Dr. Bauman classic, this blend adds savory highlights to food. Keep in a spice shaker and sprinkle on soups, salads, popcorn, cooked rice, or buttered toast.

Ingredients

4 tablespoons nutritional yeast
2 tablespoons dulse flakes
1 tablespoon granulated garlic

1 teaspoon dried oregano
1 teaspoon dried dill
1/4 teaspoon cayenne pepper

Method

Stir all ingredients together until well combined and store in an airtight container.

COOKING PEARL
Using Dried Herbs and Spices

Seasoning with dried herbs and spices means complementing, not overwhelming, the natural flavor of the food. The mark of a skilled natural chef is the ability to use herbs and spices in a synergistic way, adding flavor while increasing the metabolic activity of the body to digest and assimilate it. Consider the following when using our blends or any spice combination you create:

- More is not always better when using dried herbs and spices.

- Add dried herbs and spices when sautéing onions and other aromatics to further enhance the flavor of the dish.

- When using fresh herbs such as parsley and cilantro, add them to the dish at the end of the cooking time so they retain their vibrant color and flavor.

- Slow-cooked dishes often work better when herbs and spices are layered throughout the cooking time.

Nut Milk

Nut milks are excellent alternatives to dairy and are incredibly easy to make. Most nuts make delicious milks, but some (e.g., almonds and cashews) are especially delicious and versatile, working well in both sweet and savory recipes. While an increasing variety of nut milks are available at the grocery store, there is nothing like the fresh taste of homemade. Fresh nut milks are also healthier as they are not loaded with cane sugar, oils, and other binders like packaged varieties.

Ingredients

*1 cup nuts of choice, soaked overnight
    in filtered water (choose almonds,
    cashews, walnuts, or hazelnuts, etc.)*
6 cups filtered water
⅛ teaspoon sea salt

Flavoring Options
*2 medium, pitted dates (Medjool
    or Deglet)*
1 tablespoon vanilla extract
1 teaspoon cinnamon

Method

1. Drain soaked nuts and rinse with filtered water.

2. Add nuts, water, salt, and optional flavorings to blender and purée until smooth.

3. Using a nut milk bag or fine mesh strainer layered with cheese cloth, pour nut milk purée through bag or sieve and gently squeeze or press to strain "milk" into a bowl or pitcher. Be sure to squeeze bag or press solids against strainer firmly to extract all of the liquid.

4. Nut milk can be stored in a sealed glass jar in the refrigerator for up to 4 days.

5. The remaining solids can be spread out onto a dehydrator sheet or parchment-lined baking sheet and dried into nut meal for baking.

NOTE: For a richer nut milk, forget about straining and enjoy the puréed mixture alone or blended with fruit and Vital Scoop™ for a delicious and nutritious smoothie.

Homemade Nut Flour/Meal

YIELDS 4½ CUPS NUT FLOUR OR MEAL

Finely ground nuts make fantastic, flavorful flours that are excellent for using in baked goods, as thickeners for sauces, and for breading proteins like fish and chicken for pan frying. Some of the earliest recipes for cakes utilized almonds ground into flour to add a richness and extra deliciousness. Since nuts are abundant in oil, it is easy to over grind them into a butter instead of a flour. Following these easy steps will ensure that your flour is crumbly and not pasty.

Ingredients

1 pound frozen almonds or other nuts (preferably soaked and dehydrated)

1 to 2 tablespoons sorghum or brown rice flour (optional)

Method

1. Using 1 to 2 cups at a time (depending on how large your food processor is) process frozen nuts by using the "pulse" button in short, quick bursts to avoid turning the nuts into butter. The transformation from nuts to meal or flour is very quick so stop the food processor and check often by pinching the nut flour between your fingers. It should remain crumbly, not sticky.

2. Nut flours tend to be grainy. For a finer nut flour, add 1 to 2 tablespoons of flour. This will dry out the almonds and keep the nut flour dry and powdery. The use of either sorghum or brown rice flour keeps it gluten free.

Nut Sense

True nut flour is made from nuts that have first been blanched, then dried thoroughly. Nut meal is made from the whole nuts and is often grittier and oiler than the more refined nut flour. Both are great flour substitutes for baking and cooking. Choose nut flour when a lighter cake, muffin, or crumb is desired. For a heartier or more rustic effect, nut meal is the best choice. For example, I tend to choose nut flour for light and buttery sponge cakes or madeline-type cookies, while nut meal is best for quick breads, muffins, and spice or chocolate cakes.

Nut flours have tremendous nutritional value as well. They are loaded with quality proteins and essential fats that make them more filling and satisfying. Nut flours are also gluten free, an added benefit for those who are trying to avoid it. And let's not forget that nut flours are actually flour free. That is, they are nuts, not grains and therefore, more nutrient dense and not starchy.

Soaking and Dehydrating Nuts

To make the best quality nut meal or flour that is highly nutritious and easy to digest, soak and dehydrate nuts before freezing them in preparation for making flour.

To soak and dehydrate nuts, cover nuts with filtered water overnight. The next morning drain them well and spread them out on dehydrator sheets and dehydrate until completely dry and crispy. If you do not have a dehydrator, spread nuts out evenly on a parchment-lined baking sheet and dry in the oven overnight or for 18 to 24 hours on the lowest setting (below 150° F is ideal).

Great Nuts for Flour

Other nuts besides almonds make excellent flours. Follow the technique in the Homemade Nut Flour/Meal recipe to make any of the following:

- chestnut
- coconut (use dried, unsweetened coconut flakes)
- walnut
- peanut
- hazelnut
- macadamia nut

LIZETTE

Stock Options

Stock is nothing more than a flavored water preparation, yet it is the foundation of many delectable dishes, particularly for soups and sauces. Making stock from scratch is an essential practice for any good chef or cook, as it will enhance and heighten the flavor of many dishes. Boxed and canned stock on the supermarket shelves are no match because they are often over-cooked, over-salted, and lack character or subtlety. Making stock is like making a tea decoction – water is gently simmered with various ingredients to produce a rich and flavorful liquid that tastes like the ingredients from which it is made. Stock can be made from animal protein, bones, vegetables, herbs, and spices.

Meat

Making stock from meat and bones can be expensive but will result in a deeply delicious stock that tastes distinct and pure. An economical and convenient way to make this type of stock is to use leftover roast chicken carcasses or meaty bones from braised lamb shanks or short ribs. If made solely from fresh cuts of meat (beef, lamb, fish, poultry), the stock will impart an intense flavor but will lack body. Slowly simmering roasted bones, including the joints and parts with the most cartilage (such as the shoulder, shin, neck, and knuckle bones) will allow the gelatin from the connective tissue to dissolve into the liquid and enrich the stock. The typical ratio for preparing this type of stock is 1 part fresh meat or meaty bones to 2 parts water by weight. Water has an exact weight to volume measure, so 16 ounces in a measuring cup should weigh 1 pound.

Bones

Bones are the foundation of many basic stock recipes because they give stock weight and richness. Without bones, connective tissue, and joints, the stock will lack body and viscosity that is important especially when attempting to reduce stock into a glacé. Skin, cartilage, and bones have the most connective tissue and collagen, and as they cook over a low, simmering heat for long periods of time, the gelatin melts into the stock and thickens the liquid. Veal, beef, fish, and chicken bones are most commonly used for this type of stock. The flavor is subtle and not nearly as intense as meat stock, which makes it perfect for certain recipes. Stock made from bones needs to be simmered longer than meat stock. An ideal ratio for making excellent bone stock is 3:2 by weight. That is, 2 pounds of bones to 3 pounds (or 6 cups) of water.

Mirepoix

Considered the "holy trinity" in French cuisine, this vegetable mixture of onions, carrots, and celery is used for flavoring stocks, sauces, and many other dishes. In stocks, a mirepoix of vegetable scraps are used, since they still contain flavor and nutrients but are less desirable for eating.

Herbs and Spices

Herbs and spices are a wonderful way to add a distinctive character to a stock's flavor. In classical French cuisine, it is common to use a bouquet garni *(bundle of herbs)* consisting of fresh parsley, bay leaves, a sprig of thyme, and possibly other herbs, tied together with string. The herbs can also be placed in a square of cheese cloth and wrapped like a package, or sachet d'épices. Experiment with other herb and spice combinations to enhance different types of ethnic cuisine.

Stock or Broth?

Home cooks often use these words interchangeably, but even though the differences are slight, it is helpful to know what distinguishes a stock from a broth. Harold McGee writes in his book, *On Food and Cooking: The Science and Lore of the Kitchen,* "Stock reflects the professional cook's approach to sauce making." The word "stock" is derived from an old Germanic root meaning "tree trunk," which is related to words like "basic materials" and "source." Broth has more ancient roots, literally meaning "that which is brewed" or "the liquid in which something has boiled." Culinary schools describe the difference between stock and broth in this way. Broths have a more distinct flavor and may even have bits of meat or vegetables. Stocks are clear, richly flavored liquids and because many are made with bones, they contain gelatin.

Stock Types

Brown stock (fond brun). The brown color of this stock is achieved by roasting the bones and mirepoix, which also adds a rich, full flavor. Veal bones are the most common type used in a *fond brun.* Tomato paste is often added (sometimes thinned tomato paste is painted onto the roasting bones). The acid in the paste helps break down the connective tissue, accelerating the formation of gelatin, as well as giving color to the stock.

White stock (fond blanc), is made by using raw bones and white mirepoix composed of light-colored, unroasted vegetables like onions, garlic, celery, and either leeks or fennel, depending on the flavor direction desired. Raw chicken bones are most commonly used for *fond blanc.*

Fish stock is made with fish bones and finely chopped mirepoix. Fish stock should be cooked for 30 to 45 minutes – cooking any longer will spoil the flavor. In Japanese cuisine, a fish and kelp stock called dashi is made by briefly (3 to 5 minutes) steeping kombu and dried bonito flakes in nearly boiling water.

Chicken stock should be cooked for 3 to 4 hours.

Lamb stock should be cooked for 5 hours. To make a lamb jus, simmer roasted lamb necks and bones in chicken stock.

Vegetable stock is made only from vegetables. The type of vegetables chosen can dramatically change the flavor profile of the stock.

Glacé viande is stock made from bones, usually veal, that is reduced to 10 percent of its original volume, transforming it into a highly concentrated jelly-like consistency. A small amount of this syrupy nectar will give sauce body and heighten its flavor immensely.

Demi glacé or "half glacé" is stock that has been reduced to 25 to 40 percent of its original volume. Tomato puree or paste is often added for more flavor and an appealing color.

Preparing stock

When preparing any stock, follow these basic guidelines for the best results:

• Cover the stock ingredients with cold water before bringing to a simmer. This assists in the extraction of collagen from the bones, which may be sealed in by hot water. If hot water is used to cover meat and bones, soluble proteins will release into the surrounding liquid and coagulate into very fine particles, making the stock cloudy.

- When using raw bones for white stock, clean them by parboiling for 10 to 15 minutes. Drain the water and begin making stock.

- Simmer stock gently over low heat and do not allow to boil. As some chefs say, the stock should smile with tiny bubbles just breaking the surface, not laugh with large bubbles and gurgles. If a stock is allowed to boil, it will churn up proteins and fats into the liquid and make a murky, cloudy stock.

- Salting stock is not advised, as this can result in soups and sauces that are too salty. Unsalted stock also makes it possible to make successful glacés, such as demi glacé. If a salted stock were reduced to make demi glacé, it would be far too salty.

- Add meat to a stock before the vegetables. Animal proteins, like meat and bones, emit a foamy "scum" that rises to the surface. Skim stock free of this scum before adding vegetables and herbs.

- To skim, use a shallow spoon to carefully lift off the foam that develops on the surface of the stock. A pinch of salt added at the start of cooking encourages impurities to rise to the top.

- Sometimes fat is removed from the stock after it cools, when it has solidified and can be easily removed.

- Stock can be made ahead and cooled completely, uncovered, then covered and refrigerated in an airtight container for up to 1 week.

- Stocks stored in an airtight container, can be frozen and kept for several months. Be sure to date and label stocks clearly.

Cooling Stock Safely

In the professional cooking world, cooling food properly (particularly soup and stock) is paramount in keeping food safe and free from developing harmful bacteria. The industry term for cooling stock is called "dropping" stock, referring to dropping the temperature as quickly as possible before refrigerating or freezing. The food safety window is to reduce the temperature of stock, soup, or other perishable hot foods within 2 hours. The safe temperature is below 40° F. Any foods that languish in what is considered the danger zone – between 40° F and 140° F – are breeding grounds for all sorts of bacteria that can cause potentially serious food poisoning. Do not make the mistake of rushing the cooling process by placing hot stock in the refrigerator. Doing so will only reduce the stock to an unsafe temperature and possibly raise the overall temperature of the refrigerator, making all foods inside subject to bacterial growth.

Below is an easy, step-by-step guide to cooling stock safely.

1. Strain stock according to the recipe's instructions from one large pot to another large (but cooler) pot.

2. Plug the drain of your kitchen sink and place two 2-inch high mini loaf pans, bricks, or other similar item to use as risers for your stock pot. Put the stock pot on a platform and raise it above the bottom of the sink so water can get underneath and cool the stock much faster. This technique is called venting.

3. Fill the sink half way up with cold water. Add a few trays of ice cubes or plastic ice packs and carefully place the pot of stock in the sink, making sure it sits squarely on your makeshift "risers."

4. Remember, the safe time zone for cooling stock is 2 hours. When the stock is cool, refrigerate or freeze. Transfer stock to either a tempered glass jar or a stainless steel container that can be tightly sealed.

LIZETTE

Sources

Harold McGee (1984, 2004). *On Food and Cooking: The Science and Lore of the Kitchen,* New York, NY, USA: Scribner

Escoffier, A (1941). *The Escoffier Cook Book,* New York, NY, USA: Crown Publishers

COOKING PEARL
Making a Bouquet Garni

The cook's bouquet is a tight bundle of culinary herbs cinched together at the stem by a piece of kitchen twine. Traditionally this seasoning bouquet is composed of fresh parsley, rosemary, thyme sprigs, and a bay leaf, but other herbs can be included as well.

1. Select fresh herbs that have long stems. For a classic bouquet garni, the herbs should consist of 3 sprigs of parsley, 2 sprigs of thyme, and 1 bay leaf.

2. Tie the herbs together with kitchen twine and leave a "tail" that you can use to tie to the pot handle so the bouquet can be easily removed when straining stock.

Making a Sachet d'Épices

Mix together 1 tablespoon dried parsley, 1 teaspoon dried thyme, 6 peppercorns, and 1 bay leaf. Wrap in cheesecloth and tie with kitchen twine. Leave a "tail" of twine that you can use to tie to the pot handle so the sachet can be easily removed when straining stock.

Fresh Vegetable Stock

YIELDS 2 QUARTS

Use the freshest organic vegetables available for best results. Remember, your stock will be only as good as the ingredients you put into it. This fresh vegetable stock has a light, clean flavor ideal for most recipes.

Ingredients

1 tablespoon coconut oil
2 medium onions, peeled and
   coarsely chopped
2 stalks celery, chopped (include
   some leaves)
1 medium leek, white part only, thinly
   sliced (reserve one 5-inch piece of
   green leek leaf for bouquet garni)
2 medium carrots, scrubbed and
   coarsely chopped
3 cloves garlic
1 small rutabaga, peeled and diced
1 small fennel bulb, thinly sliced
   (reserve fronds for bouquet garni)

Bouquet Garni
4 sprigs fresh thyme
1 piece green leek leaf, about 5-inches
   long, cleaned
2 medium fennel fronds
½ bunch fresh parsley

Sachet d'Épices
½ teaspoon black peppercorns
¼ teaspoon fennel seeds
1 whole clove

Method

1. Make bouquet garni and sachet d'épices (see Cooking Pearl on previous page for guidelines).

2. In a heavy-bottomed stock pot, melt coconut oil over medium heat. Add onions, celery, leeks, carrots, and garlic and sweat for 5 minutes, until wilted. Add ½ cup filtered water and cook until tender, about 15 to 20 minutes.

3. Add remaining ingredients, including bouquet garni and spice sachet, and cover with cold filtered water to a depth of about 2 inches above the solids. Bring to a strong simmer, then reduce the heat and simmer gently for 1 hour. Do not allow the stock to boil.

4. Strain stock into a large bowl or another stock pot, using a large sieve layered with finely woven cheesecloth, to remove all sediment.

5. To cool, place container of strained stock into an ice bath. IMPORTANT: See Cooling Stock Safely, page 23.

6. Store cooled stock in canning jars or use in desired recipe. If freezing stock, be sure to leave 2 inches of head room at the top of the canning jars.

Roasted Vegetable Stock

Yields 2 quarts

Roasting brings out the natural sweetness in vegetables. When making stock from roasted vegetables, the result will be a darker, richer, more full-bodied broth.

Ingredients

1 large yam, peeled and chopped
2 carrots, scrubbed and coarsely chopped
2 stalks of celery, chopped (include leafy ends)
2 leeks, white and light green parts only, sliced lengthwise, thoroughly rinsed, and chopped into 1-inch pieces (reserve one 5-inch piece of green leek leaf for bouquet garni)
2 medium yellow onions, unpeeled, quartered
2 red bell peppers, quartered, seeded, and chopped
½ pound Roma tomatoes, quartered

1 head garlic (about 15 cloves)
3 shallots, unpeeled, halved
2½ cups cremini mushrooms, stems included
1 tablespoon coconut or olive oil
½ cup dry white wine
1 bay leaf
5 black peppercorns

Bouquet Garni
4 sprigs fresh thyme
4 sprigs marjoram
1 piece green leek leaf, about 5-inches long, cleaned
½ bunch fresh parsley

Method

Preheat oven to 350° F

1. Using a large bowl, toss yams, carrots, celery, leeks, onion, red peppers, tomatoes, garlic, shallots, and mushrooms in oil.

2. Roast vegetables in a stainless steel pan until golden brown and tender when pierced with a fork, about 40 to 45 minutes.

3. Place pan of roasted vegetables on the stove and turn both burners on if necessary to heat pan. Add ½ cup of wine and deglaze, using a wooden spoon to quickly scrape bits of the unburned vegetable matter from the bottom of the pan. Place roasted vegetables and pan juices into a large stock pot. Add filtered water to cover the solids to a depth of about 2 inches. Add bay leaf, peppercorns, and bouquet garni.

4. Bring stock to a strong simmer, then reduce heat and simmer gently for 1 hour. Do not let the stock boil.

5. After 1 hour of simmering, taste the stock. It will not be salty, but should have a full-bodied, rich flavor. If you are not planning on reducing this stock for sauce making, you may add just a bit of sea salt and black pepper.

6. When the stock has reached the desired flavor, strain through a fine-mesh sieve lined with cheese cloth into a large bowl. Press the solids to extract as much liquid as possible.

7. To cool, place container of strained stock into an ice bath. IMPORTANT: See Cooling Stock Safely, page 23.

8. Store cooled stock in canning jars or use in desired recipe. If freezing stock, be sure to leave 2 inches of head room at the top of the canning jars.

Classic Fish Stock

YIELDS 2 QUARTS

Classic fish stock (or fish fumet, as it is formally called) is a magical elixir in many applications. From a culinary standpoint, fish fumet enhances and elevates seafood based dishes and sauces. From a therapeutic consideration, the stock derived from fish bones contains replenishing minerals known in many cultures to be the perfect nourishing broth for women recovering from childbirth.

Ingredients

1 medium onion, very thinly sliced
2 stalks celery, very thinly sliced
2 leeks, white and green parts
* thinly sliced*
1 fennel bulb, thinly sliced (save fronds
* for sachet d'épices)*
2 medium carrots, very thinly sliced
½ cup dry white wine
4 pounds fish frames (bones) from
* sole, flounder, halibut, and/or turbot*
* cut into 2-inch pieces and rinsed*
* clean of any blood*
2½ quarts water

Sachet d'Épices
2 dried bay leaves
½ cup roughly chopped fresh Italian
* parsley leaves and stems*
½ cup roughly chopped fennel fronds
6 sprigs fresh thyme
1 tablespoon black peppercorns

Method

1. Heat a large 12-quart stock pot on medium heat and sauté the onions, celery, leeks, fennel, and carrots in ¼ cup of water for about 2 to 3 minutes. Cover pot and allow vegetables to steam and soften for 5 minutes. Remove cover and continue cooking until liquid has nearly evaporated.

2. Stir white wine into the vegetables to deglaze. Then, add fish bones and just enough water to cover (you will not need the full 2½ quarts of water at this point). Bring to a boil, skimming off the white foam from the top of the stock as it approaches boiling, then reduce the heat so the stock simmers. (Using a ladle and a circular motion, push the foam from the center to the outside of the pot, where it is easy to remove.)

3. Add remaining water and sachet d'épices. NOTE: if the water level does not cover the bones, add enough extra water to cover.

4. Simmer stock gently for 30 minutes, skimming off any additional foam that rises to the top. Do not overcook or allow fish stock to boil. Doing so will damage this stock's delicate flavors.

5. When the fish stock is finished simmering, remove from the heat and allow to steep for another 15 minutes. Strain twice through a fine mesh strainer lined with cheesecloth into a large bowl or clean stock pot. You may need to change the cheesecloth before straining a second time.

6. To cool, place container of strained stock into an ice bath. IMPORTANT: See Cooling Stock Safely, page 23.

7. Store cooled stock in canning jars or use in desired recipe. If freezing stock, be sure to leave 2 inches of head room at the top of the canning jars.

Roasted Chicken Bone Stock

YIELDS 2 QUARTS

Roasting bones gives this stock a deep, robust flavor perfect for savory stews, braises, and sauces.

Ingredients

2½ pounds chicken bones
1 large onion with skin, quartered
1 leek, white and pale green parts, sliced lengthwise, cleaned and coarsely chopped (reserve one 5-inch piece of green leek leaf for bouquet garni)
1 medium carrot, scrubbed and coarsely chopped
1½ pounds Roma tomatoes, halved
2 large celery stalks with leaves, coarsely chopped

6 cloves unpeeled garlic, crushed
6 black peppercorns
Pinch of sea salt
3-inch piece Parmesan cheese rind

Bouquet Garni
3 sprigs fresh thyme
2 sprigs fresh oregano
1 piece green leek leaf, about 5-inches long, cleaned
½ bunch parsley
1 bay leaf

Method

Preheat oven to 400° F

1. Roast chicken bones in roasting pan with onion, leek, carrot, tomatoes, celery, and garlic cloves.

2. Place the bones and vegetables in a stock pot. Add enough cold filtered water to just cover the bones. Add in the bouquet garni and bring to a boil, then reduce heat and simmer, uncovered, for 3 hours.

3. During the first 30 minutes or so of simmering, add a pinch of salt to the stock and then skim away the froth that develops on the surface.

4. When stock is finished, strain through a fine mesh strainer lined with cheese cloth into a large bowl. Press the solids to extract as much liquid as possible.

5. To cool, place container of strained stock into an ice bath. IMPORTANT: See Cooling Stock Safely, page 23.

6. Store cooled stock in canning jars or use in desired recipe. If freezing stock, be sure to leave 2 inches of head room at the top of the canning jars.

Good to the Bone Broth

Part of many traditional diets throughout the world, bone broths are highly nourishing and can be used to boost the flavor and nutrition profile of a variety of dishes.

Ingredients

2 pounds organic chicken
   or grass-fed beef bones, rinsed
   with filtered water
2 tablespoons apple cider vinegar
   or fresh squeezed lemon juice
2 stalks celery with leaves, diced
2 large carrots, scrubbed and diced
1 large onion, diced
1 large leek, white part only, sliced

3 cloves garlic
5 black peppercorns

Bouquet Garni
5 3-inch sprigs fresh thyme
1 piece green leek leaf, about 5-inches
   long, cleaned
½ bunch fresh parsley
1 bay leaf

Method

Preheat oven to 400° F

1. Place the bones on a baking sheet lined with parchment paper and roast until browned, about 30 minutes.

2. Place the bones in a stock pot with vinegar or lemon juice and just enough filtered water to cover them completely. Let stand for 30 minutes.

3. Bring stock to a strong simmer, then reduce heat immediately to a gentle simmer. Skim off any scum that rises to the surface.

4. Add the vegetables and bouquet garni and simmer for at least 6 hours or as long as 48 hours. (The longer the broth simmers, the better.) Add more water as needed to keep the solids barely submerged.

5. When the stock is finished, strain through a fine mesh strainer lined with cheese cloth, into a large bowl. Press the solids to extract as much liquid as possible.

6. To cool, place container of strained stock into an ice bath. IMPORTANT: See Cooling Stock Safely, page 23.

7. Store cooled stock in canning jars or use in desired recipe. If freezing stock, be sure to leave 2 inches of head room at the top of the canning jar.

Healing Mineral Broth

YIELDS 2 QUARTS

If ever there was a universal tonic for healing and rejuvenation, it is mineral broth. It is the very foundation of a cleansing, building, or balancing diet. Cook soup, grain, or legume dishes using this delicious and therapeutic broth.

Ingredients

1½ pounds onions with skins, quartered
4 celery stalks with leaves, chopped
2 carrots, scrubbed and chopped
2 parsnips, scrubbed and chopped
½ pound fresh shiitake mushrooms
1 large red beet, peeled and chopped
2½ pounds winter squash or yams, chopped into 2-inch pieces

1 small celery root, rutabaga, or turnip, chopped
1 2-inch piece dried kombu
¼ cup dried wakame
1 pound fresh greens (spinach, kale, collards, chard), washed, patted dry, and chopped
½ bunch fresh parsley
¼ cup flax seeds

Method

1. Heat a heavy-bottomed stock pot over medium heat and add the onions and celery. Add 2 to 3 tablespoons of water and cover the pan so the vegetables will release their own water content. This action is called sweating.

2. After about 5 minutes or so, remove the lid and give the onions and celery a stir; they should be slightly softened. Stir in the carrots, parsnips, and shiitake mushrooms and cover the pan again to sweat the vegetables for another 5 minutes. The vegetables will continue to soften and release their juices.

3. Add the beets, squash, celery root, kombu, and wakame. Cover with filtered water to a depth of 2 inches above the vegetables and bring to a soft boil. Reduce heat and simmer, uncovered, for 4 to 6 hours.

4. Add the fresh greens and parsley during the last hour of cooking.

5. During the last 20 minutes of cooking, stir in the flax seeds.

6. When stock is finished, strain through a fine mesh strainer lined with cheese cloth into a large bowl. Press the solids to extract as much liquid as possible.

7. Place bowl of hot stock in an ice bath to cool. IMPORTANT: See Cooling Stock Safely, page 23.

8. Store cooled stock in canning jars for up to 1 week in the refrigerator. If freezing stock, leave 2 inches of head room at the top of the canning jars.

The Magic of Mineral Broth

Back in 1968, I had the pleasure of meeting Dr. Henry Biehler, whose book, *Food is Your Best Medicine,* had been a revelation to me. In it, he recommends an alkaline mineral broth for all his patients. The broth is very simple, boiled and simmered zucchini, parsley, celery, and green beans. This mix could be strained and taken as a clear broth by the cup 3 to 4 times per day, or it could be blended into a purée resembling split pea soup and used as a vegetable side dish.

A bit later, in 1970, I worked with Dr. Paavo Airola, author of *Are You Confused, How to Get Well, How to Stay Slim, Young and Healthy with Juice Fasting,* and *Rejuvenation Secrets from Around the World.* Airola recommended a potassium broth for his patients, made from potato skins. Neither the Biehler nor Airola broths had any flavor or body.

When I began to lead fasting retreats in 1984, I built on my basic study of *brothology* to create the Bauman Broth. My basic formula is to fill a large pot with ⅓ root or starchy vegetables, ⅓ green vegetables, and ⅓ shiitake mushrooms, sea vegetables like kombu and wakame, herbs, and spices. Add flax seeds at the end for a nice source of oil and texture. If you use yams or winter squash as the base, you will have a golden amber nectar that is rich, smooth, and delicious.

I suggest that the vegetables be gently simmered for 4 to 5 hours to gain a complete extraction of the minerals and phytonutrients present, such as carotenes and flavonoids, which are not harmed by moderate heat. Feel free to add clean onion skins, vegetable peels, and/or broccoli stalks to your stock.

This broth alkalinizes and rebalances mineral stores in the body, rejuvenating you on a cellular level. I am sure Drs. Biehler and Airola would approve.

ED

*It's bizarre that the produce manager is more
important to my children's health than the pediatrician.*

MERYL STREEP

*The usual suspects, also known as nutrition bandits, are the
stimulants, sugars, pastries, pastas, processed cheeses, artificial
sweeteners, and margarine found in white-flour-laden, over-processed,
frozen, microwaved meals served in restaurants or grabbed on the
run. Such foods are formulated in laboratories to over-stimulate our
taste receptors so that we are no longer satisfied by the crunch of
a carrot, the refreshingly sweet juice of a fresh mango, or the zing
of fresh garlic. While it is easy to over eat nutrient-poor foods, you
can enjoy naturally satisfying, nutrient-rich vegetables, grains, seeds,
legumes, and lean proteins in abundance.*

DR. ED BAUMAN

Breaking the Fast
Morning Meals

Chapter 2

Breaking the Fast
Morning Meals

Breakfast – "breaking the fast" – is a very important meal, as you have probably heard. It is regenerative to have a 12-hour period between dinner and breakfast when no solid food enters the body. This enables the digestive system to fully process the food consumed the day before and eliminate any unusable material in the morning. If blood sugar stability is a problem with such a long time without food, then a small, healthy evening snack 3 hours after the main meal and at least an hour before bed would be fine. This could be yogurt and fruit or a bowl of hot cereal, each of which would also be nice for breakfast or a snack, any time of day.

First thing in the morning, begin your day by drinking 12 to 16 ounces of room-temperature filtered water or diluted herb tea with a squeeze of fresh lemon juice to taste. Sip it slowly. Feel hydration happening throughout your body.

Next, practice a morning routine that features some reflection, prayer, or meditation, followed by breathing, movement, and centering activities. This could include yoga, tai chi, walking, or any appropriate exercise.

It is best to create hunger by warming up your body with breath and movement, rather than eating because it is a "mealtime." Each person has a metabolic tendency, either slow, balanced, or fast. The goal is maintaining balance.

Whether you are a slow, balanced, or fast metabolizer, a healthy breakfast will include some combination of protein, healthy fats, and complex carbohydrates.

A slow metabolizer will not be very hungry in the morning, so a simple cleansing breakfast is usually best. This may consist of a glass of fresh fruit juice, made with a juice extractor such as a Champion or Omega juicer. You can dilute this juice with green or herbal tea and use it to make a smoothie with a variety of booster foods, such as Vital Scoop™, flax seeds, bee pollen, spices, frozen fruit, and unsweetened, whole milk yogurt. Having a fresh fruit salad with nuts and seeds added to provide protein and essential fatty acids is another fine option.

Balanced metabolizers tend to wake up moderately hungry. A hearty bowl of porridge made from a whole grain like steel cut oats, millet, quinoa, or amaranth would be a satisfying breakfast for this type of person. To make this breakfast even more substantial, top it with 2 to 3 tablespoons of nuts and seeds (such as almonds, flax, sunflower, and/or pumpkin seeds), a quarter to a half cup of organic fresh or dried fruit, and a dash of unsweetened almond, rice, or coconut milk for creaminess. This type of breakfast is a far better choice than processed cereal out of the box, which contains 2 to 6 tablespoons of sugar per serving!

If you wake up famished, you are a fast metabolizer. Being a fast metabolizer indicates a strong digestive capacity and a need for concentrated foods that will digest more slowly than fruits or grains. Fast metabolizers are best served by a healthy, hearty breakfast with more calories from protein and good fats than from complex carbohydrates. Eggs, savory soups, fish (lox or sardines) with vegetables and whole grains are excellent choices. For those who burn calories quickly due to a robust metabolism, or who require more calories for physical work or athletic activity, eating "dinner for breakfast" can be a winning strategy. Eating a breakfast burrito or including animal protein in the morning meal, along with vegetables, will help balance blood sugar and allay hunger for up to 4 hours.

Morning Beverages

Drink tea – be it black, oolong, green, or herbal – rather than coffee and you will be gaining nutrients and enjoy balanced energy throughout the course of the day. Remember that caffeine is a drug. Be moderate and go easy if you drink caffeinated beverages.

Many people look forward to starting the day with coffee, tea, or hot chocolate, typically adding refined or artificial sweeteners and often milk. These beverages contain a wide array of phytonutrients, including caffeine, antioxidants, and neuro-stimulants. When they are consumed alone or with a refined carbohydrate, such as a pastry, the effect is a rapid rise in blood sugar with a commensurate spike in insulin and energy. This quick energy spike will cause hyperactivity and physiological stress, and is typically followed by a dramatic let-down in the mid-morning or mid-afternoon.

A 7-ounce cup of coffee contains 125mg of caffeine. A cup of black tea or cocoa contains 45mg of caffeine. A cup of green tea contains 15mg of caffeine. A cup of herbal tea, such as peppermint or rooibos, contains no caffeine.

The healthiest morning choice would be to opt for a low-caffeine organic green tea and combine it with aromatic herbs such as mint, rosemary, sage, ginger, or lemon verbena to provide a mildly stimulating beverage with a refreshing finish.

Taking caffeinated beverages such as coffee with a hearty meal is less problematic, as the nutrients and calories in the meal help to offset the rapid rise in blood sugar caused by having a stimulant without food or with empty carbohydrates.

One cup of coffee per day is rarely a problem. For coffee fanatics, however, having one cup in the morning may be difficult as they depend on the energy boost later in the day and are enticed by the wonderful aroma. One way to wean oneself off excessive coffee consumption is to combine brewed coffee with a coffee substitute such as chickory or roasted dandelion. This allows you to enjoy coffee while also consuming liver-friendly, nutrient-rich herbs. You can add the herbs in equal amounts to ground coffee beans in a drip cone, French press, or espresso maker.

ED

Contents

Wake Up Beverages

Smoothies

Many people are not hungry first thing in the morning, a sure sign that they have a slow metabolism. These are the folks who often skip breakfast or have a cup of coffee and a pastry "on the go." If you fit that description, try this experiment for 1 week. Make and drink a *Vitality Smoothie* (see page 46) each morning and see how much it improves your energy flow and overall sense of well-being.

A Vitality Smoothie is a blended drink that always includes what I like to call "the healthy trinity" in nutritional terms: a protein powder, a green super-food powder, and flax seeds. These ingredients ensure a great nutritional profile, including complete protein, essential fatty acids, fiber, vitamins, and minerals in a tasty and digestible form. Add fresh or frozen fruit and your choice of filtered water, fresh squeezed juice, yogurt, milk, nut milk, coconut water, or even aloe vera juice to cover, then blend until smooth.

I often suggest making a "double batch" so you can have some more for a delicious energy boost later in the day.

Once you are in the habit of adding the healthy trinity to your smoothies, you can improvise with other ingredients, such as nuts, or coconut milk … but not the kitchen sink, please.

Teas

Tea is the world's most popular beverage, after plain water. *Camilla Senensis* is the Latin name for the tea plant, from which white, green oolong, and black teas are all derived.

Tea is unique in providing phytonutrients that bring about both alertness and calmness, as it is mildly stimulating as well as sedating.

Being a tea connoisseur is a healthy avocation, as there are so many varieties of flavorful and healing tea. Tea tastes bitter and astringent (drying), with a variety of finishing tones ranging from sour to sweet and aromatic.

Herbal Infusions

Herbal teas are not technically "tea" at all, but infusions made by steeping the roots, leaves, flowers, and seeds of various plants in hot water. Beginning the day with 2 to 4 cups of herbal tea is both cleansing and refreshing. The healing compounds found in fresh or dried herbs such as mint, thyme, rosemary, chamomile, lemon balm, and lemon verbena increase alkaline-forming minerals which help cleanse the blood and gently activate the digestive system.

Fresh Juice

Many of us grew up on frozen orange juice from concentrate that ranged from being okay tasting to pretty bad, which is what happens when fruit is not ripe and chemical free. There is nothing so refreshing as a glass of freshly squeezed organic orange or pink grapefruit juice in the morning to arouse our taste buds with their sweet, sour, and slightly bitter tastes.

The same goes for fresh organic apple, grape, and pineapple juices, or blends made in an extractor juicer and immediately imbibed.

This chapter introduces a variety of morning beverages that can stand alone as cleansing meals unto themselves or can complement heartier breakfast items. We will devote more attention to fresh juices in our Quenchers: Better Beverages chapter, page 279.

ED

Morning Sunshine Juice

SERVES 2

The fresh juices below are inspired by Bauman College's Vitality Cleansing and Rejuvenation Retreats. Each blend makes an invigorating drink first thing in the morning.

Ingredients

4 medium Granny Smith or
    Gravenstein apples
2-inch piece of fresh ginger, peeled

1 Meyer lemon, peeled and seeded
½ cup filtered water

Method

Juice apples, ginger, and lemon together and dilute with the water. Chill before serving, if desired.

Melon Strawberry Sunrise Juice

SERVES 2

Ingredients

4 cups fresh cantaloupe, peeled
    and cubed
1 cup strawberries
¼ cup fresh mint leaves

2-inch piece of fresh ginger, peeled
1 Meyer lemon, peeled and seeded
¾ cup filtered water

Method

1. Juice cantaloupe and strawberries together, followed by mint leaves, ginger, and lemon.

2. Dilute juice with water. Chill slightly before serving if desired or enjoy immediately.

Ruby Chai

Wake up to this stimulating yet non-caffeinated version of chai.

Ingredients

1 cup filtered water
8 green cardamom pods
6 whole black peppercorns
2 ¼-inch slices fresh ginger, peeled
  and diced
1 2-inch stick cinnamon

2 whole cloves
1 star anise pod
2 cups almond milk or coconut milk
1 tablespoon maple syrup
2 tablespoons rooibos (red tea)
  or 2 rooibos tea bags

Method

1. Put water and spices in a saucepan and bring to a boil. Reduce the heat to low and simmer for 20 minutes.

2. Add milk and maple syrup and heat to a strong simmer. Do not allow to boil.

3. Add the tea and turn off the heat. Allow to steep for 5 minutes, then strain chai into heat-proof mugs.

NUTRITION GEM
Chai Spice Tea

"Chai" is the term used for tea in many parts of the world. Indian spiced chai traditionally combines a high-quality black Indian tea, such as Assam or Darjeeling, with ginger, cardamom, pepper, nutmeg, cinnamon, clove, fennel seed, and a distinctive Indian herb called asofoetida – which is not in American chai blends. The tea and the spices are mixed into hot milk and sweetened with honey or a raw sugar.

Traditional Chai is a warming, digestive tonic and mild stimulant that improves circulation and has anti-inflammatory properties. It can be made without tea, steeping the spices in hot milk, or it can be made with a green or rooibos (red) tea.

The key to a great chai is for the spices to steep overnight with the tea and milk. This brings out the rich flavors and health-enhancing properties that make it a much preferable substitute for a café latte.

I do not like my chai very sweet, and by using fresh spices I can control the sweet flavor. The pre-made chai at coffee shops, especially the blended versions, are way too sweet to be considered healthy.

Learn the simple process of making your own and you can enjoy chai on a regular basis without ill effect. NOTE: Spiced chai tea makes a great liquid medium for a Vitality Smoothie. Yum!

ED

Vitality Smoothie

SERVES 1 TO 2

This is the perfect way to start the day – protein, micronutrient greens, essential fatty acids, and fiber in a glass!

Ingredients

2 cups almond or hazelnut milk
1 scoop Vital Scoop™
1 cup fresh or frozen berries of choice
2 to 4 tablespoons ground flax seeds
1 tablespoon coconut oil

Juice of ½ lemon
1 cup fresh spinach or other leafy greens
½ teaspoon Sweet Spice of Life (see page 14)

Method

1. Combine all ingredients in a blender and purée.

2. Refrigerate any leftovers, or freeze in an ice cube tray for a quick treat later in the day.

NUTRITION GEM
Vital Scoop™

I created the Vital Scoop™ to be an all-in-one health-boosting powder that folks could add to any liquid to create a tasty and nourishing smoothie. The primary ingredients are whey, flax, algae, cereal greens, fruits, fiber, and flora. Vital Scoop™ has a natural sweetness without added sugars of any kind.

You can blend the Scoop with fruits or vegetables, yogurt or kefir, add an avocado, coconut, or seeds and nuts. Voila! A meal in 5 minutes or less.

A Vital Scoop™ smoothie stores well in the refrigerator and can be frozen in popsicle molds or an ice tray to make creamsicles in the summer. The Scoop can also be added to warm milk or hot tea for a wonderful morning latte sans caffeine.

ED

Strawberry Basil Smoothie with Pomegranate White Tea

SERVES 2

Strawberries and basil make a dreamy combination. Adding white tea gives this smoothie the perfect subtle boost for a balanced recharge in the morning. Keep the strawberry top greens to add extra greens to this smoothie.

Ingredients

1¾ cups brewed white tea (2 cups 180°F water to 2 tea bags, steeped for 3 minutes)
¼ cup pure pomegranate juice

1 cup fresh strawberries, stems included
½ cup loosely packed basil leaves*
1 scoop Vital Scoop™
3 tablespoons ground flax seeds

Method

1. Combine all ingredients and blend thoroughly. Allow to sit for 10 minutes before serving.

2. OPTIONAL: Pour into popsicle molds to create a refreshing frozen treat.

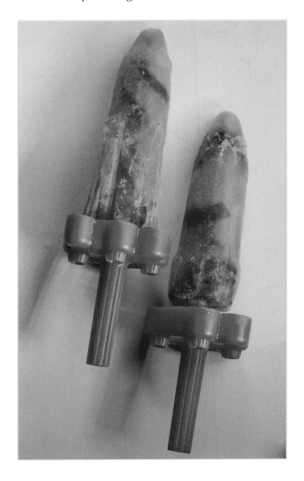

*If fresh basil is unavailable, use 2 teaspoons dried basil in 2 cups of tea.

Citrus Breeze Tonic

SERVES 2

Here is a bright and refreshing tonic for a spring or summer morning.

Ingredients

½ cup fresh lemon verbena leaves
2 cups filtered water
2 medium oranges
1 medium ruby grapefruit

½ cup frozen grapes
¼ cup fresh cranberries
1 teaspoon ground flax seeds
1 teaspoon raw honey

Method

1. In a saucepan, combine water and lemon verbena leaves and bring to a strong simmer. Lower heat and simmer gently for 15 minutes. Drain and allow to cool.

2. Juice oranges and grapefruit and place juice in a blender.

3. Add frozen grapes, cranberries, lemon verbena tea, ground flax seeds, and honey. Blend until smooth and serve immediately.

COOKING PEARL
Smoothie Boosters

Here are some ways to further enhance the flavor and nutritional value of smoothies and juices:

- Add 1 banana as a thickener

- Add frozen mangos

- Add ¼ cup aloe vera juice

- Add 1 teaspoon buffered vitamin C

- Use 1 peeled orange, ½ cup grapefruit sections, or ½-inch peeled fresh ginger instead of or in addition to berries

Egg-Free Breakfasts

Many cultures eat a warm meal of soup, grains, or stuffed pastry for breakfast. The latter is called an empanada in Mexico or a solteno in Bolivia.

Eating a substantial breakfast provides sufficient calories, nutrients, and fiber to sustain working adults and children going off to school until lunch time. Eating a whole-food breakfast at home is calming to the nervous system, which will all too soon be dealing with stressful people, problems, and modern technology that taxes our nerves and drains our nutritional reserves.

Root vegetables – such as yams, potatoes, turnips, beets, kohlrabi, and carrots – are wonderful sources of complex carbohydrates when they are baked, roasted, steamed, or sautéed with onions, garlic, ginger, and herbs. Once cooked, they can be topped with yogurt, organic cheese, or a lean protein, such as turkey bacon, or with simple sautéed vegetables for a vegan option.

Packaged cereals have been a mainstay of family breakfasts since I was a child in the 1950s. Cheerios®, GrapeNuts®, Wheaties®, Rice Krispies®, and Shredded Wheat® – actually the least sweetened of the packaged cereals on the market – became the breakfast choice for families from coast to coast.

We trusted Tony the Tiger and all the TV commercials that touted dried cereal as the perfect breakfast food, high in fiber and with nutrients added. What was not known then, and is largely unknown even now, is that dried breakfast cereal is high on the glycemic index, meaning it raises our blood sugar and insulin levels rapidly, leading to glucose instability marked by energy spikes and crashes. Whole-grain dried cereals such as high-quality granola can be adequate breakfast food with the addition of whole milk and nuts or seeds that provide good quality fat and lower the glycemic load of the meal.

Modern eaters are often in a hurry in the morning. With that in mind, planning breakfast in the evening makes good sense. Soak some whole grains overnight or cook root vegetables in the evening so you will have the makings of a healthy breakfast on hand in the morning.

You will soon find out what a great difference a proper breakfast can make in your energy level and general sense of well-being.

Ed

Tropical Fruit
and Spiced Yogurt Parfait

SERVES 2

Fresh fruit and yogurt parfaits make an easy and festive breakfast. Rather than purchasing flavored yogurts, which tend to be high in sugar, make your own by blending fresh fruits, spices, and dates or honey with plain yogurt.

Ingredients

1 cup plain whole-milk yogurt
1 large ripe banana
1 tablespoon flax seeds, ground
2 teaspoons freshly grated ginger
1 date, pitted

½ teaspoon Spice of Life
  (see page 14)
½ cup fresh pineapple, cubed
½ cup fresh mango, cubed
¼ cup seedless grapes
¼ cup flaked coconut, toasted
¼ cup raw almonds

Method

Preheat oven to 325° F

1. In a blender, purée the yogurt, banana, flax, ginger, date, and Spice of Life until smooth and creamy. Transfer to a glass container, cover, and chill until ready to use. (This can be done up to a day ahead of time; keep in the refrigerator until needed and stir to recombine if it has separated.)

2. Prepare fruits and toss together in a bowl.

3. Toast coconut flakes in a dry heavy-bottomed pan over low heat. Watch closely to avoid burning. When they turn a tan color, transfer to a cold plate.

4. Toast almonds in the oven for 5 to 8 minutes. Cool and coarsely chop.

5. Assemble each parfait in a parfait glass or other tall glass that can show off the layers. Place ¼ cup of yogurt in the bottom. Top with 2 tablespoons of fruit, a sprinkle of toasted coconut, and chopped nuts. Layer with more yogurt, then repeat with fruit, coconut, and nuts. Repeat this pattern until all ingredients are used. End with a dollop of yogurt on top sprinkled with chopped nuts and toasted coconut.

Summer Stone Fruit Salad

Serves 4

This sensational summer salad made of stone and tropical fruits is overflowing with antioxidants, especially vitamins A and C.

Ingredients

3 fresh apricots, pitted and chopped
2 fresh peaches, pitted and chopped
2 fresh nectarines, pitted and chopped
2 fresh plums or pluots, pitted
  and chopped
1 fresh mango, pitted and chopped

Juice of 1 lime
½ cup walnuts, toasted and coarsely
  chopped
½ teaspoon Sweet Spice of Life
  (see page 14)

Method

1. In a large bowl, toss the chopped fruits with the lime juice.

2. Sprinkle Sweet Spice of Life over fruit and fold gently until incorporated, then add walnuts and toss lightly. Serve as is or topped with yogurt.

Autumnal Fruit Salad

Serves 4

Reminiscent of apple pie, the delightful aroma and flavor of this dish will awaken the palate.

Ingredients

4 dried figs
1½ cup unsweetened apple juice
2 large tart green apples, cubed
   (Granny Smith is recommended)
2 large Bosc or Bartlett pears, cubed
¼ cup dried currants or raisins
¼ cup dried cranberries
Juice of ½ lemon

½ cup raw almonds, soaked overnight
   in filtered water
1 tablespoon coconut oil, melted
2 teaspoons honey
½ teaspoon Sweet Spice of Life,
   divided (see page 14)
⅛ teaspoon sea salt

Method

Preheat oven to 325° F

1. In a small saucepan over low heat, combine apple juice, figs, cranberries, and currants and simmer until fruits rehydrate and look plump. Remove fruits with a slotted spoon and set aside. Chop figs into small pieces.

2. Return apple juice to burner and simmer on low heat with ¼ teaspoon Sweet Spice of Life until juice is reduced by half and coats the back of a spoon. It should have a slightly syrupy consistency.

3. Meanwhile, chop fresh fruits and toss with lemon juice.

4. Drain almonds and toss with coconut oil, honey, salt, and ¼ teaspoon Sweet Spice of Life.

5. Toast nuts in the oven until dried and aromatic, about 10 to 15 minutes. Remove from oven and cool before chopping coarsely.

6. To assemble fruit salad, transfer fresh fruit to a large bowl and toss in dried fruit. Drizzle with apple reduction "syrup" and toss with chopped nuts. Serve as is or top with yogurt.

Fresh Fruit and Nut Breakfast Cobbler

SERVES 4

Here is a quick-and-easy cobbler recipe perfect for an energizing breakfast. Unlike typical cobblers, this one is uncooked and features an all-star cast of super foods to wake up your palate and kick start your metabolism for a great day.

Ingredients

1 medium apple (choose from Granny Smith, Pink Lady, Braeburn, Fuji)
1 teaspoon freshly squeezed lemon juice
1 Fuyu persimmon, diced
½ cup fresh pomegranate seeds (optional)
½ teaspoon freshly grated lemon zest
½ teaspoon ground cinnamon
2 teaspoons chia seeds
2 teaspoons flax seeds
1 tablespoon hemp seeds (optional)

2 teaspoons bee pollen
1 tablespoon maple syrup

Cobbler Topping
2 Medjool dates, pitted and finely chopped
2 dried black figs, soaked in warm water to soften, then finely chopped
2 tablespoons coconut flakes
1 teaspoon freshly grated ginger
½ cup walnuts or pecans, toasted and chopped

Method

1. Grate apple (with peel for added nutrients) and combine with lemon juice in a medium bowl.

2. Fold in persimmon and pomegranate seeds, if using, along with zest, cinnamon, seeds, bee pollen, and maple syrup. Set aside.

3. Using a food processor, purée dates and figs together. Add coconut flakes, grated ginger, and nuts. Process until mixture comes together. It should be somewhat crumbly but stick together when pinched.

4. Form the mixture into patties and set aside.

5. Spoon fruit mixture into 4 bowls and top with cobbler patties. Serve with a dollop of yogurt or cashew cream (recipe on next page).

Cashew Cream

YIELDS 1¼ CUPS

Ingredients

1 cup cashews, soaked for 2 hours
2 Medjool dates, pitted and chopped
½ teaspoon pure vanilla extract

¼ teaspoon freshly squeezed
   lemon juice
Pinch of sea salt
1 cup coconut milk

Method

1. Drain and rinse soaked cashews and place in a high powered blender.

2. Add dates, vanilla, lemon juice, salt, and coconut milk. Coconut milk should cover cashews to a depth of about 1 inch. If not, add filtered water to bring the liquid up to the appropriate level.

3. Purée until thick and creamy. Adjust seasoning by adding a bit more salt or maple syrup, if desired.

4. Use cashew cream as a topping for Breakfast Cobbler or a delightful addition to a bowl of fresh fruit. Store cashew cream in a tightly sealed container and keep refrigerated. Cream will stay fresh for up to 3 days.

Whole Grain Goodness

Hot cereal made from a whole grain – such as oats, rice, millet, or a mix of grains – is a better breakfast choice than packaged dry cereals, which are often heavily processed and loaded with sugar, additives, and synthetic vitamins. Whole grains have not been refined, and nothing has been added or taken away – they are truly "whole" foods. Adding a high-quality protein source and some healthy fat to a bowl of grain porridge will make a complete and satisfying breakfast.

The benefits of whole grains are hardly news these days. More and more packaged cereals and breakfast bars boldly advertise the whole grain and fiber contents. Giant food corporations know this information will persuade health conscious shoppers to buy their products, but these foods are not much different than their highly processed, sugar-laden cousins. It is simply not enough to throw a few grams of fiber and some whole grains in a box of cereal and call it healthy.

Always purchase organic whole grains that are not genetically modified (non GMO). Finally, to get the most from grains, you must prepare them so that their nutrients can be properly digested.

Gluten Grains

Whole wheat, spelt, barley, kamut, and rye grains all contain gluten, a type of protein that gives these grains structure and absorbency. In bread making, the act of kneading further develops gluten. However, one of the drawbacks of gluten-containing grains is they can be hard to digest for many people. For those who do not have serious gluten allergies, such as Celiac disease, these grains can be a healthy and enjoyable part of the diet, especially if you render them more digestible through methods such as sour leavening, soaking, or sprouting.

Gluten-Free Grains

These are the easiest grains to digest because they do not contain any gluten and have a lower level of phytates (anti-nutrients) than other grains. Buckwheat, amaranth, millet, teff, wild rice, and quinoa actually have more in common with seeds than with grains. They are also high in protein and less likely to trigger the inflammatory response than such common staples as wheat and corn.

Preparing Grains

Probably the best way to prepare grains for proper digestion and uptake of nutrients is to soak and/or sprout them. Our ancestors learned this technique by watching animals like squirrels bury their nuts in the ground and then return later to eat them when they had started to sprout. Some of the preparation methods described below were discovered by trial and error. The ancient Egyptians first tried chewing raw grains and, finding that difficult, soaked them in water to make them easier to eat. Cooking the soaked grains was the next logical step, and thus hot cereal was invented. Other cooking methods were soon discovered, such as fermenting, grinding the grains with a mortar and pestle, and baking them to make bread. The soaking, fermenting, sour leavening, or sprouting of grains neutralizes enzyme inhibitors and removes the phytates that block absorption of calcium, magnesium, iron, and especially zinc, in the intestinal tract. These minerals are needed for strong bones and teeth, and for overall health and well-being.

All grains, as well as nuts, seeds, and legumes, benefit from soaking in filtered water with an acidic medium to help predigest the grain, leading to better absorption and assimilation in the gut.

Sufficient cooking releases all the nutrients locked behind the fibery cell walls of grains so they are available for our bodies to incorporate and utilize. However, to ensure the highest absorption of nutrients from grains, it is always best to soak them.

Soaking Grains, Legumes, Nuts, and Seeds

1. Cover with filtered water (to a depth of 2 inches for legumes and 1 inch for grains, nuts, or seeds).
2. Add 1 tablespoon of liquid whey, lemon juice, vinegar, buttermilk, kefir, or yogurt for every 1 cup of grain. These acids will help neutralize anti-nutrients like phytic acid.
3. Soak grains for 12 to 24 hours.
4. To remove any possible acidic taste developed during the soaking process, transfer soaked grains to a fine-mesh strainer and rinse with filtered water for about 1 minute.

Soaking Flours

Soaking flours is a method similar to making a sponge in bread making. When soaking flour for a recipe, use only the amount of liquid and flour called for in the recipe, and no other ingredients. Buttermilk, kefir, or yogurt work particularly well, as they serve as both the acid component and a liquid ingredient. If using water as the soaking liquid, adjust the amount of acidic medium accordingly; i.e., ½ cup of flour requires ½ tablespoon whey or lemon juice, whereas 2 cups of flour requires 2 tablespoons of whey or lemon juice.

Sour Leavening

This method uses a sourdough starter made from rye flour, which takes about 1 week to make. One place to find a recipe is in Sally Fallon's book, *Nourishing Traditions* – or you can buy a good sourdough bread culture from G.E.M. Cultures (gemcultures.com).

Sourdough starters are excellent for making traditional sourdough bread, quick breads, and pancakes.

To soak flour using a sourdough starter, place 3½ cups of whole-grain flour in a large bowl, add 1 cup of sourdough starter, and cover with 2 cups of filtered water. Soak for at least 3 hours and as long as 24 hours. When finished soaking, add the remaining ingredients and proceed as called for in the recipe.

Sprouting Grains

Partially sprouting grains and then dehydrating them in a low temperature oven or dehydrator is another excellent way to make gluten-containing grains easier to digest. Sprouted and dehydrated grains can also be used for making whole-grain sprouted flours. Simply run the finished grains through a grain mill and use in recipes calling for flour. Store sprouted and dehydrated flour in a tightly sealed container in the refrigerator or freezer.

LIZETTE

Home Comfort Granola

SERVES 4 TO 6

This morning cereal delivers a generous amount of fiber and great taste! Remember to chew it well in order to assimilate all the goodness.

Ingredients

2 cups quick-cooking oat flakes
½ cup raw unsalted sunflower seeds
½ cup chopped walnuts
¼ cup flaked coconut
½ cup coconut oil, melted
⅓ cup maple syrup
1 tablespoon pure vanilla extract

2 teaspoons freshly grated ginger
1 teaspoon ground cinnamon
½ teaspoon sea salt

Topping
1 cup raw wheat germ
¼ cup raisins
¼ cup dried cherries or cranberries

Method

Preheat oven to 275° F

1. Combine oats, seeds, nuts, coconut flakes, coconut oil, maple syrup, vanilla, ginger, cinnamon, and salt in a large bowl. Stir gently with a wooden spoon until thoroughly combined.

2. Transfer mixture to two parchment-lined baking sheets, spreading out evenly.

3. Bake for 50 minutes, stirring often.

4. In the last 15 minutes of baking, add the wheat germ and dried fruit.

5. Serve with nut, rice, or coconut milk. Store leftovers in an airtight container in a dark cupboard.

Amaranth Porridge

Serves 4

Amaranth was the go-to grain of the Miwok Indians on the California Coast and considered a food of the gods by the Aztecs. When cooked, this high-protein, gluten-free grain becomes delightfully creamy with a subtle tapioca-like texture.

Ingredients

1½ cups dried amaranth, soaked overnight with 1 tablespoon whey or 1 teaspoon freshly squeezed lemon juice

1½ cups coconut milk
1½ cups filtered water
½ teaspoon sea salt
1 cinnamon stick

Method

1. Measure amaranth into a glass bowl or pitcher and cover with filtered water. Stir in 1 tablespoon of liquid whey or 1 teaspoon of lemon juice and soak overnight.

2. The next morning, drain amaranth and transfer to a pot. Add coconut milk, water, salt, and cinnamon stick and bring to a boil. Cook over low heat and stir occasionally to prevent sticking, about 10 to 15 minutes.

3. As porridge starts to thicken, begin stirring constantly. At first the amaranth and liquid will be somewhat separated, but as it continues to cook it will become more uniform and thickened.

4. When porridge is smooth and thick, add the coconut oil. Serve with any combination of the toppings below.

Cooking Pearl
From Mush to Nirvana

A bowl of porridge is like a blank canvas awaiting your creative touches. Adding a variety of toppings and seasonings that appeal to your individual taste is part of what makes "mush" a fun and satisfying meal, for kids and adults. Here are some additions that add good taste and good nutrition to the meal:

- Coconut milk or nut milk
- Dried or fresh fruit
- Maple syrup or raw honey
- Favorite nuts, seeds, or nut and seed butters
- Spices like cinnamon, nutmeg, and ginger
- Booster foods like Vital Scoop™, spirulina, maca root powder, etc.

Banana Nut Quinoa and Millet Hot Cereal

SERVES 4

Quinoa and millet are delicious when cooked low and slow in fresh almond banana milk, sweetened with dates, and spiced with cinnamon. This warming, high-protein hot cereal will sustain you through a busy morning.

Ingredients

1 cup dry quinoa, rinsed and then soaked overnight in filtered water with 1 tablespoon lemon juice or whey

1 cup dry millet, soaked overnight in filtered water with 1 tablespoon lemon juice or whey

4 cups nut milk (choose almond, hazelnut, cashew, or coconut milk for best flavor)

1 ripe banana, broken in two

2 dates, pitted and coarsely chopped

½ teaspoon ground cinnamon

2 tablespoons coconut oil or unsalted butter

1 tablespoon flax seeds (ground or whole)

1 tablespoon maple syrup (optional)

Method

1. Drain quinoa through a fine mesh sieve and run filtered water through grains for 2 minutes. Once grain has been thoroughly rinsed, transfer to a bowl and set aside. Use a rubber spatula to scrape out any grains that may have stuck to the inside of the sieve. Repeat this process with the millet and transfer it to a separate bowl until ready to use.

2. In a blender, combine nut milk with banana and dates and process until smooth. Transfer the mixture to a medium-size saucepan, add a pinch of sea salt, and bring to a gentle boil over medium heat.

3. When milk just begins to bubble, lower heat slightly and add millet. Cook on medium-low heat, stirring constantly, for about 10 minutes.

4. Add the quinoa and cinnamon and cook until grains are tender, about 8 to 10 minutes. If cereal is too thick, thin with a little filtered water.

5. Stir in coconut oil or butter. To serve, top with flax seeds and drizzle with maple syrup. Add more nut milk or yogurt, if desired.

Classic Scottish Oatmeal with a Boost

SERVES 4

This traditional, hearty oatmeal gets a nutrition boost from flax, a Vitamin C surge from ground rose hips, brain- and energy-boosting fats from pumpkin seeds, and delicious flavor with a selection of spices.

Ingredients

2 cups unsweetened almond milk
½ cup unsweetened apple juice
¾ cup Scottish oats
¼ cup raw or soaked and dried
    almonds, ground into a meal

Pinch of sea salt
2 tablespoons flax seeds, ground
1 tablespoon ground rose hips
½ teaspoon ground cinnamon
2 tablespoons coconut oil
¼ cup pumpkin seeds, lightly toasted

Method

The night before: Soak oats in 1 cup of almond milk with 1 tablespoon of whey or 1 teaspoon of lemon juice in a medium-size bowl. Cover with a clean cloth and let stand at room temperature overnight.

The next day:

1. In a medium pot, bring remaining almond milk, and apple juice to a gentle boil over medium heat.
2. Add in oats , ground almonds, and salt and stir until mixture begins to thicken.
3. Turn the heat down to low. Stir in ground flax seeds, rose hips, and cinnamon and cook for another 5 minutes. Stir in coconut oil. Top with pumpkin seeds and add raw honey or chopped fruit (fresh or dried) and more nut milk, if desired.

NUTRITION GEM
Get Your C Boost with Rose Hips

Compared to an average orange, 1 tablespoon of rose hips contain 25 percent more iron, 20 to 40 percent more Vitamin C, 25 times the Vitamin A, and 28 percent more calcium. Rose hips are also a rich source of bioflavanoids, pectin, Vitamin E, selenium, manganese, and the B-complex vitamins – not to mention trace amounts of magnesium, potassium, sulfur, and silicon. Rose hips are wonderful in tea and can be ground and added to smoothies and other recipes.

Buckwheat Flax Pancakes

SERVES 4 TO 6 (APPROXIMATELY SIXTEEN 3½-INCH PANCAKES)

These pancakes are surprisingly light and hearty at the same time. Serve with real amber maple syrup and blueberries.

Gluten-Free

Ingredients

Dry Ingredients
½ cup buckwheat flour
¼ cup sorghum flour
½ teaspoon sea salt
1 tablespoon unrefined cane sugar
½ teaspoon non-aluminum
   baking powder
2 tablespoons ground flax seeds

Wet Ingredients
¾ cup cultured buttermilk
2 large eggs or flax eggs (see Cooking
   Pearl below)
2 tablespoons unsalted butter, melted
1 tablespoon filtered water

Additions
½ cup fresh or frozen blueberries

Method

1. In a large bowl, sift together the buckwheat and sorghum flours, salt, unrefined cane sugar, and baking powder, then stir in the ground flax seeds.

2. In a separate bowl, whisk together the buttermilk and eggs. Slowly drizzle in the melted butter while whisking constantly.

3. Stir the wet ingredients into the dry with a wooden spoon, then gently fold in the blueberries. Allow batter to rest for 5 to 10 minutes while heating a cast iron pan or griddle.

4. To make pancakes, drop a small pat of butter or coconut oil onto the hot pan and spread it evenly. Ladle ¼ cup of pancake batter onto pan and cook until bubbles form and edges begin to brown, then flip and cook until bottom of pancake is golden brown.

5. Transfer each finished pancake to a baking sheet and keep in a warm oven until ready to serve.

COOKING PEARL
Flax Makes a Good Egg

For an egg-free version of our pancake recipes, you can whip up an easy flax egg. To prepare, whisk 1 tablespoon of ground flax seeds with 3 tablespoons of water for every egg. Keep in mind that without eggs, pancakes will be a little denser.

Coco Banana Baby Cakes

Serves 4 to 6 (approximately sixteen 3½-inch pancakes)

Bananas and coconut make these silver dollar pancakes a hit with children and the young at heart. Ripe bananas add just the right amount of sweetness.

Ingredients

Dry Ingredients
1¼ cups barley flour
¼ cup coconut flour (Bob's Red Mill or other brand)
½ teaspoon ground cinnamon
1 teaspoon non-aluminum baking powder
1 teaspoon baking soda
½ teaspoon sea salt

Wet Ingredients
1 tablespoon maple syrup
1½ cup coconut milk
2 tablespoons melted coconut oil
2 large eggs or flax eggs
1 ripe banana, thinly sliced

Method

1. In a medium bowl, sift together the barley flour, coconut flour, cinnamon, baking powder, baking soda, and salt.

2. In a small bowl, stir together the maple syrup, coconut milk, coconut oil, and eggs.

3. Combine the wet ingredients with the dry, stirring with a wooden spoon until well combined. Fold in the sliced bananas.

4. Heat a griddle or skillet and melt 1 tablespoon of coconut oil. Spoon or ladle pancake batter onto pan and place several banana slices on top. When surface of pancake starts to bubble and the edge turns golden brown, flip and cook on the other side until bottom of pancake is golden brown.

5. Transfer each finished pancake to a baking sheet and keep in a warm oven until ready to serve. Serve alone or with a pat of butter and drizzle of maple syrup.

Gingerbread Waffles with Spiced Applesauce

Serves 6 to 8

This delightful waffle delivers the warmth of holiday spices and the earthy sweetness of molasses. Part ginger cookie and part gingerbread, it is a breakfast treat.

Ingredients

Dry Ingredients

1½ cups barley flour
1 tablespoon organic granulated sugar
1 teaspoon baking soda
1 teaspoon non-aluminum
   baking powder
1 teaspoon ground cinnamon
½ teaspoon ground ginger
¼ teaspoon ground allspice
¼ teaspoon sea salt

Wet Ingredients

¼ cup blackstrap molasses
¼ cup maple syrup
¼ cup (½ stick) unsalted butter,
   melted
1½ cups plain whole milk yogurt
2 large eggs, separated
1½ teaspoons freshly grated ginger
Pinch of sea salt

Method

1. Sift together the barley flour, sugar, baking soda, baking powder, cinnamon, ground ginger, allspice, and salt.

2. In a medium bowl, stir together molasses, maple syrup, melted butter, yogurt, egg yolks, and grated ginger until well combined.

3. Add wet mixture to sifted dry ingredients and stir until everything is smoothly incorporated.

4. In a clean medium-size bowl, beat egg whites until foamy and add a pinch of salt. Continue beating until stiff peaks form.

5. Fold ⅓ of egg white mixture at a time into the waffle batter. The batter will be light and slightly foamy.

6. Prepare a waffle maker by heating and then brushing with a thin coating of melted butter or coconut oil. Make waffles, being careful not to overfill waffle iron with batter.

7. Serve topped with warm Spiced Applesauce (see recipe on next page), a drizzle of maple syrup, and a dollop of yogurt.

Spiced Applesauce

YIELDS 2 CUPS

All it takes to dress up applesauce is to warm it up on the stove and infuse it with a few spices. The result is a rich, thick sauce that tastes like apple pie.

Ingredients

2 cups unsweetened applesauce
1 cinnamon stick

¼ teaspoon ground ginger
½ teaspoon pumpkin pie spice

Method

1. In a small saucepan, warm applesauce over low heat with the cinnamon stick and spices for 10 minutes.
2. Remove cinnamon stick and serve over gingerbread waffles or pancakes.

Date Pecan Scones

YIELDS 12 SCONES

In every coffeehouse, the pastry case features a sumptuous selection of scones, muffins, and other pastries. The majority of these baked treats are made from all-purpose flour and white sugar. Anything labeled as "whole-grain" is usually made with a small amount of whole wheat flour added to barely meet the definition. For a healthier alternative, why not make up a batch of homemade scones using spelt flour? A relative of wheat, spelt was cultivated in Iran and southeastern Europe nearly 7,000 years ago. It has 12 percent gluten content versus the 20 to 28 percent gluten in standard wheat flour, making it very tolerable for those with mild gluten issues, unless over consumed.

Ingredients

1 large egg, beaten lightly
Unsweetened almond milk, as needed
   (see Step 1 below)
2 cups spelt flour
1 teaspoon sea salt
½ teaspoon ground cinnamon
¼ teaspoon ground ginger

1 tablespoon non-aluminum
   baking powder
6 tablespoons unsalted butter, cut into
   slim pats and frozen
½ cup coarsely chopped raw pecans,
   plus 12 whole pecans for garnish
¾ cup pitted and chopped dates
2 tablespoons fresh orange
   or lemon zest

Method

Preheat oven to 425° F

1. Break the egg into a measuring cup and add enough almond milk to make ¾ cup total liquid. Place in refrigerator to chill.

2. Meanwhile, sift spelt flour, salt, cinnamon, ginger, and baking powder together in a bowl, then transfer to the bowl of a food processor, along with the butter pieces. Pulse until small lumps of butter are evenly distributed throughout the mixture (consistency should resemble coarse crumbs).

3. Transfer the mixture to a large bowl and stir in the pecans, dates, and orange or lemon zest until well distributed.

4. Gently fold the egg and nut milk mixture into the butter and flour; there is no need to mix thoroughly.

5. Turn the dough out onto a lightly floured surface. Lightly dust a rolling pin with flour and roll the dough out into a 1-inch thick rectangle. (Alternatively, you may use your hands to pat the dough into a rectangle shape.)

6. Cut dough into 12 triangles and arrange them close together on a buttered or parchment-covered baking sheet. Place 1 pecan on top of each scone. Bake for 15 minutes, or until golden brown.

COOKING PEARL
Scone Secrets

Whole-grain scones are often accused of being tough and too dense in texture. To avoid making "bricks," follow these tips for light and buttery scones:

- Keep ingredients very cold
- Sift all ingredients to aerate flour
- Work the dough as little as possible
- Do not use too much flour for dusting when rolling out the dough
- Place scones close together on pan to encourage rising, not spreading

Plum Bran Muffins

These delicious muffins are loaded with fiber and natural sweetness.

Gluten-Free

Ingredients

Dry Ingredients
1 cup almond meal (see Making Your
  Own Nut Meal/Flour, page 18)
1¼ cup oat bran
1 teaspoon baking soda
¼ teaspoon sea salt
1 teaspoon ground cinnamon
2 tablespoons ground flax seeds

Wet Ingredients
½ cup unsalted butter, softened
2 tablespoons brown sugar
  or unrefined cane sugar
2 large eggs
1 cup whole milk plain yogurt
2 tablespoons blackstrap molasses
¼ cup maple syrup
¾ cup chopped fresh plums or dried
  pitted prunes

Method

Preheat oven to 350° F

1. Lightly grease a 12-cup muffin tin with melted butter or coconut oil, or line with unbleached paper liners and set aside.

2. Use a whisk to combine dry ingredients in a large bowl. Set aside.

3. In a medium bowl, cream the butter with the sugar until light and fluffy. Add in eggs one at a time, mixing well after each addition.

4. Add yogurt, molasses, and maple syrup and mix until smooth.

5. Add wet ingredients to dry and combine well. Fold in chopped plums or prunes.

6. Fill muffin tins halfway with batter.

7. Bake for 20 minutes, or until toothpick inserted in center of muffin comes out clean.

Flax Meal Muffins

YIELDS 12 MUFFINS

This is a tasty and hearty gluten-free muffin, perfect for a quick breakfast or mid-morning snack.

Gluten-Free

Ingredients

Dry Ingredients
¾ cup brown rice flour
¾ cup buckwheat flour
½ cup ground flax seeds (grind before
   measuring)
½ cup date or palm sugar
1 teaspoon baking soda
½ teaspoon ground cinnamon
¼ teaspoon freshly grated nutmeg
¼ teaspoon sea salt

Wet Ingredients
2 large eggs
¼ cup macademia or almond oil
½ cup unsweetened applesauce
1 cup cultured buttermilk, yogurt,
   almond milk, or coconut milk

Method

Preheat oven to 375°F

1. Lightly grease 12-cup muffin tin with coconut oil, or line with unbleached paper liners and set aside.

2. In a large bowl, whisk together brown rice flour, buckwheat flour, ground flax seeds, sugar, baking soda, cinnamon, nutmeg, and salt.

3. In a second large bowl, whisk together the eggs, oil, applesauce, and buttermilk.

4. Add flour mixture to buttermilk mixture and stir until just combined. Fold in dried fruit.

5. Spoon batter into prepared muffin tins, filling halfway. Bake until golden brown and a toothpick inserted in the center of a muffin comes out clean, about 30 minutes. Cool muffins in the pan for 5 minutes before transferring them to a wire rack to finish cooling.

Adapted by Ed Bauman from Barbra Cohn, N.E.

Apple Almond Muffins with Pecan Coconut Crumble

Yields 12 muffins

The aroma of apples and spices will fill your kitchen when you bake these muffins made from ground almonds. They make a perfect late morning or afternoon snack.

Gluten-Free

Ingredients

Wet Ingredients
2 large eggs, separated
1 large egg, whole
½ cup maple syrup
½ cup unsweetened applesauce
¼ cup coconut oil, melted

Dry Ingredients
3 cups raw almonds, soaked overnight,
  dehydrated, and ground into flour
  (see Making Your Own Nut Meal/
  Flour, page 18)
1 teaspoon ground cinnamon
¼ teaspoon ground coriander

¼ teaspoon ground ginger
⅛ teaspoon freshly ground nutmeg
⅛ teaspoon ground cloves
½ teaspoon sea salt
1 teaspoon baking soda

Crumble Top
2 tablespoons coconut oil
2 tablespoons maple syrup
Pinch of sea salt
½ cup pecans, toasted and
  finely chopped
½ cup flaked coconut, toasted

Method

Preheat oven to 300° F

1. Lightly grease a 12-cup muffin tin with coconut oil or line with unbleached paper liners and set aside.

2. In a medium bowl, whisk together the egg yolks, whole egg, maple syrup, and applesauce. Set egg whites aside.

3. Slowly drizzle coconut oil into the yolk mixture, whisking to incorporate. Set bowl aside.

4. In a separate bowl, combine almond meal, cinnamon, coriander, ginger, nutmeg, cloves, salt, and baking soda. Set aside.

5. Add wet ingredients to dry ingredients and stir until well combined.

6. In a clean medium-size bowl, beat egg whites until foamy and add a pinch of salt. Continue beating until stiff peaks form.

7. Add egg whites to batter ⅓ at a time, folding gently to incorporate after each addition.

8. Fill muffin tins halfway with batter and bake for 15 minutes while you prepare the crumble topping.

9. Melt coconut oil in a saucepan. Add maple syrup and a pinch of salt. When mixture starts to bubble, stir in chopped pecans and toasted coconut flakes.

10. After muffins have baked for 15 minutes, spoon some of the crumble on top of each one and bake for another 10 minutes.

Vital Breakfast Bars

YIELDS 12 BARS

Instead of buying protein and breakfast bars, make your own! Store-bought bars tend to be loaded with sugar and protein isolates that are difficult to absorb. When you make your own, you have full control of the ingredients and can be assured of good nutrition as well as great taste and texture.

Ingredients

1 cup lightly toasted nuts (walnuts, pecans, or almonds)
½ cup Medjool dates
¼ cup dried cherries
¼ cup dried figs
2 tablespoon ground flax seeds
2 tablespoon unsweetened carob powder or raw cocoa powder

1 scoop Vital Scoop™ (or protein powder)
1 teaspoon maca powder
½ teaspoon ground cinnamon
¼ teaspoon freshly ground nutmeg
1 tablespoon fresh orange zest
2 tablespoons filtered water (or a little more, if needed)
¼ cup unsweetened shredded coconut

Method

1. Using a food processor, grind nuts to a powder.

2. Add dates, cherries, and figs to the food processor, along with the carob or cocoa powder, Vital Scoop™, maca, spices, and zest. Pulse until mixture forms a ball. If mixture is too dry and stiff, add a bit of water.

3. Press "dough" into a shallow 9x13-inch pan or a smaller pan if thicker bars are desired. Chill in the refrigerator for 1 hour, then cut into bar shapes and carefully lift out of pan. Store in an airtight container and keep refrigerated for up to 2 weeks.

NUTRITION GEM

Maca Magic

Maca is both a starchy root vegetable and tonic herb, native to the Andes Mountains of Peru and Bolivia. The Latin name is *Lepidium peruvianum*. Maca is a cruciferous vegetable that resembles a small turnip. Most often, the maca root is sun dried and powdered. It has an earthy, smoky flavor, somewhat like carob, but with a complex and bitter aftertaste, due to its sulfur compounds. The unique soil and climate of the high mountains provide maca with an array of micro and phytonutrients that contribute to its reputation as a therapeutic food.

I first encountered maca in Peru in 1979, in a market in Pucalpa. The maca was simmered in hot water with cocoa and cinnamon. Now, I often make and eat maca balls by food processing equal parts maca, carob or cacao, flax, dates, and coconut with a drizzle of water to bind the dry ingredients. For an extra boost, add matcha green tea powder to the batch. Maca balls are an excellent pick-me-up snack that, with an *Eating For Health*™ diet and lifestyle, has helped my clients manage fatigue, depression, hormone imbalance, and blood sugar instability.

Maca does not contain caffeine, but rather contains phytosterol compounds that support the HPA (hypothalamus, pituitary, and adrenal) axis. Maca may help women control hot flashes and night sweats that accompany menopause. Men can also enjoy maca to boost energy production and support their adrenal and reproductive systems that tend to decline over time. Maca is powerful so use gradually and in moderation, starting with ½ to 1 teaspoon per day.

ED

Root 'n Tuber Home Fries

SERVES 4

Potatoes are not the only spuds to consider when making home fries, as this recipe demonstrates.

Ingredients

1 medium rutabaga, medium dice
1 large parsnip, medium dice
1 medium yam, medium dice
2 medium red potatoes, medium dice
1 teaspoon sea salt

2 tablespoons ghee or olive oil
1 large onion, medium dice
½ cup coarsely chopped fresh parsley
Sea salt and freshly ground black
    pepper to taste

Method

1. Put diced rutabaga, parsnip, yam, and red potatoes in a large pot and cover with filtered water. Add a generous teaspoon of salt and bring water to a boil. Reduce the heat to medium and cook roots until slightly tender but not mushy, about 8 to 10 minutes. Drain and set aside.

2. In a large sauté pan, melt butter or olive oil over medium heat. Add onions and a pinch of salt and sauté until softened, about 5 minutes.

3. Gently stir in root vegetables and sauté over low to medium heat until lightly browned and fork tender, with crispy skins. Season with salt and pepper and toss in chopped parsley.

NUTRITION GEM
The Truth about Taters

A myth that accompanied the Atkins high-protein diet craze was that eating potatoes contributed to weight gain. Partially true, since french-fried potatoes comprise more than 80 percent of the potatoes consumed in this country. Eliminating them certainly makes sense. However, organic potatoes and other tubers and root vegetables are excellent sources of minerals, fiber, and low-glycemic carbohydrates, as long as the skin is eaten and not just the soft fleshy part. Adding nutritional yeast to potatoes provides a nice flavor complement as well as additional B vitamins, chromium, and amino acids that help the body metabolize the carbohydrates, contributing to a more stable energy supply and a more robust metabolism.

Gallo Pinto

SERVES 6

Considered the national dish of Nicaragua and Costa Rica, Gallo Pinto is made from pre-cooked beans and rice, fried with onions and spices, then garnished with cilantro. "Gallo Pinto" means spotted rooster, which is fitting with the speckled appearance of the finished dish. Costa Ricans usually use black beans while Nicaraguans favor red. Either way, it is a delicious staple.

Ingredients

Beans
1½ cups dry black beans
1 bay leaf
3 cloves garlic, peeled
    and smashed
1 small onion, peeled
    and cut in half
1 tablespoon extra virgin
    olive oil or coconut oil

Rice
1 tablespoon extra virgin
    olive oil
1 medium onion,
    chopped finely
1 medium red bell pepper,
    diced (optional)
½ teaspoon sea salt
1 teaspoon ground cumin
½ teaspoon chile powder
2 cups long-grain brown
    rice, rinsed with
    filtered water
4 cups chicken broth,
    preferably homemade,
    or filtered water

Gallo Pinto
1 to 3 tablespoons
    coconut oil
1 small yellow or Spanish
    onion, sliced thinly
3 cloves of garlic,
    smashed, skins removed
    and minced
3 cups of cooked beans
3 cups of cooked rice
1 cup of reserved bean
    broth (use as needed)
½ cup of cilantro, chopped
    finely (optional)
½ cup of crumbled Queso
    Fresco or Feta cheese
    (optional)

Method

Prepare and Cook Beans

1. The night before cooking, put beans in a large pot or bowl and cover completely with filtered water. Add 1 tablespoon of liquid whey or lemon juice. Cover beans with a clean cloth, plate, or lid and soak overnight.

2. The next day, drain and rinse beans under cold, running filtered water. Return beans to a large stock pot with enough fresh filtered water to cover beans by 1 inch.

3. Bring to a boil over medium high heat, then reduce heat to low and add bay leaf, garlic cloves, onion, and olive oil.

4. Cover and simmer until beans are fork tender, about 3 hours. Set aside. Do not drain beans; you will need the rich bean broth when making the Gallo Pinto.

Make Rice

1. About an hour before the beans are done, heat the chicken stock or water in a sauce pan.

2. In a large skillet or chef pan, sauté the chopped onion, red pepper, and a pinch of salt in olive oil until softened, about 2 to 3 minutes.

3. Sprinkle in cumin, chile powder, and remaining salt, mixing in thoroughly to coat all of the vegetables.

4. Add the rinsed brown rice and cook until it begins to smell slightly toasty.

5. Add hot chicken stock and bring to a boil, then reduce the heat to very low and simmer, covered, for 50 minutes, or until rice has absorbed all of the liquid.

6. Transfer rice to a large bowl and set aside.

From Rice and Beans to Gallo Pinto

1. In a large skillet, heat coconut oil on medium high heat.

2. Add onions and a pinch of salt and sauté until softened. Add garlic and continue cooking until aromatic.

3. Add 3 cups each of strained beans and rice and sauté together on medium heat. When pan is dry, deglaze with a little bean broth and cook until broth evaporates.

4. Continue cooking rice and beans until all flavors marry well together. About 10 minutes. Serve immediately. Add chopped cilantro and crumbled Queso Fresco (Mexican cheese) or Feta cheese.

Nutrition Gem
Rice and Beans
The Wisdom Behind a Latin American Staple

In many countries in the world, animal protein is a luxury. To provide their large families with calories, nutrients, and dietary fiber, mothers in these places have relied on three primary foods: beans, corn, and squash. In most cases, vegetables and herbs, such as chile, parsley, cilantro, onion, garlic, oregano, and cumin are added to these rather bland food staples to make them taste great and to enhance digestibility.

A traditional Latin American diet is often local, seasonal, and natural. In some areas, quinoa, amaranth, or spelt is grown as a staple grain. When a whole grain is combined with a legume, such as pinto or kidney beans, the meal delivers a complete protein, as well as ample B vitamins and minerals, such as magnesium and potassium. Adding seeds or nuts to this combination, such as sunflower seeds or almonds, delivers fatty acids important to hormone health, brain function, and healthy skin. I have often noticed a glow on the faces of traditional women who cook with local, whole foods and eschew refined foods, sugar, and alcohol.

Ed

Egg Dishes

A New Answer to an Old Question:
Which came first, the chicken or the egg?

Nutritionists have gone back and forth on the benefits of eggs for a long time. There is no question that eggs are a rich source of cholesterol, and in the 1970s it was commonly held that eating dietary cholesterol was a major contributor to elevated blood cholesterol. This was thought to be a primary risk factor for cardiovascular disease, the number one killer in the Western world.

Over time, more scrutiny has been applied to the cholesterol issue and good (HDL) and bad (LDL) cholesterol have been identified. Beyond that, scientists realized that the greatest health risk was posed by highly oxidized cholesterol compounds. It was further observed that eggs from chickens fed an organic diet, including omega-3 fatty acids, and allowed to range freely around the yard, were substantially more nutrient-rich and of greater health value than eggs from factory-confined chickens given feed containing antibiotics and growth hormones, as well as grains containing pesticide residues.

In short, the assumption that dietary cholesterol causes cardiovascular disease has been thoroughly investigated by researchers and shown to be false.

This is a new spin on the classic question: which came first, the chicken or the egg? In this instance, it is the health of the chicken that affects the quality of the egg, which in turn effects the health of the individual eating the eggs. When the egg is from a healthy bird, it is an impressive food from a nutritional perspective. Eggs contain a wide array of healthful nutrients, including protein, healthy fats, and fat-soluble vitamins and minerals.

We suggest purchasing organic eggs if available in your area and affordable for you. Requirements for eggs to be sold as organic vary from state to state. Many eggs labeled "organic" come from hens that are not confined to a small cage – an extra bonus. Called free-range, these chickens are allowed some room to roam, and some even get daily outdoor access. However, free-range hens do not always produce organic eggs and organic eggs are not always free-range. Thankfully, there is a large market of consumers for both free-range and organic eggs, so the practice of raising chickens that will fit both descriptions is rapidly growing.

Organic eggs, and those labeled free-range, generally cost more because hens that are not fed hormones will naturally produce fewer eggs, and free-range hens may lay some eggs on the ground, which are not legally allowed to be sold in some countries. Also, free-range chickens require more space, meaning lower overall egg production for the producer. The price of organic feed factors into the equation too, since it is more expensive than other types of chicken feed.

Eating eggs along with vegetables balances out the rich protein and fat of the egg with the dietary fiber and fluid present in plant foods. Cooking eggs slowly on low heat and in water (such as poaching) rather than on high heat, protects the sensitive cholesterol in the egg from being oxidized so you can enjoy the full benefits of one of nature's great foods.

ED

Salmon Asparagus Omelet

YIELDS FOUR 3-EGG OMELETS

There are many ways to make an omelet, and if you have ever watched Julia Child preparing the classic French flat omelet with her special long-handled pan, you might well become intimidated with the whole idea and just settle for scrambling. After all, omelet making is serious business in the culinary world. When chefs are being considered for a job at a fine restaurant, one of the most basic and telling tests is how well they execute the omelet. But do not let this fact deter you from trying this recipe. This omelet is a delicious breakfast, rich in protein, beneficial antioxidants, and valuable omega-3 fatty acids. And the omelet making part is actually quite fun once you get into the rhythm of the process.

Ingredients

2 tablespoons ghee or butter
1 cup diced yellow onion
½ cup diced red bell pepper
1 cup sliced cremini mushrooms
½ pound asparagus, ends trimmed
  off, cut on the diagonal into
  ½-inch pieces
12 tablespoons filtered water
  (2 tablespoons per omelet)

1 teaspoon minced fresh thyme leaves
1 tablespoon minced fresh parsley
12 large eggs
Sea salt and freshly ground
  black pepper
12 thin slices naturally smoked
  wild salmon
¼ cup goat or cream cheese
Chopped fresh dill for garnish
  (optional)

Method

1. Heat large sauté pan over medium heat and add ghee or butter. Swirl pan to distribute butter evenly across pan.

2. Add onions and sauté until they are translucent.

3. Add red bell pepper and a pinch of salt to pan and continue sautéing on medium-low heat until onions are soft and evenly browned.

4. Gently stir in mushrooms, asparagus, and a tablespoon of water. Vegetables will begin to steam. Cook until asparagus is bright in color and fork tender, about 5 minutes.

5. Stir in fresh herbs and transfer the mixture to a heat-proof bowl. Set aside. Clean sauté pan to use for making omelets.

To prepare omelet:

1. Crack 3 eggs into a medium bowl. Add 2 tablespoons of water and season with salt and pepper. Whisk gently with a fork or whisk until yolks are broken and combine evenly with the whites. Do not over beat.

2. Heat a large sauté pan over medium heat, then add 1 to 2 tablespoons of butter or ghee and swirl the pan to coat the bottom evenly.

3. When the butter begins to foam, pour the egg mixture into the center of the pan and tilt the pan to spread the eggs evenly across the bottom.

4. Cook over medium heat to allow eggs to set slightly, about 1 minute. When edges of omelet begin to set, gently lift the edges of the omelet slightly with a spatula. Gently work the spatula around the entire perimeter of the omelet to prevent the eggs from sticking to the bottom of the pan.

5. When the underside is golden brown in color and lifts easily from the pan with the spatula, the omelet is ready to fill and fold.

6. To fill omelet, spread ¼ of the asparagus and mushroom mixture across one half of the omelet, leaving a ¼-inch space around the edge so the filling will not spill out when folded.

7. Layer two slices of smoked salmon on top of the vegetable filling and dollop 2 rounded teaspoons of goat cheese or cream cheese on top.

8. Using the spatula, gently lift the unfilled side of the omelet and fold over top of the filling. Lightly press the omelet with the back of the spatula to ensure that the fold stays together.

9. Transfer to a plate and sprinkle with fresh dill if desired.

COOKING PEARL
Making the Perfect Omelet

- Beating a tablespoon or so of water with the eggs results in a fluffier omelet, but is not strictly necessary.

- Many omelet recipes call for butter. Butter prevents the omelet from sticking to the pan while enhancing the flavor of the omelet. Using clarified butter – ghee – is a delicious alternative to regular butter. Coconut oil and olive oil are other good choices.

- Chopped vegetables may be sautéed in a little butter or olive oil before adding.

- To give cast iron or stainless steel lined pans a reliable non-stick surface, sprinkle a layer of salt in the bottom of the frying pan and turn the heat up high. Cook the salt and shake it around the pan until the salt browns. Remove the salt from the pan by wiping the bottom and sides with a paper towel.

Poached Eggs Three Ways… with Wilted Greens, Shiitakes, and Caramelized Onions

Poaching eggs is hands-down the best way to prepare them for optimal flavor and nutrient value. The runny yolk is considered the perfect sauce for whatever else is on the plate: smooth, luxurious, and perfectly balanced.

Ingredients

2 tablespoons ghee or olive oil
1 medium onion, thinly sliced
3 cloves garlic, minced
2 cups sliced fresh shiitake mushrooms
  (stems discarded)
1 pound baby spinach
¼ cup Feta or other crumbly cheese
  (optional)

Poached Eggs
1 teaspoon light vinegar (rice wine,
  white wine, or apple cider)
4 large eggs
Sea salt and freshly ground black
  pepper to taste

Method

1. Add 1 tablespoon of ghee or olive oil to a heated sauté pan and sauté onions on low heat until golden and caramelized.

2. Meanwhile, in another large sauté pan, melt remaining ghee or olive oil and begin sautéing garlic on medium to low heat. Add mushrooms and continue sautéing. When mushrooms begin to release their liquid, add spinach leaves and 1 tablespoon of filtered water. Cover the pan and allow spinach to wilt.

3. Remove pan from heat and squeeze the juice of ½ lemon over spinach mixture. Place into a bowl and stir together with caramelized onions, adding salt and pepper to taste. Set aside.

4. Poach eggs as described in the Cooking Pearl on the next page. Add salt and pepper to taste.

5. When done, remove eggs from poaching water with a slotted spoon, drain briefly, and place on a small bed of spinach, caramelized onions, and mushrooms.

6. Serve on Polenta Flax Rounds (see recipe, page 87) or sprouted whole-grain toast.

How to Poach an Egg

- Start with a saucepan that is at least 3 inches deep and fill it ¾ of the way with filtered water. Bring to a simmer and add 1 teaspoon of white vinegar, which will keep the whites together.

- Crack an egg into a small dish or bowl. Carefully slide the egg from the dish into the simmering water. The white may swirl around or drift in different directions. This is okay, just let the egg poach.

- When the white looks firm (not hard) and the yolk is opaque, gently lift the egg out of the water with a slotted spoon. Transfer to a paper towel to blot dry and then to a plate.

Tomatillo Power

Tomatillos are darling looking fruits that pack a tangy and vibrant nutritional profile. They resemble small green tomatoes wrapped like little presents in a papery husk, and dangle from a bushy, annual plant like Japanese lanterns. In Spanish, tomatillo means "little tomato." They originate in Central and South America and were cultivated in Mexico by the Aztecs. Tomatillos are also referred to as jamberry or husk tomato.

Many people who enjoy Mexican food might recognize the sauces and salsa made from tomatillos more than the fruit itself. Dishes like salsa verde and salsa cruda acquire their distinctive, tart, and lemony flavor from the tomatillos, which are best used when green. Tomatillos pair well with cucumbers, onion, cilantro, and tomatoes. They can be used raw or for more intense flavor roasted or stewed.

Tomatillos contain high amounts of pectin, which helps to thicken sauces. They are also loaded with vitamin C, K, lycopene, potassium, flavonoids, and folate. To keep them fresh for a longer period of time, remove the husk and store them in a paper bag.

Poached Eggs with Guacamole Tomatillo Salsa

SERVES 4

This is guacamole with personality. The tomatillos have a lemony tang and the cilantro freshens the creaminess of the avocado. A sauce like this will bring zest to any morning meal.

Ingredients

5 medium fresh tomatillos, peeled
   and quartered
1 tablespoon extra virgin olive oil
Sea salt and freshly ground
   black pepper
1 small jalapeño chile, seeded
   and minced
1 cup fresh cilantro leaves, roughly
   chopped
½ cup finely chopped onion

1 ripe avocado, pitted and chopped
½ teaspoon sea salt, or a little more,
   to taste

Poached Eggs
1 teaspoon light vinegar (rice wine,
   white wine, or apple cider)
4 large eggs
Sea salt and freshly ground black
   pepper to taste

Method

Preheat oven to 350° F

1. Toss quartered tomatillos with olive oil, salt, and pepper and roast in the oven for 20 minutes or until softened.

2. Remove from the oven and place in a blender; process until smooth.

3. Pour tomatillo purée into a bowl and add jalapeño, cilantro, and onion. (This can either be a coarse, chunky salsa or a smoother one; blend if a smoother consistency is desired.)

4. Halve the avocado lengthwise and remove and discard the pit. Scrape the flesh into a bowl and mash with a fork. Stir in tomatillo mixture until well combined. Serve with homemade tortilla or Polenta Flax Rounds (see recipe, page 87) or use as a sauce to top eggs, enchiladas, or beans.

Poach Eggs as shown in the Cooking Pearl, page 83.

Poached Eggs with Roasted Bell Peppers, Olives, and Feta

SERVES 4

For a taste of the Mediterranean, serve this wonderful combination.

Ingredients

1 red bell pepper, halved and seeded
1 yellow or orange bell pepper, halved and seeded
1 tablespoon extra virgin olive oil
¼ cup Kalamata olives, pitted and chopped
⅓ cup crumbled Feta cheese
6 basil leaves, chiffonade
1 teaspoon extra virgin olive oil

Sea salt and freshly ground pepper to taste

Poached Eggs
1 teaspoon light vinegar (rice wine, white wine, or apple cider)
4 large eggs
Sea salt and freshly ground black pepper to taste

Method

Preheat oven to 350° F

1. Brush pepper pieces with olive oil and place face down on a parchment-lined baking sheet. Bake until skins blister and loosen from the flesh, about 20 minutes.

2. Remove peppers from the hot oven and put in a glass baking dish. Cover tightly and set aside to steam for about 10 minutes. Remove peppers from the dish and rub off the loosened skins. Slice the peppers into thin strips.

3. In a medium bowl, toss the peppers with the olives, Feta cheese, and basil. Add the olive oil and a bit of salt and pepper. Serve with poached eggs on polenta rounds or spoon over scrambled eggs.

Poach Eggs as shown in the Cooking Pearl, page 83.

Polenta Flax Rounds

SERVES 4 TO 6

This recipe is based on a traditional Caribbean dish, but is modified for healthy eating.

Ingredients

2 cups milk or unsweetened nut milk (cashew, almond, or hazelnut are delicious options)
2½ cups filtered water
1 teaspoon sea salt
1½ cups polenta or fine cornmeal
4 tablespoons extra virgin olive oil
2 tablespoons flax seeds, ground

¼ cup freshly grated Parmesan cheese (optional)
2 tablespoons pitted and finely chopped olives (choose your favorite variety)
Sea salt and freshly ground black pepper to taste

Method

1. Bring milk, water, and salt to a boil over medium-high heat. Pour in the polenta in a steady stream, stirring constantly, until incorporated. Reduce heat to medium and stir energetically with a wooden spoon or whisk until the polenta is very creamy and comes away from the sides of the pan. Add a bit more water from time to time if the mixture gets too thick but the grains are not yet tender.

2. When the polenta is done, remove it from the heat and stir in the oil, flax seeds, grated cheese, and olives. Add salt and freshly ground pepper to taste.

3. Spread polenta out on a well-greased jelly roll pan (or baking sheet with ½-inch sides), cover with parchment paper or plastic wrap, and chill in the refrigerator until set, about 30 minutes to an hour.

4. Use a biscuit cutter or glass to cut out rounds of the firm polenta.

5. Heat a pan or griddle and add 1 to 2 tablespoons of butter or olive oil, coating evenly. Place polenta rounds in the pan and cook on each side for 1 to 2 minutes, or until lightly browned.

Torta Verde

SERVES 4 TO 6

This dish is reminiscent of the "Tortilla Espanola" served in Spain – not to be confused with the thin corn wrapper of Mexican food fame. A traditional Spanish Tortilla, typically served as tapas or as a simple breakfast, is made with eggs, thinly sliced potatoes, salt, and pepper. In this rendition, we have added greens, herbs, onions, spices, dulse, and Manchego cheese to create a delicious and health-promoting dish perfect for brunch with friends. You might even want to try this dish for lunch or dinner.

Ingredients

3 tablespoons ghee or butter
3 medium red potatoes, sliced paper
  thin (about 1/8-inch thick)
1/2 medium onion, diced
6 rainbow chard leaves; leaves
  chiffonade and stems wiped clean
  and diced
2 cloves garlic, minced
8 large eggs
1 teaspoon sea salt

1/4 teaspoon paprika
1 teaspoon garlic powder
1 teaspoon dulse seaweed
1 cup fresh cilantro leaves
1 cup chopped fresh spinach
1 tablespoon extra virgin olive oil
1 tablespoon unsalted ghee or butter
1/3 cup grated Manchego cheese
Sea salt and freshly ground black
  pepper to taste

Method

1. Melt 1 tablespoon ghee in a large skillet over medium heat and add sliced potatoes in one layer. Sprinkle with a bit of salt and cook for 1 to 2 minutes on each side, or until lightly browned and tender. You may need to cook potato slices in batches and add extra ghee to the pan. Transfer finished potatoes to a plate or baking sheet layered with paper towels to blot out excess fat.

2. Wipe out skillet and melt another tablespoon of ghee. Add onions and sauté for 2 minutes. Add a pinch of salt and the diced chard stems and cook until vegetables are softened, about 5 to 8 minutes.

3. Add minced garlic and continue sautéing for another minute. Gently add the chopped chard leaves and cook until wilted. Transfer vegetable mixture to a large bowl and set aside.

4. Combine eggs, salt, paprika, garlic powder, and dulse in a blender and blend until lightly whipped. Add cilantro and spinach and blend until eggs turn a brilliant green color.

5. Fold egg mixture into sautéed vegetables until well combined.

6. Return the large sauté pan to medium-low heat. Add olive oil and ghee (or butter) and when ghee is melted, swirl it around the pan to coat evenly, then arrange cooked potatoes on the bottom.

7. Pour egg and vegetable mixture on top of potatoes and top with grated cheese. Shake the pan gently to settle the eggs and create an even layer.

8. Cook uncovered on medium-low heat until eggs are slightly firm. Cover the skillet and continue cooking until torta is set, about 10 minutes.

NUTRITION GEM
Greens and Eggs, but Hold the Ham

Dark leafy greens offer a flavor range from sweet to bitter and peppery to earthy. Their taste, texture, and nutrient content depend on the time of year, where they were grown, and their maturity when picked.

Greens are an outstanding complement to any egg or animal protein dish as they:

- Add fiber to eggs, which contain no fiber at all

- Compliment eggs in flavor and texture

- Provide a concentrated source of chlorophyll, which enriches the blood

- Are a terrific source of vitamins, minerals, and phytonutrients such as lutein, beta-cryptoxanthin, and beta-carotene

- Are rich in calcium, potassium, magnesium, iron, folic acid, and vitamin C

- Can help prevent cardiovascular disease and diabetes

- Improve circulation and immune function

- Have antitumor, anti-inflammatory, and antioxidant properties

Eggs en Cocotte

SERVES 4

Eggs (or Oeufs) en Cocotte is a classic French dish that looks fancy and involved but is remarkably simple to make for a quick morning breakfast or for Sunday brunch.

Ingredients

1 tablespoon finely chopped onion
2 tablespoons unsalted butter, divided
1 tablespoon extra virgin olive oil
¼ cup finely diced red bell pepper
1 clove garlic, finely chopped
Sea salt and freshly ground black
  pepper to taste

2 cups chopped spinach or Swiss
  chard leaves
4 large eggs
2 green onions, thinly sliced
¼ cup heavy cream

Method

Preheat oven to 350° F with rack in middle

1. Cook onion in 1 tablespoon butter and olive oil in a 12-inch heavy skillet over medium-low heat, stirring until softened, about 2 minutes. Add red pepper and garlic, season lightly with salt and pepper, and cook, stirring for 1 minute. Transfer to a medium bowl and set aside.

2. Wipe the pan clean with a paper towel and return to heat. Add a bit of oil, spinach, ¼ teaspoon salt, and ⅛ teaspoon pepper. Cook, turning with tongs, until spinach is wilted.

3. Drain spinach in a colander, pressing with a wooden spoon to remove excess liquid, then coarsely chop. Combine drained spinach with red peppers and onions.

4. Divide spinach, red pepper, and onion mixture among ramekins, or other small, ovenproof dish.

5. Crack 1 egg into each ramekin and season lightly with salt and pepper and a sprinkle of chopped green onion.

6. Spoon 1 teaspoon cream over each egg.

7. Cut remaining tablespoon butter into 8 small pieces and dot each egg with butter.

8. Put ramekins in a shallow baking pan. Pour warm water into the baking dish until it is halfway up the sides of the ramekins.

9. Carefully place the baking dish in the oven. Bake eggs for 15 to 20 minutes, or until set and golden on top.

10. Remove from the water bath. Garnish with extra green onions and serve in ramekins.

Huevos Revueltos con Ejotes
(Scrambled Eggs with Green Beans)

Serves 4

Gently scrambled eggs with green beans is a classic Central American breakfast. The idea is similar to the Mexican staple Nopalitos con Huevos (cactus with eggs). Both are quite tasty.

Ingredients

1 tablespoon unsalted butter
½ onion, thinly sliced
1¼ teaspoons sea salt, divided
1 garlic clove, mashed and minced
1 pound fresh string beans,
   ends removed, chopped into
   1-inch pieces

¼ cup plus 2 tablespoons
   filtered water
6 large eggs
¼ cup Cotija cheese (hard, dry
   Mexican grating cheese, similar to
   Parmesan)

Method

1. Heat a pan over medium heat and add butter. When melted, add the sliced onions and sauté until translucent. Add ¼ teaspoon of salt then the garlic and continue cooking another minute.

2. Add green beans and another ½ teaspoon salt and sauté for 5 minutes. Add ¼ cup water and continue cooking vegetables until green beans are bright and tender, about 5 more minutes. Transfer to a plate and set aside.

3. Wipe the pan clean with a paper towel and return to heat. Add another tablespoon of butter. While butter is melting, whisk the eggs with the water, remaining ½ teaspoon of salt, and pepper until frothy. Pour the eggs into the hot pan and wait until the eggs just begin to set before scrambling gently.

4. Fold the warm green beans in with the eggs and cook until heated through, but do not overcook the eggs in the process. Sprinkle with crumbled Cotija cheese if desired and enjoy.

Most people are willing to admit that the foundation of health is adequate nutrition. Few people however, have studied the subject of nutrition sufficiently to recognize the fact that most of our ill health today is directly the result of malnutrition, by which we are actually starving to death among plentiful supplies of supposedly good foods.

ROYAL LEE, D.D.S.
NOVEMBER 10, 1946

When food is understood and appreciated as an instrument of personal healing and sharing with community, it becomes more than our daily bread. Nourishing ourselves becomes a wise, mature, and loving act of awareness cultivated through daily practice. Periodic fasting, cleansing, intentional eating, and serving others less fortunate is what I would call Spiritual Eating.

ED BAUMAN, Ph.D.

Lunch Break
Mid Day Delights

Chapter 3

Lunch Break
Mid Day Delights

"Say, what's up? Let's meet for lunch. Where should we go?" The conversation usually revolves around various restaurants: Mexican, Chinese, pizza, or the deli counter. Unfortunately, finding healthy restaurant food is challenging because many restaurants are more concerned with surviving as a business than with providing top quality ingredients.

As an alternative to grabbing a bite at the nearest lunch place, the *Eating For Health*™ system can give you great ideas on what to eat mid day whether you are at work, on the go, or at home.

In some parts of the world, lunch is the main meal of the day and dinner is lighter fare. Time is allowed for a leisurely meal at mid-day, followed by a rest, a walk, or free time at home. This pause after eating allows the body to fully digest a big meal, which provides energy for the rest of the afternoon and evening. All of this makes good health sense.

Deciding whether your lunch will need to be light (cleansing), moderate (balancing), or more substantial (building) will depend on your metabolism and choice of diet direction. It is not wise to eat a heavy meal for lunch if you have a slow metabolism, as it will likely cause you to feel sluggish later on. Conversely, if you have a fast metabolism and eat a small, light lunch, you will be hungry very soon after eating and may find yourself snacking or thinking obsessively about food, unable to maintain concentration on the task at hand. Practicing conscious nutrition (mindfulness of your dietary needs) will help you to maintain good energy throughout the day.

The key to a nutritionally balanced meal is a proper ratio of vegetables to proteins. If a meal has 3 ounces of animal protein, it is best to consume 6 to 9 ounces of fresh vegetables with it to maintain proper acid-alkaline balance. This also ensures a healthy amount of vitamins, minerals, and antioxidants in the daily diet. Starch at lunch can consist of root vegetables or whole grains for sustained energy throughout the afternoon.

The recipes that follow are designed to meet a variety of needs. Some are quick and easy, while others take a little more time and rely on a few simple Slow Food preparations, such as soaking grains or legumes the night before. When considering easy lunch options, do not forget the beauty of leftovers. Make a batch or two of South American stew for a Sunday lunch with friends for instance, and enjoy another round of this exotic dish for lunch another day. For quicker fare, look to the salad ideas, or use one of our delicious spreads as a vegetable dip or for sandwiches.

Ed

Contents

Persimmon, Pomegranate, and Pecan Salad

SERVES 6

The fresh fruits in this salad are a delightful study in contrasts; the persimmons are brilliant orange and candy sweet, while the pomegranates are bright red and tart. The combination is truly tantalizing and vibrant.

Ingredients

Seeds of 1 large pomegranate,
   about ½ cup
4 ribs of celery, with leaves
2 small Fuyu persimmons
   (the crunchy kind)
½ cup pecan halves, toasted
4 cups mixed baby salad greens,
   washed and spun dry

1 large lemon, peel grated into long
   tendrils using a zester or vegetable
   peeler (do not include any of the
   white pith beneath the skin)
3 tablespoons extra virgin olive oil
Fresh lemon juice to taste
Sea salt and freshly ground black
   pepper to taste
¼ to ½ cup crumbled Feta cheese
   (optional)

Method

1. Remove the seeds from the pomegranate as described in the Cooking Pearl on next page and place in a large salad bowl. There should be about ½ cup.

2. Cut the celery on the diagonal into paper-thin slices and put into a salad bowl, along with any celery leaves, finely chopped.

3. Core the persimmons, cut them vertically into quarters and then cut each quarter crosswise into ¼-inch slices.

4. Add the persimmon to the bowl, along with the toasted pecans, salad greens, and strands of lemon peel.

5. Drizzle in the oil, squeeze in some lemon juice and season with salt and pepper to taste. Toss to combine and sprinkle with cheese, if desired. Serve immediately.

Adapted from Jill Abrams, N.C.

COOKING PEARL
Removing Pomegranate Seeds

An easy (and not so messy) way to remove pomegranate seeds from the husk of the fruit is to make a shallow cut near the blossom end of the fruit, then submerge the pomegranate in a bowl of water and pull the fruit apart with your fingers. The seeds will sink to the bottom of the bowl. Drain and enjoy as a refreshing snack or add to recipes as directed.

Cauliflower Couscous

SERVES 6

The cauliflower preparation mimics the texture of couscous in this grain-free recipe. For extra visual appeal, three different types of the vegetable are used, a white, yellow, and purple cauliflower. When combined with incredible flavor popping ingredients like olives, parsley, cilantro, and currants, you may never go back to traditional couscous again.

Ingredients

½ head each of white, yellow, and purple cauliflower
½ cup currants, soaked 15 minutes, then drained
3 carrots, finely diced
¼ cup finely chopped flat parsley
¼ cup finely chopped cilantro

1 tablespoon apple cider vinegar
1 tablespoon balsamic vinegar
2 tablespoon fresh orange juice
2 teaspoon ground coriander
½ teaspoon sea salt
¼ teaspoon white pepper
½ cup olive oil

Method

1. Remove core and stems of cauliflower and cut into pea-sized pieces. Alternatively, you can cut the cauliflower into chunks and pulse in a food processor until it resembles grainy crumbs. Place in a large mixing bowl.

2. Add currants, carrots, parsley, and cilantro and mix well.

3. In a small bowl, whisk the apple cider vinegar, balsamic vinegar, and orange juice together with the ground coriander, salt, and white pepper. Drizzle in the olive oil while whisking constantly until dressing is emulsified.

4. Add dressing to cauliflower couscous mixture and fold thoroughly until well combined. Allow flavors to marinate together for 30 minutes in the refrigerator.

5. Before serving, season to taste with salt and pepper. Garnish with chopped fresh parsley.

Recipe by Jennifer Una, Natural Chef

Carrot, Jicama, and Apple Slaw with Minty Citrus Marinade

SERVES 6

This recipe features jicama in grated form, which changes the texture from crunchy to light and airy. The addition of grated carrots, tart apples, and a splash of rice vinegar make this salad a refreshing treat.

Ingredients

4 medium carrots, peeled and grated
1 pound whole jicama, peeled
   and grated
2 apples, peeled and grated
1 tablespoon freshly squeezed
   lemon juice

1 lime, juiced
2 tablespoons unseasoned rice vinegar
¼ cup avocado oil or extra virgin
   olive oil
¼ cup fresh mint leaves, chiffonade
Sea salt to taste

Method

1. First, make the dressing. In a large bowl, whisk together lemon juice, lime juice, and vinegar with the oil until emulsified and season to taste with salt.

2. Grate carrots, jicama, and apple into bowl with dressing.

3. Toss everything together along with the mint and serve immediately.

Fruitless Waldorf Salad

SERVES 8

Here is a crunchy and satisfying salad perfect for lunch or a healthy snack.

Ingredients

Vegetables and Nuts
1 cup diced jicama
1 cup diced celery
1 cup diced cooked beets
1 cup diced carrots
1 cup chopped walnuts

Dressing
¼ cup omega-3 Flaxonnaise
  (see recipe, page 138)
1 cup plain whole milk yogurt
Juice of 2 medium lemons
¼ cup maple syrup
1 teaspoon ground cinnamon

Method

1. Place all the chopped vegetables and nuts in a large bowl.

2. Place dressing ingredients in a small bowl. Whisk to combine well or put in a jar and shake until emulsified.

3. Drizzle the dressing over the vegetables and nuts and stir to combine.

NUTRITION GEM
Jicama

Jicama is a crispy, sweet, edible root that has been cultivated in Mexico and South America for centuries. It has a sweet flavor and crunchy texture that is a hit in salads, salsas, and vegetable platters. Jicama is actually a legume, and it grows on vines that may reach 20 feet in length. Small to medium-sized roots of 3 to 4 pounds in weight are the most flavorful. Before eating, peel the coarse brown skin of the jicama and enjoy the glistening white pulp inside. Jicama is excellent raw and can be eaten plain or lightly steamed, with a pinch of salt, chile, and a twist of lime. Jicama is a great source of potassium, vitamin C, bioflavonoids, and fiber – making it a super snack, dip companion, and appetite quencher.

Fresh Gingered Beets

SERVES 4

These richly flavored beets are good as a side dish or on salad greens.

Ingredients

1 pound raw beets, peeled and diced into
   1-inch cubes
1½ tablespoons extra virgin olive oil
1 tablespoon red wine vinegar
½-inch piece of fresh ginger root, peeled
   and minced
1 clove garlic, minced
⅛ teaspoon freshly ground black pepper
Splash of tamari soy sauce
⅛ teaspoon sea salt
1 tablespoon minced fresh mint* (optional)

Method

1. Steam diced beets for 5 to 7 minutes. Test them for doneness by pricking with a fork. When beets can be easily pierced with a fork, transfer them to a bowl and set aside.

2. In a small bowl, whisk together the olive oil, vinegar, ginger, garlic, black pepper, tamari, salt, and mint, if using.

3. Pour the dressing over the cooled beets and marinate for 1 hour in the refrigerator. For a stronger flavor, marinate for several hours more or overnight.

4. Before serving, remove beets from the refrigerator and allow to come to room temperature.

*When mincing or chopping mint leaves, do so just before serving, otherwise leaves will oxidize and turn black.

Fresh Asparagus Salad with Meyer Lemon and Walnuts

SERVES 4

This is a perfect spring salad. It is simple, attractive, easy to make, and has a deliciously tart and minty flavor. Select young, slender asparagus spears with an even green color on the majority of the stem. Some asparagus varieties will have a beautiful, light purple tint to them.

Ingredients

1 pound fresh asparagus, tough ends snapped off and discarded, cut into 1-inch pieces
1 tablespoon of sea salt
Juice of 2 medium Meyer lemons
2 tablespoons finely chopped fresh mint

1 medium red bell pepper, julienned
3 cups chopped romaine lettuce
1 medium red onion, halved then thinly sliced
1 cup raw walnuts

Method

Preheat oven to 325° F

1. Prepare an ice bath by filling a mixing bowl halfway with ice and covering it with water.

2. Bring 2 quarts of water and sea salt to a boil. Add the asparagus and cook for 3 to 4 minutes until they turn bright green and are tender-crisp. Using a slotted spoon or tongs, carefully transfer the asparagus from the pot to the ice bath. Remove when they are cold, about 1 minute. Drain well.

3. In a bowl, combine the asparagus with the lemon juice, mint, red peppers, and red onions. Toss lightly and refrigerate until well chilled, about 3 hours.

4. Meanwhile toast walnuts in the oven for 8 minutes. Cool a bit, then chop and set aside.

5. To serve, place romaine on a chilled platter and top with marinated vegetables and walnuts.

COOKING PEARL

Blanching and Shocking

Blanching and shocking are easy techniques cooks use to keep vegetables crisp and tender, while preserving texture, color, and flavor.

To blanch and shock successfully, follow these steps:

1. Bring a large pot of water to boil. Add a tablespoon of sea salt to the water for added flavor. Salt also helps brighten the color of vegetables during the blanching process.

2. While waiting for the water to boil, fill a large bowl with cold, filtered water and ice cubes.

3. When water comes to a boil, add vegetables, being careful not to plop them in the pot to avoid splashing water. To do this safely, simply place the vegetables in a bowl and gently tip the bowl into the pot, allowing the vegetables to slide into the water slowly, or use tongs to place the vegetables into the water.

4. Be sure the vegetables are submerged in the boiling water so they blanch evenly. When the vegetables brighten in color, they are ready.

5. Carefully scoop out the vegetables with a slotted spoon or sieve and immediately place them in the iced water bath.

6. Transfer cooled and blanched vegetables to a bowl until ready to use. Blot them gently and thoroughly with a clean towel.

Tips for Successful Blanching

Although blanching is an easy cooking technique, it is also easy to overcook. Follow these simple guidelines and your blanched veggies will be tender, crisp, and brightly colored:

- **Watch closely.** Once the color of the vegetable brightens, take out and shock in ice cold water.

- **Add a few vegetables at a time.** Adding too many vegetables will slow the blanching process by cooling the water. This can result in dull and limp vegetables.

Carrot Seaweed Salad

SERVES 4

The subtle sweetness and crunch of carrots and the savory saltiness of seaweed are perfectly matched in this salad. A simple blend of apple cider vinegar and honey brings everything together in this mineral-rich sensation.

Ingredients

½ cup arame seaweed
1 cup grated carrots
1 teaspoon apple cider vinegar

½ teaspoon honey
¼ teaspoon chopped fresh dill

Method

1. Cover arame with filtered water and soak the seaweed for 30 minutes, then drain and rinse.

2. In a large bowl, whisk apple cider vinegar and honey together until well combined.

3. Add drained arame and carrot to the dressing and toss lightly to distribute evenly. Add dill and toss again before serving.

NUTRITION GEM
Sea Vegetables

Sea vegetables, also collectively called seaweed, are large, edible algae that can be harvested and eaten in soups, salads, and many other dishes. Seaweed is one of the most nutrient-dense foods on the planet, rich in minerals and trace elements not found in land animals or plants. Very low in calories, sea vegetables are a wonderful snack food that naturally boost your metabolism.

I enjoy eating dried seaweed such as hiziki, dulse, or arame broken up into pieces with almonds in a snack mix. The salty, pungent flavor is a nice contrast to the sweet and oily taste of nuts.

ED

Chopped Deviled Egg Salad

SERVES 4

This turbo charged egg salad is a medley of satisfying protein, great quality fats, energizing minerals, and booster foods. Use as a filling for sandwiches, top on whole-grain crackers, or on a bed of crisp lettuce greens.

Ingredients

6 eggs, hard cooked, peeled
   and chopped
2 avocados, pitted, skins removed,
   and diced
½ cup celery, diced
⅔ cup red pepper, diced
¼ cup of extra virgin olive oil
2 tablespoons of yogurt, sour cream,
   kefir, or mayonnaise

2 tablespoon of nutritional yeast
2 tablespoons Dijon mustard
1 teaspoon toasted and crushed
   cumin seeds
¼ teaspoon sea salt or more to taste
1 tablespoon fresh dill, chopped
1 tablespoon whole flax seeds
Freshly ground pepper
Paprika (optional)

Method

1. Combine chopped eggs, avocados, celery, and red pepper in a medium bowl.

2. In a small bowl, whisk olive oil, yogurt, nutritional yeast, mustard, cumin seeds, and salt.

3. Pour over egg and avocado mixture and fold together until all ingredients are thoroughly combined.

4. Add chopped fresh dill and flax seeds. Stir together lightly. Finish with a little more sea salt if desired, freshly ground pepper, and a few sprinkles of paprika if using.

5. Serve on whole-grain bread, with crackers, or cut raw vegetables.

Land and Sea Salad

SERVES 2

Eat this salad when you want to balance, build, and cleanse – all at the same time.

Ingredients

2 ounces salmon, tuna,
    or sardines (fresh, flash-frozen,
    or canned in spring water)
2 ounces cooked skinless chicken
    or turkey breast
2 cups fresh baby salad greens
½ cup grated carrot
½ cup cucumbers, peeled, seeded
    and thinly sliced
¼ cup fresh sunflower, clover, and/or
    broccoli sprouts
½ small red onion, cut in half
    and thinly sliced
1 medium red or yellow bell pepper,
    seeded and sliced into thin rings
2 tablespoon flax seeds, whole
    or ground
Sprinkle of kelp powder (optional)

Salad Dressing
⅓ cup red wine vinegar
½ cup extra virgin olive oil
1 clove garlic, minced
1 tablespoon minced fresh basil
2 teaspoons minced fresh
    oregano leaves
2 teaspoons minced fresh
    thyme leaves

Method

1. Poach, steam, or grill the fish and bake or grill the chicken or turkey.

2. Chop, slice, or flake the meat.

3. In a bowl, whisk together the vinegar, oil, garlic, basil, oregano, and thyme. Set aside.

4. Place all of the salad ingredients, except the meat, in a large bowl and toss gently with the dressing. Divide equally among 2 plates and top each serving with a portion of the fish and chicken.

108   FLAVORS OF HEALTH

Dressings for Any Occasion

Store-bought salad dressings are pricey and never deliver the fresh flavor or health benefits of homemade. A great salad dressing has several key components: a premium oil, such as extra virgin olive oil; an acid such as fresh lemon or lime juice, or vinegar such as balsamic or red wine vinegar; an emulsifier, such as prepared mustard or ground flax seeds; a raspberry or date, or some organic cane sugar or maple syrup, to balance out the sharpness of the sour flavor; some pungent herbs, such as thyme, oregano, marjoram, or dill; and a pinch of sea salt to enhance all the flavors.

Consider the ingredients of the salad when deciding what dressing to make. With a salad of pungent, bitter greens, a mildly sweet dressing would be a good fit. For a salad containing salmon or chicken, something with a bit of garlic or ginger would be helpful to the digestive process.

Commercial dressings generally deliver too many calories and too few nutrients to be healthful. A well-crafted homemade dressing, conversely, is made with excellent ingredients that enhance the salad's flavor and nutrition profiles. Salad dressings made with high-quality oil and a protein – such as miso, yogurt, Feta, or blue cheese – provide enough taste and nutrition for a main-meal salad as well as the typical side salad.

Toss the dressing with the salad just before serving so the leaves and vegetables do not get soggy. Do not over-dress: Two tablespoons of dressing to a handful of salad greens (about 1½ cups) is a good rule of thumb. Keep some of the salad mix undressed for your next meal and refrigerate it in a plastic bag with a paper towel to absorb excess moisture.

Ed

Blue Cheese Dressing

YIELDS 1¼ CUP

Here is a traditional favorite made with yogurt and olive oil for a healthy twist.

Ingredients

½ cup blue cheese
1 cup whole-milk yogurt
2 tablespoons minced chives
  or green onions
2 tablespoons extra virgin olive oil

2 tablespoons freshly squeezed
  lemon juice
1 teaspoon honey
Sea salt and freshly ground pepper
  to taste

Method

1. Crumble blue cheese into a blender and add in the remaining ingredients. Purée until smooth.

2. Taste and add additional salt and black pepper, if needed.

COOKING PEARL
Blue Cheese Dressing Pairings

Blue cheese dressing pairs beautifully with thick, crunchy wedges of Iceberg lettuce, a classic combination dating back to the 1950s, but here are some other ways to enjoy it.

- Mix green and red leaf lettuce with radicchio, frisee, and other more bitter greens for a refreshing, crunchy treat.

- Include grated green apples and/or cabbage.

- Use as a dip for raw vegetables like carrots, zucchini, jicama, celery, and radishes.

- Grate or shred carrots, radishes, kohlrabi, and cabbage. Toss with blue cheese dressing and some herbs like tarragon, chevril, or parsley.

Viva Italia Dressing

YIELDS 1¾ CUPS

This salad dressing is quite versatile. You can vary the flavor by using different types of vinegar.

Ingredients

½ cup vinegar (apple cider, sherry, or balsamic)
¼ cup filtered water
2 cloves garlic, minced
1 teaspoon Dijon mustard
1 teaspoon nutritional yeast
1 teaspoon flax seeds
1 teaspoon dulse flakes

1 cup extra virgin olive oil
1 tablespoon finely chopped fresh parsley*
1 tablespoon finely chopped fresh basil*
1 teaspoon finely chopped fresh oregano*

Method

1. In a blender, combine vinegar, water, garlic, mustard, nutritional yeast, flax seeds, and dulse flakes. Purée.

2. With blender on low speed, slowly add olive oil in a thin stream.

3. When dressing is emulsified, pour into a mason jar and add the parsley, basil, and oregano. Season to taste with sea salt and freshly ground pepper.

4. Store in the refrigerator for up to 3 days if using fresh herbs or up to 1 week if using dried herbs. Before serving, cap the jar tightly and give the dressing a good shake to recombine the ingredients.

*If fresh herbs are unavailable, use 1 teaspoon each of parsley and basil and ¼ teaspoon of oregano. Finish with a pinch of sea salt and freshly ground black pepper.

French Boost Dressing

YIELDS 1¾ CUPS

This salad dressing is a very zesty and flavorful vinaigrette.

Ingredients

2 ripe Roma tomatoes, puréed
    in blender
¼ cup filtered water
½ cup vinegar (champagne, apple
    cider, rice, or balsamic)
2 cloves garlic, minced
1 teaspoon Dijon mustard
1 teaspoon nutritional yeast

1 teaspoon flax seeds
1 tablespoon red wine (optional)
1 cup extra virgin olive oil
1 tablespoon fresh parsley
1 teaspoon dried basil
1 teaspoon dried oregano
Pinches of sea salt, paprika, and freshly
    ground black pepper

Method

1. In a blender, purée the tomatoes with the water until smooth.

2. Add vinegar, garlic, mustard, nutritional yeast, flax seeds, and red wine.

3. With blender on low speed, slowly add olive oil in a thin stream.

4. When dressing is emulsified, pour into a mason jar and add fresh parsley, basil, and oregano. Give the jar a shake and season to taste with salt and pepper.

5. Store in the refrigerator for up to 3 days. Before serving, cap the jar tightly and give the dressing a good shake to recombine the ingredients.

Poppy Seed, Orange, and Tahini Dressing

YIELDS 1 CUP

Fresh orange juice and flecks of poppy seed bring exotic and slightly floral elements to this dressing. Try it on crunchy lettuces or use it as a sauce for sautéed winter greens.

Ingredients

⅓ cup sesame tahini
⅓ cup whole-milk cow or goat yogurt
½ cup freshly squeezed orange juice
3 tablespoons brown rice vinegar
2 teaspoons toasted sesame oil

2 garlic cloves, peeled
2 tablespoons fresh poppy seeds
⅛ teaspoon ground fennel seeds
Sea salt and freshly ground black
    pepper to taste

Method

1. Purée tahini, yogurt, orange juice, brown rice vinegar, toasted sesame oil, and garlic cloves together in a blender until very smooth.

2. Add poppy and fennel seeds and blend a bit more. Taste and season with salt and pepper as desired.

3. Store in the refrigerator for up to 3 days. Before serving, cap the jar tightly and give the dressing a good shake to recombine the ingredients.

Sesame Tahini

Tahini has a special place in my heart and in my health history. When I worked at Home Comfort restaurant in the early 1970s, I was on my feet from 8 a.m. until 10 p.m. most days. I was able to sit down in the mid afternoon between lunch and dinner service, but that was about it. Gradually, I noticed that my legs were becoming quite swollen and achy. At first, I thought it was just wear and tear, but it became so aggravated that one day I went to the urgent care center. When they checked it out, they determined that I had a blood clot on my inner right calf. This is called phlebitis.

I was given a shot of coumadin, a blood thinner, that cleared out the clot, at which time my leg returned to normal. I was advised to continue on this medicine for the rest of my life.

Being just 25 years old at the time, I looked into alternatives and read that sesame tahini was an excellent source of vitamin E, minerals, and bioflavonoids that are strengthening to weak capillaries, which contribute to a breach of a vein that can cause the body to clot as a protective measure against hemorrhaging.

I began to make tahini and applesauce pudding every day, and also made sure not to stand on my feet for such long hours. I have a mark where the clot was but, nearly 20 years later, there have been no further cardiovascular or circulatory issues.

Tahini is a wonderful source of calcium, magnesium, B vitamins, and protein, making it a wonderful food for vegetarians and omnivores alike. It tastes great on toast with a healthy fruit purée and has many delicious uses in cooked dishes, as well.

Ed

Soups and Stews

One whiff of a savory aromatic soup and appetites come to attention… An inspired soup puts family and guests in a receptive mood for enjoying the rest of the menu.

Louis P. De Gouy, The Soup Book (1949)

I remember eating canned soup growing up. Campbell's French Onion, Chicken Noodle, Hearty Beef Stew, Cream of Mushroom, and – best of the lot – Progresso's Italian Minestrone. Even as a boy of about 10 years old, I thought these soups were only okay, not outstanding.

A little later, I encountered a homemade matzo ball soup made from fresh chicken, with the chicken meat in the soup along with fresh vegetables. Wow, what a difference! I asked my mom if I could make a homemade soup, and she said, "Well, I guess so." That was one of my earliest cooking experiences, making wonderful, rich corn and potato chowder under my mom's watchful eye. I even helped clean up, which was a sign of great professional potential to come.

Fortunately, my mom did not say "no" to my cooking when I was young, saying it was too messy, or we did not have enough time, or there was not enough money to buy fresh ingredients.

I started reading the *Joy of Cooking* to get a few ideas, then put it down and started cooking to taste, a sure indication that I was on my way to being a Natural Chef.

Later on, when I had become a vegetarian in my early twenties, I loved to make lentil vegetable soup and, my all-time favorite, mushroom barley with lots of garlic and fresh herbs, cooked on a wood-burning Home Comfort stove at our organic farm in western Massachusetts. To accompany the homemade soup, I would whip up some homemade garlic bread (even ground the flour by hand for the whole-grain bread), and make Parmesan-herb croutons from dry bread that was a day or two old.

After making a soup or a stew from scratch, you will never again enjoy eating soup out of a can. It is just not the same. The beauty and fun of making soups and stews is that you can add just about anything you have on hand in the realm of vegetables, grains, tubers, mushrooms, and proteins. The only limit is your imagination.

For me, the key to a great soup is to start by sautéing a couple of garlic cloves per person, along with half an onion per person, then some herbs and spices such as ginger, curry, and green herbs to create an amazing aroma. When these ingredients are beginning to brown, I add filtered water – or homemade stock if I have some on hand – as the cooking liquid.

From there, I braise the animal proteins if they are part of the dish and begin adding the slower cooking foods, such as soaked legumes and root vegetables, to the soup pot. Next come the less dense vegetables, leafy greens, and more herbs and spices. I often add flax seeds to my soup to thicken the broth a bit. I am nuts about adding seeds to all kinds of dishes.

A vegetable soup can be delicate rather than hearty, with a nice herb broth, finely chopped vegetables, and miso for flavor. Miso is a fermented soy paste that can be white, yellow, red, or brown. The darker the miso, the longer it has been fermenting and the stronger its flavor. I like using lighter miso for warm-weather soups and the darker ones for cold-weather soups.

A stew is similar to a soup but is less brothy. As such, it is heartier and can be served over brown rice or gluten-free noodles made of quinoa or buckwheat.

Soups and stews can be ongoing projects: revive them after a day or two by adding fresh vegetables like celery or carrots and additional herbs and spices, such as thyme or garlic.

Soups and stews are very economical and can be either the centerpiece or side dish of a meal. They store well in the refrigerator or freezer and can be taken to work or school for lunch in a thermos, which keeps them warm, or in a container that can be reheated in a toaster oven.

Consult the stock chapter on page 20 to learn how to make wonderful broths, including vegetable and chicken stocks.

Making and eating soup or stew on a regular basis is a boon to your own and your family's health and well-being.

ED

COOKING PEARL
How to Make Silky Smooth Soup

Making puréed soups as silky and smooth as those served in fine restaurants requires something more than the trusty and time-saving immersion blender. One essential tool is a good blender (like a Vitamix), or food processor, and a sieve or chinois. The latter is a funnel shaped, fine-mesh sieve. To make silky soup, first ladle the soup into the blender or food processor, filling no more than two-thirds full. Begin puréeing at low speed, then increase to high speed until well blended. You will need to do this in batches. Return puréed soup to the pot by passing it through a fine-mesh sieve or chinois. Use a wooden spoon if necessary to press the soup through the sieve.

Tomato and Red Pepper Soup with Red Miso

SERVES 6

Tomatoes are high in the cancer-protective antioxidant lycopene, which becomes more concentrated and potent when cooked. Miso adds a rich complementary flavor.

Ingredients

1 tablespoon coconut oil or ghee
2 medium onions, chopped
4 stalks celery, diced
2 medium carrots, diced
1½ tablespoons minced fresh ginger
¾ cup mirin (seasoned, rice wine)
2 pounds ripe tomatoes, red or heirloom, seeded and chopped (or 2 1-pound cans or packages of whole tomatoes)
1 small head of garlic, roasted (see next page)
1 pound red bell peppers, roasted and peeled (see next page)

6 to 8 cups vegetable broth, preferably homemade
Tomato paste, as needed
1 teaspoon freshly ground black pepper, or to taste
⅔ cup red miso
Sea salt and pepper to taste

Garnish
2 teaspoons minced fresh ginger
½ cup plain whole milk yogurt
¼ teaspoon nutritional yeast
3 green onions, very thinly sliced

Method

1. Heat a stock pot over medium heat and add the oil or ghee. Add the onions, celery, and carrots. Reduce heat to low, cover, and sweat vegetables for about 15 minutes. Do not allow the vegetables to brown. Add the ginger and stir for another few minutes.

2. Deglaze the pan with the mirin and then add the tomatoes, roasted garlic, and red peppers. Sweat for another 15 minutes.

3. Add the vegetable broth, starting with about 6 cups. Bring to a simmer and cook for 45 minutes to an hour. Taste. If the tomato flavor is not strong enough, add a tablespoon or two of tomato paste. Season with pepper to taste. Do not add salt yet.

4. Turn off the heat, using an immersion blender, purée the soup until smooth. If the soup needs thinning, more stock can be added. Adjust seasoning, if necessary.

5. Pour a cup of soup into a bowl and whisk in the red miso until smoothly incorporated. Pour this mixture back into the soup. Taste and adjust seasonings as necessary.

6. Combine the ginger with the yogurt and nutritional yeast. Garnish each serving of soup with a few slivers of green onion and a swirl of the yogurt mixture.

COOKING PEARL
Roasting Vegetables to Maximize Flavor

Peppers

Preheat to 375° F

To roast bell peppers, cut them in half and discard the stem, seeds, and white membrane. Place the peppers cut side down on a parchment-lined baking sheet and bake in oven until skins blister and loosen. Transfer the roasted peppers to a bowl and top with a plate, or place in a paper bag and fold it closed. Set aside for 10 minutes or so to further steam and loosen the skins, then peel away the skins. Once the skins are removed, the peppers are ready to be sliced or diced into your favorite dishes.

Garlic

Preheat to 375° F

Select a large, firm bulb of garlic. Slice off stem end (not root end) of garlic to barely expose the cloves. Layer a square of foil with a square of parchment paper and place garlic bulb in the center. Drizzle about 2 to 3 teaspoons of olive oil on the exposed cloves. (Other oils such as coconut or sesame may be used instead.) Wrap bulb securely in parchment-lined foil. Roast until cloves are very tender; about 1 hour. When done, the garlic cloves will be quite soft, like room temperature butter. Allow to cool slightly, then squeeze out the garlic pulp, discarding the papery husk. Roasted garlic imparts an intense, aromatic, and almost buttery flavor. Use it to enhance the flavors of any savory dish.

Roasted Garlic, Sweet Onion, and Almond Soup

SERVES 4

This recipe is inspired by a classic Spanish soup – a white gazpacho known as Ajo Blanco made with garlic, almonds, white bread, vinegar, and oil. Served warm instead of cold, this version trades the day-old bread with slow roasted onions and garlic scented with thyme and rosemary.

Ingredients

4 medium garlic bulbs
4 large Vidalia onions or yellow onions
4 medium shallots
2 tablespoons almond oil, divided
1 teaspoon dried thyme, divided
2 teaspoons dried rosemary, divided
1 tablespoon butter or ghee
3 tablespoons sherry vinegar
4 cups chicken or vegetable stock

Sea salt and pepper to taste
⅓ cup fresh chervil, chopped finely

Crispy Herbed Almonds
1 cup almonds, blanched
    and skins removed
½ teaspoon sea salt, divided
1 teaspoon dried thyme
1 teaspoon dried rosemary
1 tablespoon butter or ghee, melted

Method

Preheat oven to 350° F

1. Line a baking sheet with a sheet of parchment paper.

2. Quarter onions, leaving skins on, and place them in a large bowl with separated shallot cloves.

3. Toss onions and shallots with 1 tablespoon of almond oil, 1 teaspoon of thyme and 2 teaspoons of rosemary. Reserve remaining herbs for toasting almonds.

4. Place onions and shallots on the baking sheet.

5. Cut the stem end off of each garlic bulb and drizzle with almond oil.

6. Place garlic bulbs on baking sheet.

7. Cover all of the vegetables with an additional sheet of parchment paper and then line the top with a sheet of aluminum foil. Crimp the edges of the foil over the baking sheet to form a large packet.

8. Roast onions, shallots, and garlic in the oven for about 1 hour or until garlic cloves are very soft. Onions and shallots should also be soft and slightly caramelized.

9. While vegetables are roasting, prepare almonds.

Crispy Herbed Almonds

Preheat to 325°F

1. Bring a medium saucepan of water to boil and add ¼ teaspoon of salt to the water. Add almonds and blanch until almond skins look wrinkled.

2. Carefully remove almonds with a slotted spoon and place in a bowl of cold water. Remove almond skins by gently pinching almond between thumb and index finger. The skins should slip off easily.

3. Transfer skinned almonds to a small bowl and toss with 1 tablespoon of melted butter, the remaining thyme and rosemary, and ¼ teaspoon of salt.

4. Spread almonds on a parchment-lined baking sheet and bake for 8 to 10 minutes or until almonds are lightly toasted.

5. Remove almonds and transfer to a cold plate. Set aside.

Finish Soup

1. When vegetables are roasted, remove them from the oven. Remove the skins of the onions and shallots and squeeze the garlic cloves from their peels.

2. Set an 8-quart pot on the stove and bring to medium heat. Add 1 tablespoon of butter. Once melted, add roasted onions, shallots, and garlic and cook on medium high heat until vegetables start to sizzle.

3. Deglaze pan with sherry vinegar and cook for another 2 minutes.

4. Add chicken broth and bring soup to a boil. Reduce heat and add ½ cup of the herbed almonds and simmer for about 10 minutes.

5. Remove soup from heat and allow to cool slightly before ladling into a blender.

6. Purée soup until very smooth.

7. Rinse and dry out soup pot and set a fine mesh sieve over the pot. Slowly pour soup from blender through sieve, using a wooden spoon to gently stir and press soup through the sieve.

8. When all of the soup has been passed through the sieve, turn heat back on to gently warm soup. Taste and add sea salt and pepper if desired.

9. Serve immediately. Top each serving of soup with a few remaining almonds and a bit of chopped chervil. For an added treat, drizzle with a bit of olive oil or a dollop of créme fraîche if desired.

Thai Coconut Milk Soup with Spaghetti Squash

SERVES 8

This is a lovely, aromatic, and hearty soup for a lunch, brunch, or any celebratory meal.

Ingredients

1 medium spaghetti squash
2 tablespoons coconut oil, melted
1 pound cooked chicken, cubed
¼ cup tamarind paste or ½ cup dried apricots soaked in filtered water to soften
1-inch piece fresh galangal, thinly sliced (or ginger, if galangal is not available)
2 small Thai chiles, seeds removed, chopped finely
1 large red onion, cut in half and thinly sliced
4 sticks lemongrass, ends trimmed off and outer leaves removed
10 kaffir lime leaves, torn in half (use lemon basil if kaffir lime leaves are not available)

6 cloves garlic, minced
1 large bunch fresh cilantro, stems finely chopped and leaves reserved
3 14-ounce cans coconut milk
6 cups vegetable stock, preferably homemade (see stock recipe, page 25)
1 pound fresh shiitake mushrooms, stems removed, sliced
3 tablespoons Thai fish sauce
1 teaspoon curry powder
1½ cups cherry tomatoes, smashed
Juice of 1 lime
2 green onions, thinly sliced
1 tablespoon nutritional yeast, or to taste
Sea salt and freshly ground black pepper, to taste

Method

Preheat to 350° F

1. Slice spaghetti squash in half, remove and discard seeds, and brush with 1 table-spoon of melted coconut oil.

2. Place squash cut side down on a baking sheet lined with parchment paper. Bake for 35 minutes, or until squash is tender when pierced with a fork.

3. Meanwhile, prep the other ingredients. To prepare the lemongrass, smash the pale, bulb end to release its floral, lemony aroma and roughly chop it into 2-inch lengths, discarding the tough, dry part of the stalks.

4. When the squash is finished baking, remove it from the oven and allow to cool, then use a fork to scrape the squash into strands.

5. Transfer squash to a bowl and toss with remaining 1 tablespoon coconut oil and salt to taste.

6. Place the chicken in a large, heavy-bottomed saucepan and add tamarind, galangal, chiles, red onion, lemongrass, kaffir lime leaves, garlic, and cilantro stems. Cover with filtered water and bring to a boil over medium-high heat, then reduce heat to medium-low and simmer for 30 minutes.

7. Add the coconut milk, stock, shiitake mushrooms, fish sauce, and curry powder. Bring back to a simmer and cook for 30 minutes over medium-low heat.

8. Add spaghetti squash, tomatoes, and cilantro leaves to the soup. Taste and season with salt, pepper, and lime juice according to your taste.

9. Remove lemongrass pieces and kaffir lime leaves before serving. Ladle into bowls and garnish with sliced green onions and a sprinkle of nutritional yeast.

Using Lemongrass

Lemongrass is a tough perennial grass blade used widely in Thai and Vietnamese cooking. It is an extremely aromatic and potent herb with a strong lemony, floral scent that combines beautifully with garlic, chilies, and cilantro. To coax out its special flavor and aroma, smash the white, bulbous portion of the lemongrass stalk with a mallet or bruise it by whacking against a counter. Hints of lemon and floral aromas will immediately fill the air.

Since lemongrass is very pungent, a little goes a long way. It tends to remain tough even after long, slow cooking, so for soups and curries it is best to cut the lemon grass in large pieces after bruising so it can be easily removed before serving.

For a stronger lemongrass flavor, chop the tender parts of the lemongrass very finely so fibers will break down more easily during cooking.

NUTRITION GEM

Lemongrass Spells Relief

Lemongrass is rich in a substance known as citral, the active ingredient in lemon peel. This substance is known to aid digestion and relieve spasms, muscle cramps, rheumatism, and headaches. It makes a great herb tea as well as a delicious ingredient for flavoring soups and sautéed dishes.

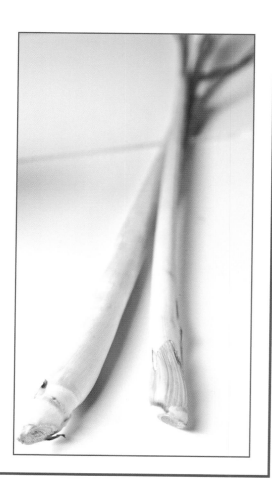

Jolly Green Gazpacho

SERVES 4

Cold soups like gazpacho are a refreshing and rejuvenating lunch option, perfect for a hot summer day. Most gazpacho recipes are tomato-based but to work more green foods into the day, this version is loaded with peas, avocado, cucumber, zucchini, tomatillos, and even green grapes.

Ingredients

¼ cup fresh or frozen peas, blanched
1 large avocado, sliced in half, pitted
   and peeled
1 cup chopped, English cucumber,
   seeds removed
1 cup chopped, zucchini
3 small tomatillos, husks removed
   and chopped
½ medium yellow pepper, chopped
½ medium jalepeño pepper, seeded
   and chopped

¼ cup green grapes
2 to 3 cloves garlic, peeled
1 medium lime, juiced
1 tablespoon fresh mint leaves
   (about 5 mint leaves)
2 tablespoons fresh cilantro leaves
1 green onion, chopped
1 cup coconut water
2 tablespoons extra virgin olive oil
Sea salt and pepper to taste

Method

1. Prepare an ice bath by filling a large bowl with filtered water and plenty of ice cubes. Set aside.

2. Fill a small pot with filtered water and stir in 1 teaspoon of sea salt. Bring to a boil. Add peas and blanch until they turn bright green. Using a slotted spoon, transfer peas into the ice bath to shock. Drain and set aside.

3. Add peas and remaining ingredients to a blender and purée until smooth. Add salt and pepper to taste.

4. Transfer mixture to a bowl and chill in the refrigerator for 30 minutes to 1 hour. To serve, ladle into chilled bowls or glasses.

NOTE: For a cold and slushy gazpacho, add 4 to 5 ice cubes to blended ingredients.

South American Black Bean and Yucca Stew

SERVES 6

This colorful stew is inspired by indigenous Latin American ingredients such as yucca, corn, beans, and quinoa. It is loaded with antioxidants from the carrot and tomato juices. The beans are cooked with the Mexican herb, epazote. This herb not only imparts a distinctive Latin American flavor, it also improves digestion and eliminates the gassy tendency associated with beans. The combination of the beans and quinoa, a staple food in Peru and Bolivia, creates a complete protein meal.

Ingredients

Beans

1 cup black beans,
   soaked overnight with
   1 tablespoon of liquid
   whey or lemon juice
A few sprigs fresh epazote,
   or 1 tablespoon dried
   epazote, available in
   Hispanic grocery stores
1 bay leaf
3 cloves garlic, smashed
   and peeled
1 tablespoon extra virgin
   olive oil
Sea salt to taste

Yucca

3 cups peeled yucca root,
   cut into 1-inch cubes
Juice of 1 medium lime
1 tablespoon extra virgin
   olive oil
Sea salt to taste

Stew

1 tablespoon coconut oil
1 cup diced onions
3 cloves garlic, chopped
1 tablespoon chile powder
1 tablespoon dried
   Mexican oregano
1 teaspoon dried cumin
3 cups canned diced
   tomatoes, drained,
   juice reserved
½ cup uncooked quinoa,
   rinsed
1 cup fresh carrot juice
4 cups vegetable stock,
   preferably homemade
   (see stock recipe,
   page 25)
1 cup fresh green beans
   cut into 1-inch pieces
   (or diced zucchini
   when in season)
2 cups corn kernels, fresh
   or frozen
Fresh lime juice to taste
Sea salt and freshly
   ground black pepper
   to taste

Method

Preheat to 350°F

Cook Black Beans

1. Drain the soaked beans and place in a soup pot with the epazote, bay leaf, and garlic. Cover with water to a depth of about 2 inches. Bring to a boil over medium-high heat, then reduce to a simmer. Cook on low heat until the beans are tender but not falling apart; about 2 hours.

2. After the first 30 minutes of cooking, add the olive oil to the beans. When beans are nearly fork tender, add salt to taste. (Keep adding salt, a small pinch at a time, tasting as you go, until bean water tastes delicious.)

3. When beans are tender, remove them from the heat and discard the epazote sprigs and bay leaf. If using dried epazote, it is fine to leave it in.

While Beans Are Cooking, Prepare Yucca

1. To prepare yucca, carefully peel the thick skin with a knife or sturdy vegetable peeler. Slice into 1-inch thick discs. You will notice a thick spine in the center of each disc. Cut your cubes around this hard center.

2. Add yucca to a medium stock pot and cover with 1 quart of water. Bring to a boil and reduce heat to a simmer. Cook until just fork tender, about 10 to 15 minutes. Keep a close eye on it and be careful not to overcook or it will get mushy. Drain and place on a sheet pan to cool.

3. When yucca has cooled, place it in a bowl and toss with the lime juice, olive oil, and sea salt to taste. Set aside.

To Complete the Stew

1. Heat oil in a large stock pot or Dutch oven and sauté the onions for about 5 minutes.

2. Add the garlic, chile powder, oregano, cumin, and tomatoes and cook another 1 to 2 minutes, until aromatic.

3. Add the quinoa, reserved tomato juice, carrot juice, and vegetable stock and bring to a boil. Reduce heat to very low and simmer, covered, 10 minutes.

4. Using a slotted spoon, transfer the beans to the quinoa mixture. Add 1 cup of bean broth, or more if needed to barely submerge the other ingredients. Simmer another 15 minutes to meld flavors.

5. Add the green beans (or zucchini) and corn and simmer until vegetables are tender but still *al dente,* about 5 minutes.

6. Add the yucca before serving. Season to taste with the lime juice, salt, and pepper.

Adapted from Bauman College Natural Chef Culinary Cookbook

NUTRITION GEM
Yucca: The Full-Spectrum Root

One look at yucca and you might think you mistook a tree branch for a vegetable. The outer skin is brown, thick, and waxy; more like tree bark than peel. Remove this outer layer and the flesh is white and starchy, similar to a rutabaga.

Yucca (also spelled yuca) is known by other names, too, including manioc and cassava. Pronounced "yoo-ka," not "yucka," it is a staple food of Latin America, the Caribbean, Africa, and Asia and is usually eaten boiled, steamed, and in flour form as a thickener.

Yucca is more caloric than a potato, but its nutritional profile is impressive. It is loaded with potassium, vitamin C, and iron and is a good source of thiamin and vitamin B6. In fact, indigenous people in Latin America were known to thrive on yucca alone when other food was scarce.

Because of its tough outer skin, it is easier to peel yucca with a knife rather than a vegetable peeler. Once peeled, yucca suddenly looks less alien, but be sure to remove the tough, fibrous spine in the center of the root before serving.

Be sure to choose yucca roots that are very firm. If it gives when pressed or feels slightly mushy, it is not fit to eat.

Hearty Lentil, Chicken, and Vegetable Soup

Serves 8

Here is Mom's chicken soup, only more nutritious. If you are recovering from an illness, infection, or exhaustion, drink 1 or 2 cups of this immune-enhancing broth every day. You can freeze single servings in small freezer bags and reheat them when you need a pick-me-up.

Ingredients

Soup Base
1 cup dried lentils
½ chicken with bones, skin removed and trimmed of fat
1 cup diced winter squash
1 tablespoon freshly grated ginger
1 tablespoon freshly grated turmeric, or 1 teaspoon dried if fresh is not available
8 cups mineral broth, vegetable, or chicken stock, preferably homemade (see stock recipes, pages 25–32)

Vegetable Flavors
2 tablespoons extra virgin olive oil

1 bulb garlic (about 15 cloves), peeled and coarsely chopped
2 medium onions, finely diced
2 medium red bell peppers, finely diced
6 fresh shiitake mushrooms, stems removed, sliced
1 cup fresh kale leaves, chiffonade

Minerals and Seasonings
2 tablespoons curry powder, divided
2 teaspoons granulated seaweed (arame, hiziki, or dulse)
½ cup miso of choice
1 bunch fresh thyme, chopped
1 bunch fresh parsley, chopped
1 bunch fresh cilantro, chopped
1 bunch fresh dill, chopped

Method

1. Place ingredients from Soup Base list in a large pot over medium-high heat. Bring to a boil, then reduce the heat to medium-low and simmer gently for 2 hours. Take care not to let the soup boil.

2. During the last half hour of simmering time, heat a large skillet over medium heat. Add the olive oil, garlic, onions, bell pepper, mushrooms, and kale. Stir in 1 tablespoon of curry powder and sauté until the vegetables are tender, about 5 minutes.

3. When the simmering time is up, transfer the chicken to a plate. When cooled, pick off the meat in shreds.

4. Add the sautéed vegetables, chicken, thyme, seaweed, and remaining curry powder. Cook for another 15 minutes until flavors meld together nicely.

5. Ladle 1 cup of broth into a bowl and allow to cool for about 5 minutes. Then, gently whisk in miso. Set aside.

6. Meanwhile, toss parsley, cilantro, and dill into pot of soup. Stir until the herbs wilt.

7. Remove soup from the burner and stir in the bowl of soup mixed with miso. Adjust seasonings to taste and serve immediately.

Big Soup Heals

When I was growing up, my Nicaraguan grandmother, who lived with us, would make us a giant pot of chicken soup – the same "la sopa" her own mother had made to keep her and her seven sisters and little brother strong and healthy. She would affectionately call the concoction "Big Soup." A fitting name, as it contained two quartered chickens, large chunks of carrots, celery, onions, potatoes, chayote and banana squash, sliced cabbage, and a couple ears of chopped corn on the cob. She tossed in bay leaf, parsley, peppercorns, and other herbs – whatever she had on hand – and let it simmer on low heat until the chicken was falling off the bones. Sometimes (if she was in the mood) she would add a little rice, chopped tomatoes, or zucchini. Before serving, she would add a touch more sea salt and pepper and a squeeze of fresh lime juice to round out the flavors. Then she would ladle the chunks of chicken and vegetables along with the thin, flavorful broth into giant bowls. A bowl of soup and a side of freshly made, warm corn tortillas completed our Big Soup meal.

When I was young, I was never that excited about this meal. It was warm and comforting and I loved the tortillas, but it seemed so simple and the chunky vegetables were so unwieldy as I struggled to cut them into small pieces without splashing broth out of the bowl! It was not until years later that I truly came to appreciate my grandmother's Big Soup. Sure the vegetables were kind of rustic, but they tasted wonderful; never overcooked and mushy. But the biggest mystery was the broth itself – how did she get it to taste so rich and flavorful?

The broth in my grandmother's Big Soup was essentially the same as broths made the world over and used to make countless traditional foods. Whatever else it might contain, her stock pot always included bones. The slow cooked broth was simply a bone broth which has been a source of sustenance for human beings for centuries. Cultures throughout the world have their own version of Big Soup – whether it is the Pho in Vietnamese cuisine, a pot of Borscht, or a piping hot bowl of "New York Penicillin" – the queen of chicken soups. These nourishing broths use the bone and marrow from beef, lamb, or fish.

Science now confirms the healing powers of chicken broth and soup in general, but our grandmothers intuitively knew these things long before modern science gave us the technology to describe them. If my grandmother were alive today, she'd probably shrug and roll her eyes at all the excitement these days over bone and mineral broths. "Just cook the food. Do not make it too fussy," I can hear her saying. Despite her modesty, I thank her dearly for passing on her "Big Soup" wisdom. It is a great reminder that keeping foods simple and authentic is always the best approach. Big Soup and bone broths have that in common.

LIZETTE

Spreads and Dips

In these economic hard times, it is a great savings to prepare healthy, delicious, versatile foods. How often have you purchased an 8-ounce container of hummus at the store, for instance, for somewhere between $4 and $7? The cost of making your own is only about 20 percent of what it costs to buy the commercial product, and that includes using top-of-the-line ingredients, such as organic beans and extra virgin olive oil rather than the canola oil typically used in store-bought versions. You can also use exactly the amount of cayenne or garlic you like when you make a spread or dip from scratch, and you do not need to add preservatives to extend the shelf life. Finally, bean spreads like hummus are super-easy to prepare and make great high-protein snacks.

What makes dips and spreads so popular is that they can be eaten in so many ways: on a cracker, chip, or vegetable stick; in a sandwich, wrap, or burrito; or even right out of the container with a spoon.

As when comparing soups and stews, the main difference between a spread and a dip is the consistency. A spread is thicker and heartier, a dip more runny.

A nut butter, such as almond butter, is a spread. It is all ground nuts, with no added water. An almond butter dip, on the other hand, would be thinned out with other ingredients, such as yogurt or water. It is softer, smoother, and lighter.

Hummus consists of garbanzo beans, sesame tahini, lemon juice, garlic, and spices such as cumin or chile. Often, it is served with a drizzle of olive oil on top, along with chopped herbs and pine nuts. You can substitute other beans such as tofu, edamame (fresh whole soybeans), or cooked black, red, or white beans for the garbanzo beans to invent other kinds of "hummus." Likewise, other nut butters, or whole soaked nuts or seeds, could be used instead of tahini.

Imagine almond, cashew, peanut, or sunflower butter mixed with edamame or pinto beans. Another acid could be used in place of fresh lemon juice. Try orange or pineapple juice, or apple cider or rice vinegar.

If you have not explored the wide array of possibilities in making your own dips, you are in for a treat.

Dips and spreads have a base ingredient or set of ingredients that make up a complete protein, such as the beans and seeds in hummus and its variations. The landmark book, *Diet for a Small Planet,* by Frances Moore Lappé introduced the concept of complementary vegetable proteins. By combining a whole grain, such as rice or corn, with a legume, such as lentils or kidney beans, the limited amino acids in each join forces and become whole proteins. This is a nutritionally sound approach, but it should be noted that Lappé and a host of nutritionists now believe it is not necessary to eat all amino acids in the same meal. If various protein-containing foods are eaten over the course of a day or so, the body can easily make the "complete" proteins it needs for essential bodily functions.

Animal foods such as meat and dairy products contain all eight essential amino acids, so mixing a vegetable such as spinach with some yogurt, for instance, also creates a complete protein dip.

Dips and spreads make great snacks as well as appetizers. Have fun combining foods with different tastes, textures, and consistencies to create hunger-quelling spreads that you can keep in the refrigerator and enjoy all week.

Ed

Herb and Pistachio Paté

YIELDS 2½ CUPS

My husband came up with this amazingly delicious nut paté during one of our catering gigs. It was a huge hit and it will wow guests at your next cocktail party. The paté works great as a topping on crackers, makes a terrific spread on crostini, or even as a dip on a vegetable platter.

Ingredients

1 cup pistachio nuts, toasted
2 tablespoons flax seeds, soaked in ¼
    cup water (will yield approximately
    ½ cup gummy flax seeds)
¾ cup sun dried tomatoes, soaked
⅓ cup sun dried tomato water
5 Cerignola olives, pitted
1 cup basil leaves, tightly packed
⅓ cup chives, chopped
1 medium garlic clove, peeled
⅓ cup diced red onion

¼ teaspoon sea salt
¼ teaspoon freshly ground
    black pepper
¼ cup extra virgin olive oil
2 tablespoons apple cider vinegar

Garnish
⅓ cup tightly packed fresh basil leaves,
    chiffonade
1 cup minced fresh chives

Method

Preheat oven to 325°F

1. Toast pistachios in the oven for 10 minutes, or until aromatic. Transfer nuts to a plate to cool.

2. Drain sun dried tomatoes, reserving liquid.

3. Add all of the ingredients to a blender and purée together until thoroughly incorporated. It may be necessary to start and stop the blender while puréeing to make sure all ingredients come together evenly.

4. Top paté on crackers and garnish with basil and chives, or serve paté as a dip with freshly cut, crunchy vegetables, pita slices, bread, or crackers.

Recipe by Geoffrey Marx

Flaxonnaise

YIELDS ⅓ CUP

Mayonnaise is about as American as hot dogs and apple pie; and with that image, those who might want to eat healthier may decide this spread is no good. Despite the unhealthy reputation, mayonnaise is still one of the most popular sandwich spreads, a creamy addition to cole slaws, chicken and tuna salads, and believe it or not, a secret ingredient in many sushi rolls. Most commercial mayonnaise spreads have poor quality ingredients and are a sad testament to one of French cuisine's most supreme emulsion sauces. This recipe is a "tip of the hat" to a favorite spread with an added nutritional kick. You guessed it, flax. Make a batch or two and use to your healthy heart's content. Enjoy!

Ingredients

1 large egg yolk
2 teaspoons fresh squeezed lemon juice
½ teaspoon Dijon mustard

¼ cup extra virgin olive oil
2 tablespoons flax oil

Method

1. Whisk together the egg yolk, lemon juice, and mustard.

2. While whisking constantly, slowly drizzle in the olive oil, until the mixture emulsifies. Follow with the flax oil and continue whisking until the sauce is smooth and glossy.

3. Flaxonnaise can be kept in a tightly sealed, glass container for up to 3 days.

Mock Chopped Liver

YIELDS 1 CUP

You will not believe how good this spread is! It is a vegan Jewish nosh, high in potassium, B vitamins, and protein.

Ingredients

2 tablespoons extra virgin olive oil
1 medium onion, diced
½ teaspoon sea salt
2 cups green beans
½ cup raw walnuts

¼ cup flax seeds
2 tablespoons red miso
¼ cup finely chopped fresh parsley
Sea salt and freshly ground pepper
   to taste

Method

1. Heat a wide, heavy-bottomed pan over medium low heat and add olive oil. Add onions and sauté, stirring occasionally, for 10 minutes.

2. Sprinkle ½ teaspoon of salt on the onions and cook on low heat until they are soft and golden brown, stirring often, about 40 minutes.

3. Meanwhile, bring a medium saucepan of filtered water to boil. Add a generous pinch of salt to the water and then add the green beans. Cook until soft, about 8 minutes. Drain and set aside.

4. Place the caramelized onions, green beans, walnuts, flax seeds, and miso in a food processor and purée. Taste and season with salt and freshly ground pepper.

5. Transfer to a bowl and garnish with finely chopped parsley.

Yam and Seed Spread

YIELDS 2 CUPS

An unusual, delicious, and exotic spread that will delight the senses with its savory and sweet notes. Try it on flatbread, crackers, or whole-grain bread, or simply enjoy by the spoonful.

Ingredients

2 pounds of yams
¼ cup sunflower seeds
¼ cup sesame seeds
¼ cup poppy seeds
¼ cup flax seeds

¼ cup plain whole milk yogurt
½ teaspoon ground cinnamon
½ teaspoon ground coriander
½ teaspoon freshly grated ginger
½ teaspoon sea salt

Method

Preheat oven to 450° F

1. Bake the yams until very soft, about 45 to 60 minutes.

2. Separately grind sunflower, sesame, poppy, and flax seeds to a fine meal. NOTE: A coffee grinder designated as a nut and seed grinder works great for this process.

3. When the yams are finished baking, remove them from the oven and allow to cool slightly for about 10 minutes. Peel and compost the skins and mash the yams in a medium bowl.

4. Add the ground seeds, yogurt, cinnamon, coriander, ginger, and salt and stir well to combine.

5. Enjoy as a sandwich filling, dip, or spread. Store spread in a tightly sealed container in the refrigerator for up to 3 days.

COOKING PEARL
Great Garnishes

There are many ways to enhance a basic spread or dip. Here are a few ideas:

- Add ½ cup peeled, seeded tomatoes, fresh or canned

- Garnish with a dollop of yogurt and fresh chopped dill

- Sprinkle nutritional yeast and a pinch of cayenne on top

Tahini Applesauce Spread

Yields 1½ cups

This sweet spread can be eaten as a pudding or on whole-grain bread.

Ingredients

½ cup toasted sesame tahini
1 cup unsweetened applesauce
¼ cup raisins

1 teaspoon ground cinnamon
1 teaspoon lemon zest (Meyer
 lemon preferred)

Method

1. Stir the tahini and unsweetened applesauce together until well combined.

2. Add the raisins, cinnamon, and lemon zest. Serve immediately or store in a tightly sealed container in the refrigerator for up to 2 weeks.

Spinach and Beet Green Hummus

YIELDS 3 CUPS

This popular Middle Eastern dip, traditionally made with chickpeas and tahini, gets a dose of greens as well as a new bean for an even healthier version of the classic. Instead of chickpeas, white beans are blended with tahini, olive oil, and garlic, along with freshly sautéed onions, spinach, and beet greens.

Ingredients

½ cup olive oil, divided
1 small onion, diced
3 cloves garlic, minced
½ teaspoon cumin
⅛ teaspoon chili flakes
1½ cups fresh spinach, packed tightly
1 cup beet greens, packed tightly

2 cups cooked white beans
⅓ cup roasted tahini
¼ cup lemon juice
2 tablespoon lime juice
Sea salt and pepper to taste
Extra virgin olive oil for drizzling
1 tablespoon pine nuts or pumpkin seeds, toasted

Method

1. In a sauté pan, heat 2 tablespoons of olive oil over low heat and add onions. Sauté until soft and translucent; then add garlic and a pinch of salt. Sprinkle in cumin and chili flakes. Sauté another minute.

2. When garlic, onions, and spices become intensely aromatic (after 1 minute or so of cooking) add spinach and beet greens, turning leaves gently into onions and garlic until wilted. Remove from heat and set aside.

3. In a food processor, add beans, tahini, and remaining olive oil. Blend until smooth.

4. Gradually add sautéed spinach mixture in three batches and blend until smooth.

5. Add lemon and lime juices a little at a time until hummus reaches desired flavor profile. Season with salt and pepper.

6. To serve, transfer hummus into a serving bowl. Drizzle with a little olive oil and top with toasted pine nuts or pumpkin seeds. Enjoy with flatbread and freshly cut raw vegetables.

Multi-Grain Flatbread

YIELDS ENOUGH DOUGH FOR TWO 12-INCH ROUND FLATBREADS

This vegan and gluten-free flatbread is delicious, versatile, and easy to make. Its complex, herby flavor and satisfying texture are as good as any flatbread made with white flour, and it takes less time to make.

Ingredients

½ cup brown rice flour
½ cup teff flour
½ cup chickpea flour
6 tablespoons ground flax seeds
1 tablespoon palm sugar
1 teaspoon xanthan gum
½ teaspoon sea salt

½ teaspoon non-aluminum
   baking powder
¼ teaspoon baking soda
1 tablespoon extra virgin olive oil plus
   a bit more
1 teaspoon apple cider vinegar
1 cup filtered water
2 teaspoons minced fresh
   rosemary leaves

Method

Preheat oven to 350° F

1. In a large bowl, combine flours with the flax seeds, sugar, xanthan gum, salt, baking powder, and baking soda.

2. Make a well in the center of the flour mixture and add olive oil and apple cider vinegar. Pour in half the water and stir until well combined, adding a bit more water if necessary, until a dough forms. Dough will be slightly sticky to the touch.

3. Shape dough into two discs and wrap in plastic wrap. Refrigerate for 30 minutes.

4. Unwrap dough one disc at a time and place on a sheet of parchment paper on a large, flat surface. Place a sheet of plastic wrap over dough and roll out evenly to approximately ⅛-inch thickness. If dough is rolled out thinner, flatbread will have a cracker-like texture. Remove plastic wrap and slide sheet of parchment with flatbread onto baking sheet. Follow the same procedure with the other disc of dough.

5. Brush dough with olive oil and sprinkle with sea salt and herbs. Bake for 15 minutes. Allow to cool for 5 minutes before cutting into serving pieces. Flatbread can be made ahead and refrigerated in freezer bags for up to 1 week. Simply toast or warm in the oven before using.

Buckwheat Gruyere Crackers

<small>YIELDS APPROXIMATELY 24 CRACKERS</small>

Store-bought crackers simply do not compare to these amazing and delicious gluten-free crackers. Make a large batch and enjoy them for snack time, lunch time, or any time. These crackers can even be dressed up for canapés. Top them with one of our spreads and a few sprigs of micro greens and wow your friends and family at the next party or potluck.

Ingredients

2 tablespoons coconut oil
1 large egg, at room temperature
1 tablespoon warm water
¾ teaspoon sea salt
½ cup brown rice flour
¼ cup buckwheat flour

2 tablespoons ground flax seeds
2 tablespoons tapioca flour
⅛ teaspoon xanthan gum
⅛ teaspoon freshly ground
   black pepper
2 cups grated Gruyere cheese

Method

Preheat oven to 350° F

1. Melt the coconut oil in a small pan over low heat, then remove from heat and allow to cool slightly.

2. Whisk egg in a small bowl. Add water and then slowly whisk in the melted coconut oil. Set aside.

3. In a large bowl, whisk together all of the dry ingredients: salt, brown rice and buckwheat flours, ground flax seeds, tapioca flour, xanthan gum, and black pepper.

4. Mix cheese into dry ingredients, taking care to distribute it evenly.

5. Make a well in the center of the flour mixture and pour in the egg mixture. Mix well until a solid dough ball forms.

6. Cut dough ball in half, shape each half into a disk, and wrap each one tightly with plastic wrap. Chill in refrigerator for 40 minutes.

7. To roll out crackers: Place a 9x13-inch piece of parchment paper on a clean, hard surface and place one disc of dough at a time on the parchment. Unwrap dough and place the same plastic wrap or another larger piece over dough. Roll out dough between parchment and plastic wrap until ⅛-inch thick, or as thin as possible before dough begins to crack and tear.

8. If dough does crack, press with fingers to "heal" the imperfections. For best results, do not remove plastic wrap cover as you attempt to fix imperfections in the dough. This dough tends to break a bit around the edges, but this is fine.

9. Once dough is rolled out to the desired thickness, use a sharp knife or pizza cutter to score dough into desired shapes.

10. Move parchment with scored dough onto a baking sheet and bake for 25 minutes or until golden brown. Allow to cool for about 10 minutes and then break into pieces. Store in an airtight container in the refrigerator for up to 2 weeks.

Adapted from Bauman College Natural Chef Culinary Cookbook

South of the Border Flax Crackers

Yields approximately eighty 1½-inch round crackers

These crisp and zesty grain-free crackers will dazzle and delight munchers, party monsters, and midnight snackers. They are perfect for school lunches and picnics too!

Ingredients

1 cup flax seeds, soaked in 2 cups of pure, filtered water
½ cup sun dried tomatoes, soaked in 1 cup pure, filtered water
¼ cup sun dried tomato soaking water
1 cup fresh corn kernels
2 medium tomatillos, chopped (optional)

2 cloves garlic, peeled
2 green onions, white and green parts chopped roughly
½ cup cilantro, chopped
1½ teaspoon sea salt
½ teaspoon cumin powder
½ teaspoon chili powder
2 tablespoons lime juice

Method

1. Pour soaked flax seeds into a large bowl and set aside.

2. Drain sun dried tomatoes, reserving tomato water to use as needed in recipe.

3. Add tomatoes to a blender with sun dried tomato water, corn, tomatillos, garlic, green onions, cilantro, salt, cumin powder, chili powder, and lime juice. Blend ingredients until combined but not smooth. A few small chunks will add texture to the cracker.

4. Fold blended vegetable and spice mixture with soaked flax seeds.

5. Measure ½ tablespoons of the flax mixture onto Teflex sheets from your dehydrator, or sheets of parchment paper. Using the back of a spoon, spread the flax mixture into a ⅛-inch thick circle. Repeat until dehydrator sheet is filled (see Flax Cracker Tip, next page).

6. Dehydrate crackers in a dehydrator on 125° F or in an oven on the lowest temperature setting possible (no more than 150 to 170° F) for about 18 hours, until crisp.

COOKING PEARL
Flax Cracker Tips

Making flax crackers is a little like dolloping cookie dough onto a baking sheet. However, you will not need to worry about the flax mixture spreading as it dehydrates. Instead, the cracker will shrink slightly as it loses moisture from dehydrating; so feel free to place the flax cracker rounds ¼ inch apart from each other.

When removing crackers from Teflex sheets or parchment paper, carefully lift the edge of the cracker with your fingers or use an offset spatula.

Crackers should be stored in an airtight container and will stay fresh for up to 1 week. Sometimes the crackers do soften over time. If this happens, simply place the crackers back in the dehydrator or in a warm oven until they become crisp again; about 20 minutes in a dehydrator on the lowest setting and about 10 minutes in a warm oven.

Gluten-Free Pizza

Pizza does not have to be a junky fast food. It has all the potential for being a superbly delicious and terrific balancing meal. Sans gluten-containing flour, this crust holds its own against the standard version. All you need is a great sauce, yummy cheese, and some well-chosen toppings. Enjoy!

Ingredients

¾ cup tapioca flour
½ cup brown rice flour
⅓ cup chickpea flour
⅓ cup sorghum flour
1 teaspoon xanthan gum
1 teaspoon fine-grain sea salt
½ cup whole milk or nut milk (almond
   or hazelnut work well)
¼ cup filtered water

2¼ teaspoons active dry yeast
   (1¼-ounce package)
2 teaspoons date sugar or honey
2 large egg whites, lightly beaten
2 tablespoons extra virgin olive oil
   (plus extra for brushing onto pizzas)
Fresh grated cheese of choice
Toppings of choice: mushrooms,
   olives, artichoke hearts, sun-dried
   tomatoes, fresh tomatoes, etc.

Tomato Sauce (see recipe on page 150)

Spinach Basil Pesto (see recipe on page 151)

Method

Preheat oven to 400°F at least 45 minutes ahead of time if using pizza stone, or 20 minutes if using a baking sheet.

Cut two 12-inch square sheets of parchment paper.

1. In the bowl of an electric mixer, whisk together the tapioca, brown rice, chickpea, and sorghum flour, with the xanthan gum and salt.

2. In a small saucepan over moderate heat, stir together the milk and water and heat until warm but not hot to the touch, about 1 minute (the mixture should register between 105°F and 115°F on a candy thermometer). Remove pan from heat and stir in the yeast and date sugar or honey.

3. Add milk–yeast mixture, beaten egg whites, and 2 tablespoons of the oil to the dry ingredients and, using the paddle attachment in a stand-up mixer, beat at medium speed until the dough is very smooth and thick, about 5 minutes, scraping the bowl occasionally.

4. Remove the racks from your oven and place a pizza stone or heavy inverted baking sheet on the bottom. Have ready two 12-inch squares of parchment paper.

5. Divide the dough between the squares and form each half into a ball. Coat each ball with 2 teaspoons of oil, then use oiled fingertips to pat and stretch each ball out into a 9-inch diameter round, ¼-inch thick, with a ½-inch thick edge. Loosely cover rounds with plastic wrap and let rise in a warm, draft-free place until each crust has expanded to 10 inches or so in diameter, about 20 minutes.

6. Transfer one crust with parchment to the preheated pizza stone and bake until top is puffed and firm and underside is lightly browned and crisp, 5 to 10 minutes.

7. Carefully transfer baked crust to a rack to cool. Bake second crust in same manner.

NOTE: Baked crusts can be made ahead and frozen, wrapped in plastic wrap, for up to 1 month. Thaw in 350° F oven until hot, 4 to 5 minutes, before topping and broiling.

Top and broil pizzas

1. Preheat the broiler in your oven.

2. Prepare your toppings of choice. Vegetables like mushrooms can be used raw or sautéed.

3. Transfer baked crusts to two large baking sheets. Brush 1 teaspoon olive oil over each crust. Spread each with tomato sauce, if desired, leaving a ½-inch border bare of sauce around the outside, then scatter desired toppings evenly over the sauce. Drizzle a bit more olive oil over pizzas.

4. Broil pizzas about 4 inches from the heat, rotating as needed for even browning, until cheese is bubbling and browned in places and the crust is golden brown, about 4 to 8 minutes. Scatter with chopped fresh basil and serve immediately.

Tomato Sauce

YIELDS APPROXIMATELY ¾ CUP SAUCE

Tomato sauce should have an intense freshness, and this version delivers.

Ingredients

2 tablespoons extra virgin olive oil
3 cloves garlic, minced
1 large onion, minced
¼ cup tomato paste
½ pound Roma tomatoes, blanched,
    peeled, seeded, and puréed

2 teaspoons dried basil
1 teaspoon dried oregano
¼ teaspoon dried marjoram
Sea salt and freshly ground black
    pepper to taste
Filtered water, if needed

Method

1. Heat the oil in a skillet over medium heat. Sauté the garlic and onion over medium to low heat until translucent, about 5 minutes.

2. Add the tomato paste and tomatoes. Stir and cook until thickened.

3. When sauce begins to bubble slightly, turn heat to low and stir in herbs, salt, and pepper. Cook for a few minutes longer until flavor of herbs comes through in the sauce. Taste and adjust seasonings if necessary. Thin sauce with a little water if it is too thick.

COOKING PEARL

Removing Tomato Skins

To peel tomatoes effortlessly, you must blanch them first. Using a paring knife, score the bottom of each tomato with an "X." Immerse each tomato in a pot of boiling water for 15 seconds. When you notice the skin wrinkling or curling, lift the tomato out with a slotted spoon and dunk in an ice bath to cool before peeling.

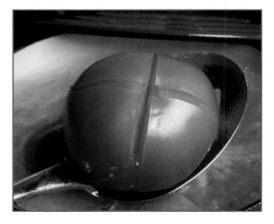

Spinach Basil Pesto

YIELDS 1 CUP

Pesto is not only a delectable sauce, it is a great way to get more greens in your diet. Authentic pesto is a combination of basil, pine nuts, olive oil, garlic, Parmesan cheese, and a splash of lemon juice ground together in a mortar and pestle. There is definitely more than one way to mash up a pesto sauce and in this version, we have thrown in some spinach leaves and swapped out expensive pine nuts for walnuts. Enjoy this sauce on pizza or flatbread, on chicken, or as a dip for vegetables.

Ingredients

1 cup of loosely packed basil leaves
1 cup loosely packed spinach leaves
¼ cup walnuts (raw, unsalted)
3 small garlic cloves, minced
1 tablespoon of lemon juice

½ cup finely grated Parmesan cheese
¼ cup water
⅓ cup extra virgin olive oil
Sea salt to taste
Freshly ground pepper to taste

Method

1. Wash basil and spinach leaves and pat dry.

2. In a food processor, blender, or mortar and pestle, grind together basil, spinach, walnuts, garlic cloves, and cheese. Add water to bring everything together.

3. Gradually add in olive oil and process until smooth. Add salt and freshly ground pepper to taste.

Skillet Tempeh Reuben

Serves 8

Because it is fermented, tempeh is easier to digest than some other soy products. The caraway seeds in this meat-free Reuben mimic the flavor of the corned beef on rye bread. The raw sauerkraut is excellent for improving digestion. To preserve enzymes and lactobacilli, add the sauerkraut at the very end, just before serving the dish.

Ingredients

2 packages (8 ounces each) soy tempeh, crumbled
3 tablespoons tamari soy sauce
2 tablespoons Dijon mustard, or more to taste
2 tablespoons light sesame oil
2 tablespoons vegetable stock

1 medium red onion, thinly sliced
12 ounces sauerkraut (raw and unpasteurized, if available)
Sea salt, to taste
2 teaspoons whole caraway seeds, toasted

Method

1. Place the crumbled tempeh in a steamer basket inside a high-walled saucepan and pour in water just up to the bottom of the steamer. Cover and steam for 20 minutes. Transfer tempeh to a medium bowl.

2. Whisk together the tamari and mustard. Add this sauce to the tempeh, stirring to combine. Cover bowl with a plate and allow tempeh to marinate for 1 hour.

3. Heat the sesame oil in a heavy skillet or sauté pan over medium heat. Add onions and sauté until soft, 5 to 10 minutes.

4. Deglaze pan with stock, then add the tempeh. Stir to warm through and remove from heat.

5. Stir in the sauerkraut and caraway seeds. Taste and season with salt and pepper, if desired, before serving as is or on your favorite whole-grain bread.

Adapted from Bauman College Natural Chef Culinary Cookbook

Cabbage Rolls Stuffed with Kasha and Raw Sauerkraut

SERVES 6

Stuffed cabbage rolls have been a popular comfort food in European Jewish cooking for thousands of years. Most often stuffed with a variety of meats, grains, and vegetables, this roll takes on a new role. Kasha, which is hearty and earthy, stands in for the meat, and tangy raw sauerkraut and Dijon mustard gives the whole dish a deliciously pungent bite.

Ingredients

1 cup uncooked kasha
2 cups vegetable stock, preferably homemade (see stock recipe, page 25)
2 teaspoons plus 1 tablespoon extra virgin olive oil
¼ cup raw unsalted pumpkin seeds
1 cup raw sauerkraut
¼ cup plus 3 tablespoons Dijon mustard
1 tablespoon nutritional yeast
1 teaspoon dulse flakes
Sea salt and freshly ground pepper to taste

1 head green cabbage, separated into whole leaves (Savoy cabbage makes the prettiest cabbage roll)
Sea salt and freshly ground pepper to taste

Mustard Sauce
6 tablespoons Dijon mustard
2 tablespoons honey
2 tablespoons olive oil
Sea salt and pepper to taste

Method

Cabbage Rolls

1. Bring stock to a boil in a medium saucepan. Add the kasha and olive oil and reduce heat to low, cover, and cook for 15 minutes. Without disturbing the lid, remove the pan from the heat and continue to steam, covered, an additional 10 minutes. Transfer kasha to a large bowl.

2. Toast pumpkin seeds in a small skillet over medium heat until they begin to pop and become aromatic. Transfer to a plate to cool.

3. Add the sauerkraut, mustard, nutritional yeast, dulse flakes, and toasted pumpkin seeds to the cooked kasha. Season with salt and pepper to taste.

4. Using a large pot, steam whole cabbage head until tender, about 15 minutes. Carefully lift cabbage from pot with tongs or two large spoons and gently remove the individual leaves, blotting each with a clean towel. The leaves should come away from the cabbage head with little effort. Once the leaves become difficult to remove, return cabbage to the pot and continue steaming until all of the leaves can be removed. NOTE: Depending on how tight the cabbage head is, you may have to return it to the steamer to loosen leaves several times. If this is necessary, steam in 5 minute increments, taking out cabbage and removing as many leaves as possible, then returning to steamer if necessary.

5. To stuff and roll cabbage, place one leaf at a time on a flat surface and place a spoonful or two of kasha filling in the center of the leaf. Tuck in the sides of the leaf and roll. Place each cabbage roll seam side down onto a serving platter.

Sauce

In a medium bowl, whisk together mustard, honey, and olive oil until well blended. Season with salt and pepper. Drizzle sauce over cabbage rolls before serving.

Ceviche

SERVES 6

Ceviche is a popular dish in many of the coastal regions of Latin America, where seafood is plentiful. The fish is "cooked" in the lime juice and mixed with a variety of seasonings, creating a simple and refreshing dish. Use the freshest and best quality fish available.

Ingredients

1 cup freshly squeezed lime juice
½ cup finely diced red onion
4 cloves garlic, minced
½ teaspoon sea salt
1 pinch cayenne pepper

1 teaspoon chopped fresh oregano
1 tablespoon chopped fresh parsley
2 tablespoons chopped fresh cilantro
¼ cup extra virgin olive oil
2 cups medium diced raw white fish
    (see Cooking Pearl below)

Method

1. Combine all ingredients except the fish in a glass bowl and mix well.

2. Add the fish and cover tightly with plastic wrap. Allow to marinate in the refrigerator for about 1 hour. Turn several times while marinating to distribute juices.

3. When fish has an opaque appearance, it has been adequately marinated and is ready to eat.

4. To serve, spoon into a small bowl and top with chopped cilantro. Serve with homemade tortilla chips.

COOKING PEARL
Always Use the Best Quality Fish

Choose only wild-caught fish that are listed "safe" from heavy metals and other toxins and are not on the list of endangered fish species. See montereybayaquarium.org/cr/seafoodwatch.aspx for more information about sustainable seafood.

Chicken Satay
with Almond Flax Sauce

SERVES 6

Satay, made with peanuts and chicken, is a traditional Indonesian recipe that is quite popular in American Thai restaurants. The twist in this version is all about the accompanying dipping sauce, where almonds and flax seeds take the place of peanuts.

Ingredients

1 cup plain whole milk yogurt
1 teaspoon freshly grated ginger
1 teaspoon minced garlic
1 tablespoon curry powder
1½ pounds skinless and boneless chicken breasts, cut into strips
¼ cup coconut oil, melted (for oiling grill; use more if necessary)

20 dried rosemary stalks or wooden skewers, soaked in water for 30 minutes
4 to 5 large lettuce leaves (butter lettuce or large red, or green leaf lettuce preferred)
¼ cup finely chopped cilantro
Almond Flax Sauce (recipe follows)

Method

1. In a medium bowl, combine yogurt, ginger, garlic, and curry powder; stir well.

2. Place chicken in the yogurt marinade and gently toss until well coated. Cover and set aside to marinate in the refrigerator for up to 2 hours.

3. Thread chicken onto the soaked skewers, working each skewer in and out down the middle of a chicken strip so that it stays in place during grilling.

4. Place a grill pan over medium heat and brush it with coconut oil to prevent the meat from sticking. Grill the chicken skewers for 5 to 7 minutes on each side, until nicely seared and cooked through.

5. Serve the chicken on a platter lined with lettuce leaves and cilantro, accompanied by a small bowl of Almond Flax Sauce (see recipe, next page).

Almond Flax Sauce

YIELDS 3 CUPS

This is a delicious, spicy sauce loaded with healthy omega-3 fats from flax seeds. Flax also has great thickening qualities, which make for a terrific consistency perfect for a creamy sauce to go with chicken satay or steamed vegetables.

Ingredients

1 cup dry roasted, unsalted almond butter
½ cup flax seeds, ground into a fine powder
¼ cup tamari soy sauce
2 teaspoons red chile paste, such as sambal
Juice of 2 medium limes

2 Medjool dates
½ to 1 cup hot filtered water
¼ cup almonds,* chopped,
　for garnish

Method

1. Combine almond butter, flax seeds, tamari sauce, red chile paste, lime juice, and dates in a food processor or blender. Purée until very smooth.

2. While the motor is running, drizzle in the hot water to thin out the sauce. You may not need it all; the sauce should be thick and creamy but thin enough to drizzle, if desired.

3. Pour the sauce into an attractive serving bowl and garnish with chopped almonds.

---

*To make almonds easier to digest, soak overnight in filtered water, then rinse and dehydrate or dry until nuts are crispy. Another option for added flavor is to toast nuts in a 325°F oven for 8 minutes.

Flax-tastic

Flax has been my favorite seed since I came across it 25 years ago. Turns out, flax dates back to ancient Egypt and is mentioned several times in the Bible as a healing plant.

Flax is a seed with either a dark brown or golden outer husk. Brown flax seeds have a greater amount of the precious omega-3 fatty acids than any other land food. Only algae and deep ocean fish contain higher concentrations. Omega-3s have soothing, calming, and anti-inflammatory properties, and allow our bodies' receptors for neurotransmitters and hormones to better receive and respond to the chemicals that various processes produce. I have known people who began to eat flax seeds on a daily basis and saw their blemishes disappear, skin and hair become more lustrous, PMS symptoms diminish, blood sugar stabilize, and excess weight melt away.

Flax contains fibers called lignans, which add bulk to the bowel to improve elimination. Unlike most other fibers, which dry out the intestine, flax helps to moisturize it. It can help to heal leaky gut syndrome, a condition that develops when chronic gastrointestinal aggravation develops, caused by toxic bile, food allergies, or an imbalance in gut flora.

Flax seeds can be soaked in water, tea, broth, or juice and then added to smoothies, baked goods, soups, dressings, or sauces. When ground into a meal or powder, it makes a good binder with other ingredients. It can even be used as an egg substitute in baking. However, if retaining flax seeds' omega-3s are the goal, then do not heat above 300° F, as oxidation caused by heat will destroy this nutrient (but you will still get soluble and insoluble fiber). If you cannot have eggs and you want to use flax eggs in your baking (see Cooking Pearl, page 62), just make sure you get your omega-3s elsewhere. Remember, you do not need to get everything from everything all the time – think versatility and variety.

I prefer soaking flax and other seeds to grinding, as this hydrates them and allows for slow, deliberate chewing. Good digestion comes from being a chew chew train and committing to the process of masticating our food.

The work of Dr. Bernard Jensen, including *Nature Has a Remedy* and numerous other books, taught me to chew plant foods until they become liquid in order to assimilate all their beneficial compounds. It is a practice I recommend to all my students.

ED

The only real stumbling block is fear of failure.
In cooking you've got to have a what-the-hell attitude.

Julia Child

One of the very nicest things about life is the way
we must regularly stop whatever it is we are doing
and devote our attention to eating.

Luciano Pavarotti and William Wright
Pavarotti, My Own Story

Dinner
A Gathering Time

Chapter 4

Dinner
A Gathering Time

After a long day, there is nothing better than sitting down to a lovely homemade dinner with family and friends. When I was growing up in the 1950s, we always had a family dinner. Only once a week or less did we go out to dinner as a family. Fast forward 50 or 60 years. Now most families eat on the run, going out or bringing in prepared foods for dinner.

In an ideal situation, many people contribute to the making of the evening meal and all sit down together to enjoy the fruits of their labors. One person makes a main dish, someone else a side dish, a third makes the salad, others bring hearty bread, beverages, or a dessert.

Imagine the dinner table free of the clutter of the day, laid out with a tablecloth, candles, flowers, and place settings. Several dishes are served that cater to the eating styles of each family member. Perhaps dad wants meat while mom or one of the children is vegetarian. What to do?

My suggestion is to encourage dad to purchase grass fed, free-range, hormone-free meat, such as lamb. Mom and the kids can make a delicious ethnic vegetable stew, casserole, or stir-fry. Everyone can enjoy a variety of side dishes, which could include baked, braised, steamed, or raw vegetables, with a salad and dressing on the table as well. Good fats in the meal could include nuts and seeds in the salad, a high-quality oil in the homemade salad dressing, and perhaps a soup or dessert that uses coconut or nut milk.

After a long day, it is wonderful to be home and enjoy a warm and colorful evening meal with loved ones. It does not have to be excessive, especially if bedtime looms in the next 3 hours. Like all meals and snacks, it is nutritionally sound to have a quality protein, fat, several colorful vegetables, and gluten-free starches during the meal.

Cooking a pot of brown rice, quinoa, or buckwheat, or preparing whole-grain noodle products made from these ingredients, will provide a naturally sweet, chewy, and filling comfort food.

I suggest water or herb tea as the dinner beverage, which makes a great palate cleanser.

If overeating, the most prevalent eating issue I work with as a nutrition consultant, is a problem for any family member, I have several suggestions:

1. Say grace before meals.
2. Be more attentive to chewing your food.
3. Put your eating implement down between bites and focus on breathing and tasting the food.
4. Exercise some portion control, having a single serving of each dish but not returning for seconds or thirds just because it tastes so good.
5. Have a cup of tea at the end of the meal, or hot water with lemon, which signals to your body that you are finished eating solid food.
6. Say another grace, giving thanks for the nourishing food you have been blessed to enjoy; and last but not least…
7. Clear the dinner table and do the dishes, a wonderful digestive tonic.

The recipes that we are presenting in this section could be eaten at any time of day, not just for dinner, as they are all well balanced, nourishing, and nicely spiced.

When making a meal, cook enough so there will be leftovers to take with you to work or eat at home the next day, or to put into your freezer for a future mealtime when you do not have time to cook from scratch.

Do not short change your life by eating out or bringing food home more frequently than making your own meals. The joy of cooking for yourself and your loved ones is a marvelous affirmation of your love for them and your commitment to be well.

Ed

To make a salad is to be a brilliant diplomatist –
the problem is entirely the same in both cases.
To know exactly how much oil one
must put with one's vinegar.

OSCAR WILDE

Contents

Miso Shallot Vinaigrette

This elegant, Asian-inspired dressing is perfect with tender salad greens and crunchy Napa cabbage. You can also use it as a marinade for fish. It can be stored in a covered jar for up to 2 weeks in the refrigerator.

Ingredients

½ cup white miso
½ cup thinly sliced shallots
¾ teaspoon sesame seeds
¼ teaspoon garlic powder
⅛ teaspoon allspice powder
½ tablespoon freshly grated ginger
Pinch of cayenne
1 tablespoon orange or tangerine zest

1 teaspoon togarashi (optional,
   see below)
1½ teaspoons unrefined cane sugar
Juice of 1 lemon
¼ cup unseasoned rice vinegar
½ teaspoon toasted sesame oil
1 cup grapeseed oil
Sea salt and freshly ground black
   pepper to taste

Method

To Make Togarashi

Grind together equal parts of dried hot chile, Szechuan peppercorn, hemp seed, sesame seeds, poppy seeds, dried orange peel, and roasted nori. (Commercial togarashi blends are available at Asian markets and some well-stocked supermarkets.)

To Make Dressing

1. In a blender, combine the miso, shallots, sesame seeds, dried spices, ginger, zest, togarashi, sugar, lemon juice, rice vinegar, and sesame oil, and purée.

2. Add the oil in a thin stream with motor running until dressing is emulsified. Taste and season with salt and pepper as desired.

166   FLAVORS OF HEALTH

Raspberry Vinaigrette

YIELDS APPROXIMATELY 1 CUP

This salad dressing pairs beautifully with mesclun, also referred to as gourmet salad mix. A popular combination includes arugula, dandelion greens, frisee, mizuna, oak leaf lettuce, mache, radicchio, and sorrel.

Ingredients

½ cup raspberries or black raspberries
½ cup champagne or brown
  rice vinegar
½ cup freshly squeezed orange juice
1 teaspoon Dijon mustard
1 cup extra virgin olive oil
Sea salt and freshly ground black
  pepper to taste
1 tablespoon poppy seeds

Method

1. In a blender, combine raspberries, champagne vinegar, orange juice, and Dijon mustard and blend until smooth.

2. While blender is still running, add the oil in a thin stream until dressing is fully emulsified. Taste and season as desired with salt and pepper.

3. Pour dressing into a canning jar and add the poppy seeds. Cap the jar tightly and give dressing a good shake to evenly distribute the seeds.

Lemon Mint Vinaigrette

YIELDS APPROXIMATELY 2 CUPS

A cool and lemony dressing perfect for tender leafy greens like butter lettuce, mache, or mesclun.

Ingredients

1 cup boiling water
½ medium lemon, seeds removed
20 fresh mint leaves, or enough to
  tightly pack ¼ cup

¼ cup champagne or white wine
  vinegar
½ teaspoon honey
¾ cup grapeseed oil
Sea salt and freshly ground pepper
  to taste

Method

1. Pour the boiling water into a bowl and add the lemon half. Stir and let steep for 30 minutes. Chill the lemon water and the lemon.

2. Once chilled, place lemon, ½ cup of the lemon water, mint leaves, vinegar, and honey in a blender. Purée.

3. Strain the mixture through a fine mesh strainer and return strained liquid to the blender.

4. Pour in the oil gradually, while blender is running on the lowest setting, until dressing is emulsified. Season with salt and freshly ground pepper to taste. Refrigerate until ready to serve.

5. Stir well before serving, or place in a jar with a tight-fitting lid and shake until well-combined.

COOKING PEARL
Selecting Lemons

When lemons are on your shopping list, select medium-sized fruits with an even yellow color, ones that feel heavy for their size. Lemons are ripe when they give to a little pressure. Most hard lemons will soften at room temperature over the course of a few days. Hard lemons yield very little juice.

Green Salad
with Mustard Dill Vinaigrette

Serves 4 to 6

When an elegant but no-fuss salad is in order, this is the one to turn to again and again. The flavors work well with just about any entrée.

Ingredients

8 cups chopped or torn salad greens
  of choice

Vinaigrette
1 tablespoon finely minced shallot
1 teaspoon Dijon mustard
1 tablespoon nutritional yeast

1 clove garlic, minced
2 teaspoons fresh dill, minced
1 teaspoon raw honey (optional)
¼ cup apple cider vinegar
¾ cup extra virgin olive oil
Sea salt and freshly ground black
  pepper to taste

Method

1. In a large bowl, whisk together the minced shallot, mustard, nutritional yeast, minced garlic, dill, and raw honey (if using) with apple cider vinegar.

2. While whisking, slowly drizzle in the olive oil until the dressing is emulsified.

3. Season with salt and freshly ground pepper to taste. Toss dressing with salad greens and serve.

Greens, Rosemary Walnuts, and Chopped Apple Salad

Serves 4 to 6

The bright and creamy green apple dressing and buttery, rosemary flavored walnuts make this salad a perfect accompaniment for hearty, simple fare. Serve alongside roast chicken, salmon, or a frittata and it's a meal.

Ingredients

6 cups mixed greens
1 large tart apple
½ lemon, juiced
1 cup chopped Rosemary Walnuts*
2 tablespoons flax seeds
¼ cup dried cranberries (optional)

Dressing
1 medium green apple, quartered
    and cored
2 tablespoons apple cider vinegar
1 green onion, finely chopped
¼ cup minced fresh parsley
2 tablespoons filtered water
½ cup extra virgin olive oil
Sea salt and freshly ground pepper
    to taste

Method

1. Wash and dry greens using a salad spinner.

2. Chop apple into bite-sized pieces and put in a glass bowl. Cover with filtered water and the juice of ½ lemon to keep them crisp and prevent oxidation (browning). Set aside along with prepared walnuts, flax seeds, and cranberries.

Make Dressing

1. Combine apple, vinegar, green onion, parsley, and water in a blender. Purée until smooth (mixture will appear somewhat grainy).

2. With the blender running on slow speed, add the oil in a slow stream. Stop and scrape down the blender jar as needed. Blend until smooth and emulsified. Taste and adjust seasoning, if needed. If dressing is too thick, add a little filtered water to make thinner.

3. Gently toss salad greens with the apples, walnuts, flax seeds, and enough dressing to lightly coat the leaves. Sprinkle on additional flax seeds and Rosemary Walnuts (see recipe, next page).

*For best results, prepare walnuts at least 2 days ahead (see recipe, next page).

Rosemary Walnuts

YIELDS 4 CUPS

Nuts add a satisfying crunchy texture to salads and are a fantastic and nutritious snack. Walnuts have a pleasant taste on their own but once you taste Rosemary Walnuts, you will have to implement serious portion control. The process of soaking and drying nuts makes them lighter and crunchier. Toasting further enhances the walnut's flavor, as does a dosing of butter, rosemary, sea salt, and a spike of cayenne. Try this extraordinary treat.

Ingredients

4 cups raw walnut halves
2 teaspoons sea salt
Filtered water to cover
¼ cup butter

¼ cup dried rosemary
1 teaspoon sea salt
1 teaspoon cayenne pepper

Method

At least 2 days ahead

1. Place walnut halves in a medium-sized glass bowl and cover with filtered water. Add 2 teaspoons salt and stir gently. Allow to soak for 8 hours.

2. The next day, drain walnuts in a colander and dry in a dehydrator, or spread evenly on a parchment-lined baking sheet and dry in the oven on the lowest temperature setting possible (no more than 150 to 170° F) for 12 to 24 hours or until nuts are dry and crisp. Turn nuts occasionally during drying time.

Make Rosemary Walnuts

Preheat oven to 325° F

1. Spread prepared walnuts on a parchment-lined baking sheet and toast in the oven for 8 minutes, turning over half way through so they cook evenly.

2. While the nuts are toasting, melt the butter in a small saucepan and stir in the rosemary. Allow the rosemary to infuse with the butter over low heat for 2 to 3 minutes. Stir in the salt and cayenne pepper.

3. Remove the walnuts from the oven and transfer them to a large bowl.

4. Pour the rosemary butter over the walnuts and toss gently until well coated.

5. Spread the walnuts out on a parchment-lined baking sheet and return to the oven until aromatic, about 10 minutes. Walnuts can be stored in an airtight container in the refrigerator for up to 1 week.

Nutrition Gem
Walnuts

Walnuts are wonderfully nutrient-dense. They contain a substantial amount of protein, as much as any animal food by weight, plus a variety of healthful oils, including monounsaturated fats, good for the heart and brain; and omega-3 fatty acids, rarely found in plant foods, which support cell membranes and also nourish and protect the brain. Walnuts are a powerful source of minerals, especially magnesium and zinc, and provide B vitamins to help us manage stress and stay calm under duress.

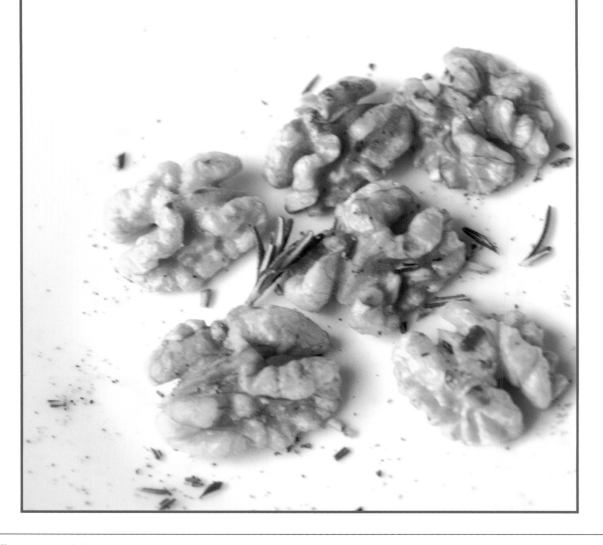

Avocado Caesar

SERVES 4

Avocados take the place of egg yolk in this Caesar dressing. The result is a creamy, light green dressing. Toss it with crisp romaine leaves or any favorite salad green. Add homemade croutons or toasted nuts for added crunch.

Ingredients

6 cups of chopped romaine leaves

Dressing
1 small to medium avocado, pitted
2 large cloves of garlic, finely chopped
2 small anchovy fillets
1 tablespoon sherry vinegar
2 tablespoons lemon juice
⅓ cup extra virgin olive oil
Sea salt and freshly ground pepper
    to taste
Up to ¼ cup of filtered water
    to thin dressing

Optional toppings
2 tablespoons of toasted
    pumpkin seeds
½ cup croutons made from whole-
    grain sourdough or gluten-free
    bread cubes
¼ cup grated Parmesan cheese

Method

1. Cut avocado in half and remove pit. Scoop avocado out and place in a blender along with chopped garlic, anchovies, vinegar, lemon juice, and olive oil. Purée ingredients until very smooth.

2. Dressing will be thick and creamy. Taste and season with salt and pepper. Blend again.

3. To thin dressing, add a little filtered water, 1 tablespoon at a time, blending a bit after each addition. Avoid making dressing too watery. Doing so will dilute flavors and prevent dressing from coating leaves well enough.

4. Just before serving, toss dressing with chopped romaine leaves. Top with toasted pumpkin seeds, croutons, and grated Parmesan cheese if desired.

Forbidden Rice and Greens with Harvest Fruits

SERVES 8

This autumnal salad is a perfect accompaniment to any festive meal. Forbidden rice granules are inky black and look elegant combined with a confetti of vibrant kale greens, sparkling pomegranate seeds, and orange segments. Pecans, shiitake mushrooms, and water chestnuts also enter the mix, along with a fresh raspberry champagne vinaigrette. Kale is a wonderful, nutrient-dense green that is typically cooked before eating. In this recipe, kale is enjoyed raw after being massaged with a little sea salt, making the leaves tender and delicious.

Ingredients

1 cup forbidden (black) rice, cooked
    and cooled
1 ¾ cups filtered water
1 ¼ teaspoon sea salt, plus a pinch
    or two, divided
½ small red onion, thinly sliced
1 tablespoon olive oil
1 tablespoon apple cider vinegar
1 teaspoon unrefined cane sugar
    or other unrefined sugar
Pinch of red chili flakes
1 large bunch Lacinato (Dino) kale,
    stems removed, cut into a
    fine chiffonade
1 cup thinly sliced shiitake mushroom
1 cup oyster mushrooms, thinly sliced
1 cup canned water chestnuts, sliced

½ cup pomegranate seeds
    (see Removing Pomegranate Seeds,
    page 99)
¾ cup orange or mandarin segments,
    preferably supremed (see How to
    Supreme Citrus, next page)

Dressing
½ cup fresh or frozen raspberries
⅓ cup champagne vinegar
2 teaspoons freshly squeezed
    lemon juice
1 tablespoon freshly squeezed
    orange juice
¼ cup extra virgin olive oil
Sea salt and freshly ground pepper
    to taste
½ cup pecans, toasted and chopped

Method

1. Wash rice several times, drain and put into a bowl with 1 ¾ cup water. Soak 1 hour.

2. Put rice, soaking water, and salt in a heavy-bottomed pot and bring to boil. Cover with a tight-fitting lid and reduce heat to low. Cook for 35 minutes.

3. Let pan sit undisturbed for 10 minutes. Fluff rice with a fork and transfer rice to a parchment-lined baking sheet and spread out to cool.

4. Place the onion in a small bowl and add apple cider vinegar, olive oil, sugar, chili pepper, and salt. Toss well and allow to marinate while preparing the rest of the salad.

5. Place chopped kale and mushrooms in a large bowl. Drizzle with a little olive oil and sprinkle with salt. Massage the mixture with your hands, kneading and squeezing until vegetables begin to wilt. Set aside.

6. Add cooled rice to kale mixture and combine well. Add onion, water chestnuts, pomegranate seeds, and oranges. Toss to combine.

7. In a blender, purée raspberries with champagne vinegar, lemon juice, and orange juice. While blender is running on low, add olive oil gradually and blend until emulsified. Add salt and pepper to taste.

8. Fold the dressing into the salad, just enough to coat the ingredients. Toss in the pumpkin seeds and serve.

COOKING PEARL
How to Supreme Citrus

Salads and desserts using citrus fruits can look much fancier when using the supreme cut instead of just peeling the fruit into segments. To supreme citrus fruit, all the skin, pith, membranes, and seeds are removed to reveal a beautiful, jewel-like segment.

To supreme:

- Begin by making a shallow cut on the bottom and top end of the citrus fruit. This cut will make a flat edge so the fruit can be held steady.

- With a sharp paring or chef knife, carefully cut away the peel, all the way to the juicy flesh.

- When all the peel and pith are removed, hold the fruit in one hand and carefully cut each segment away. The first cut is the trickiest. To do it successfully, hold the knife at an angle and make a careful slice between the segment and its membrane. This will get easier as you keep removing segments because you will be able to guide your knife edge between the membrane and the segment.

- As you keep removing segments, fold each membrane over onto itself as the fruit becomes smaller. See picture.

- Be sure to hold the fruit over a bowl to catch the juice.

Jicama and Cucumber Salad with Orange Lime Marinade

SERVES 8

Known as the "Mexican potato," jicama is a refreshing and cooling vegetable with a terrific crunch. In this salad, it is combined with cucumber and a citrus vinaigrette to create a fantastic accompaniment to zesty Mexican or Latin American dishes, or anything with a bit of spice.

Ingredients

½ cup freshly squeezed orange juice
2 tablespoons freshly squeezed lime juice
2 tablespoons extra virgin olive oil
¼ teaspoon ground coriander
½ teaspoon pure chile powder
¼ teaspoon sea salt

1 pound jicama, peeled and cut into ¼-inch julienne
1 medium cucumber, peeled, sliced in half lengthwise, seeds removed and cut into ¼-inch julienne
3 tablespoons minced fresh cilantro leaves

Method

1. First, make the dressing. In a large bowl, whisk together the orange juice, lime juice, olive oil, coriander, chile powder, and salt. Set aside.

2. Place jicama pieces in the dressing as you finish cutting them. Set aside to marinate at room temperature for about 1 hour.

3. Just before serving, cut the cucumber into julienne and add into bowl with dressing and jicama slices. Toss until well-coated with dressing.

4. Toss in cilantro leaves and serve atop a red cabbage leaf, if available.

Vegetarian Entrées

I had the great fortune of being the vegetarian chef in two restaurants I brought to prominence in the 1970s: Home Comfort in Greenfield, MA, and the Diamond Sutra in San Francisco, CA. In each of these, I created seasonal, tasty, satisfying main courses that did not depend on animal protein. These started out as daily specials, and then, due to their popularity, became menu staples.

I studied with the great Michio Kushi, a main promulgator of macrobiotics. Kushi stated that if the world chewed brown rice 50 times (together) we would usher in an era of world peace. Those of us who ate this way were peaceful, caring, and mindful, but unfortunately, the idea that finding complete proteins in balanced vegetarian meals or "Meatless Mondays" has not become the universal staple that Kushi, Frances Moore Lappé, and John Robbins have advocated to improve the health of people and the planet.

When Frances Moore Lappé's book, *Diet for a Small Planet,* came out, it changed the way health-oriented people ate. No longer was meat the perfect protein. Lappé reminded the public that by combining whole grains with legumes, all the essential amino acids were present and accounted for. This perspective lent credence to whole-grain, Japanese-influenced macrobiotic diets, vegetarian, vegan, and living food cuisine.

Any combination of the following contain the amino acids, or protein building blocks, our bodies need for growth, repair, and to support a robust metabolism:

- Legumes, whole grains, and vegetables

- Legumes with nuts and seeds or their "butters," such as sesame tahini or almond butter

- Single whole grains, nuts, seeds, or vegetables with booster foods such as nutritional yeast, seaweed, algae, or miso

The recipes in this section are complete vegetarian dishes that are delicious and satisfying on their own or a wonderful accompaniment to a meal including quality animal protein. Bon Appétit!

ED

Moroccan Lentils with Garnet Yams and Chard

SERVES 8

This recipe uses a complex and exotic Moroccan spice blend known as Ras El Hanout (see recipe, next page). Delicate and somewhat peppery, French green lentils give this hearty stew a satisfying texture.

Ingredients

2 tablespoons ghee

2 medium onions, small dice

2 medium carrots, scrubbed and medium diced

2 large garlic cloves, minced

1 tablespoon cumin seeds, toasted and ground

1 teaspoon minced fresh ginger

1 teaspoon Ras El Hanout (recipe on next page)

½ teaspoon cayenne pepper

1 teaspoon sea salt

3 whole tomatoes, peeled and chopped

1 pound yams, peeled, medium diced

5 cups vegetable stock, preferably homemade (see recipes, page 25 and 26)

2 cups uncooked French green lentils

1 bunch chard, preferably "rainbow," chopped roughly or chiffonade

¼ teaspoon freshly ground black pepper

½ cup chopped cilantro

¼ cup Italian parsley

2 lemon wedges

Method

1. In a Dutch oven or 8-quart stock pot, melt ghee over medium-high heat. Add onions and sauté until translucent.

2. Add a pinch of sea salt to the onions and give them a quick stir. Add carrots and continue cooking until carrots brighten and become slightly tender, 10 to 15 minutes.

3. Quickly stir in the garlic, cumin, ginger, Ras El Hanout, cayenne, and salt and cook on low heat until aromatic, 2 to 3 minutes.

4. Stir in tomatoes and yams until all ingredients are well distributed.

5. Add stock and lentils. Return the pot to medium low heat, cover, and simmer until lentils and yams are tender but not mushy, about 30 minutes.

6. Stir in chopped chard 10 minutes before serving. Adjust seasonings to taste.

7. Serve topped with chopped cilantro, parsley, and a squeeze of lemon.

Ras el Hanout

Most recipes for this spice blend include cardamom, nutmeg, anise, mace, cinnamon, ginger, various peppers, and turmeric, but 30 or more ingredients might be used. The literal translation from Arabic is "head of the shop" or "best of the shop." Many Moroccans use this spice blend in their daily cooking as well as for more festive, specialty dishes.

Ingredients

2 teaspoons ground ginger
2 teaspoons ground cardamom
2 teaspoons ground mace
1 teaspoon ground cinnamon
1 teaspoon ground allspice
1 teaspoon ground coriander seeds

1 teaspoon ground nutmeg
1 teaspoon turmeric
½ teaspoon ground black pepper
½ teaspoon ground white pepper
½ teaspoon ground cayenne pepper
½ teaspoon anise seeds, ground
¼ teaspoon ground cloves

Method

1. Combine all of the spices in a bowl and stir until well combined. Transfer to a glass jar and store in a dry, dark place. It keeps well for several months.

2. Use Ras El Hanout to season tangines, stews, meat, poultry, fish, and vegetables.

Hominy and Tomatillo Pozole

SERVES 6

Here is a lighter, meatless version of Pozole, a customary Mexican style stew that has been popular since pre-Hispanic times. Prepare it a few days in advance and the flavors will meld together harmoniously over time. For extra protein, add crumbled, steamed tempeh.

Ingredients

¾ cup raw unsalted pumpkin seeds

1½ pounds fresh tomatillos, husks discarded, and quartered

5 cups vegetable stock, preferably homemade, divided (see recipes, page 25 and 26)

2 medium serrano peppers, seeded and minced

2 cloves garlic, minced

1½ tablespoons extra virgin olive oil

4½ cups hominy, canned or dried hominy, soaked and pre-cooked (see Cooking Pearl, next page)

½ teaspoon sea salt, or to taste

Toppings

3 green onions, sliced thinly

1 avocado, peeled and diced, tossed with freshly squeezed lime juice

1 lime, cut into 6 wedges (1 per serving)

1 large tomato, diced

¼ cup minced fresh cilantro

Method

1. Toast pumpkin seeds in a dry sauté pan over medium-low heat. Immediately transfer to a plate or bowl to cool. When cool, use a mortar and pestle or small food processor to grind them to a fine meal. Set aside.

2. Place tomatillos in a blender. Add 2 cups of vegetable stock, the chiles, ground pumpkin seeds, and garlic. Purée.

3. Heat oil in a Dutch oven or heavy-bottomed 8-quart stock pot over medium-high heat. Pour in tomatillo purée and cook for 5 minutes, stirring frequently. Reduce to low heat and cook for 10 minutes, occasionally stirring to prevent sticking.

4. Add remaining 3 cups vegetable stock, cooked hominy, and salt to pan. Increase heat to medium-high and cook for 15 minutes, stirring occasionally.

5. Prepare the toppings and place in little bowls so people can help themselves and garnish the pozole to their individual taste.

Cooking Dried Hominy

Dried hominy, also known as maize mote or nixtamale, is made from dry corn that is "peeled" by soaking and cooking it with calcium oxide (called cal in Spanish or quicklime in English).

Dried hominy takes some time to cook, so it is best to soak it overnight with filtered water and a tablespoon of liquid whey or lemon juice.

The next day, rinse the hominy well through a fine mesh strainer and place in a large pot. Cover with 2 inches of filtered water lightly salted with sea salt. Bring to a boil and reduce heat to medium. Cook until the corn is soft and starts to "pop," about 2 to 3 hours. Stir occasionally and add additional water if needed.

When hominy is soft but still retains its shape, drain and spread evenly on a baking sheet to cool down quickly. Allowing hominy to cool in the cooking pot may cause it to clump together. When hominy is finished cooling, use in desired recipe or simply serve with a little fresh squeezed lime juice, a drizzle of olive oil, and sea salt and pepper to taste.

Sea Palm Fettuccine with Cilantro Pesto

Serves 4

If you think sea vegetables are not for you, then try this faux pasta dish. Yes, it is unusual and unexpected, but it is also absolutely delicious.

Ingredients

2 cups filtered water for soaking
2 ounces dried sea palm fronds
¼ cup pine nuts
2 teaspoons ghee
4 cloves garlic, minced
2½ cups filtered water,
*   room temperature*

2 red bell peppers, julienned
2 carrots, julienned
Sea salt to taste
1 cup of Cilantro Pesto
*   (see recipe, page 184)*
Cilantro for garnish

Method

1. Heat 2 cups of water and pour over sea palm fronds to cover. Soak until they are softened, about 15 minutes. Drain and shake out excess water.

2. Toast pine nuts in a dry sauté pan on medium heat until aromatic, about 3 to 5 minutes. Shake the pan frequently to keep nuts from burning.

3. Heat a skillet or wok over high heat and add ghee. When ghee is melted, swirl pan to coat the bottom and lower the heat to medium.

4. Add garlic to the pan and sauté for 30 seconds. Add sea palm and toss with garlic for 3 minutes. Add water and simmer until tender, about 20 minutes.

5. During last 10 minutes of simmering, stir in red bell pepper and carrots.

6. Remove from heat and transfer sea palm and vegetables to a large bowl with tongs or a large, slotted spoon. Fold in Cilantro Pesto sauce. If sauce is too thick, add a little of the cooking liquid to thin out so that vegetables are coated evenly. Adjust seasonings with salt and pepper to taste. Top with fresh, chopped cilantro and pine nuts before serving.

Sea Palm

Sea Palm *(Postelsia palmaeformis)* is versatile, mild, delicious, and succulent. Unique to the Pacific Coast of North America, it grows like a miniature palm forest on the tidal rocks. It is high in trace minerals and valuable marine saccharides. Most commercial sea palm is harvested off the coast of Mendocino, California. The "fronds" are carefully picked by hand to avoid disrupting their reproductive cycle and are then sun dried. In that area, the plant can be harvested at low tide. Before cooking and eating hand-harvested sea palm, soak it in a half cup of apple cider vinegar in a sink of water for 10 minutes to neutralize unfriendly bacteria.

Before using in a recipe, rinse off the surface salt on the fronds. It is also a good idea to reduce salty seasonings in your dish to compensate for the salty nature of the sea palm. You can use it in all styles of whole food cuisine, including soups, salads, and sautés, but finding new uses for it is one of the most delightful aspects of cooking!

Sea Palm fronds are delicious in vegetable sautés, casseroles, salads, beans, pickled dishes, or in crispy toasted condiments or snacks.

Cilantro Pesto

YIELDS 1 CUP

A pesto is based on some kind of greens combined with a nut or seed and a fat. Usually the word "pesto" calls to mind the classic Italian combo of basil, olive oil, and pine nuts. This version is an invitation to experiment with other herbs, nuts or seeds, and oils. In this case, our pesto trades basil for cilantro, and pine nuts for pumpkin seeds. The result is nothing short of amazing.

Ingredients

1 cup raw unsalted pumpkin seeds
2 cups fresh cilantro leaves
2 tablespoons extra virgin olive oil
3 cloves garlic

¼ cup filtered water or more,
  as needed, to make pesto smoother
Sea salt to taste
Juice of ½ lemon, used to taste

Method

1. Toast pumpkin seeds in a dry sauté pan over medium heat for 1 to 2 minutes or until they start to plump slightly and pop. Shake pan from time to time to prevent burning.

2. Combine toasted pumpkin seeds, cilantro, olive oil, garlic, and water in a blender and purée until smooth. Add more water if necessary to bring ingredients together.

3. Add lemon juice and salt to taste. Use pesto for Sea Palm Fettuccine (see recipe, page 182), on whole-grain pasta, chicken, fish, in soups, or over sautéed vegetables.

 NUTRITION GEM

Cilantro and Coriander: An Herb and Spice in One

Coriander is considered both an herb and a spice, since both its leaves and its seeds are used as seasonings. Fresh coriander leaves are more commonly known as cilantro and resemble Italian flat leaf parsley. Both plants belong to the *Umbelliferae* family and are excellent sources of chlorophyll, magnesium, potassium, fiber, vitamin C, beta carotene, and bioflavonoids.

The culinary use of coriander and cilantro can be traced back to 5,000 BC. It is native to the Mediterranean and Middle Eastern regions, and has been used in Asian countries for thousands of years.

Early physicians, including Hippocrates, used coriander for its medicinal properties, including as an aromatic stimulant. Coriander's use as a food also dates back hundreds of years, and cilantro has long been featured in the culinary traditions of Latin American, India, and China.

The fruit of the coriander plant contains two seeds that, when dried, are used as a spice. They have a fragrance and flavor reminiscent of both citrus peel and sage. Coriander seeds are available in whole or ground forms.

Cilantro leaves are protective against mercury accumulation and helpful in its removal. The contention that cilantro is a powerful chelation agent is based on the research of Dr. Yoshiaki Ombre. In 1995, Ombre observed that patients had lower than normal levels of mercury in their urine after consuming Vietnamese soup, which includes large amounts of cilantro (also called "Chinese parsley"). He followed up on this accidental finding and discovered that giving cilantro to patients with mercury poisoning for several weeks successfully eliminated the toxin from the body.

Storing Cilantro

Cilantro leaves should be deep green in color and free from yellow or brown spots. Fresh cilantro stalks are best stored with roots still attached in a glass of water. Cover the leaf ends loosely with a plastic vegetable bag and keep this "bouquet" in the refrigerator. If the roots have been removed, wrap the coriander leaves in a damp cloth or paper towel and refrigerate them in a plastic bag.

Eggplant Manicotti

SERVES 4

Hold the noodles, pass on the starch, and embrace the idea of vegetable based "pasta" with this delicious manicotti.

Ingredients

*1 large eggplant, cut lengthwise
    into ⅛-inch slices*
Sea salt
1 cup whole milk ricotta cheese
2 tablespoons extra virgin olive oil
¼ cup chopped parsley
*2 tablespoons currants or chopped
    raisins, rehydrated in warm,
    filtered water*

1 tablespoon pine nuts
2 cloves garlic, minced
*2 tablespoons freshly squeezed
    orange juice*
*Tomato Herb Concassé (see
    following recipe)*
*Black Olive Béchamel (see recipe
    on page 188)*

Method

Preheat oven to 350°F

1. Preheat the grill or boiler. Lay the eggplant slices in a single layer on a clean tea towel or a few layers of paper towels. Sprinkle both sides liberally with salt and let stand for at least 30 minutes to allow the bitter juices to drain off. Rinse the eggplant slices under cold water and pat dry. Brush the slices with 1 tablespoon of olive oil and grill or broil until soft and slightly charred, about 3 minutes per side.

2. Combine the ricotta, parsley, currants, nuts, and garlic in a bowl. Add the remaining 1 tablespoon olive oil and orange juice and mix well.

3. Place 1 cooked eggplant slice on a flat surface. Place about ½ tablespoon of filling at one end of the slice. Flatten the filling slightly with the back of your spoon. Roll the slice starting at the stuffing end and place the roll seam side down on a lightly oiled casserole dish. Repeat the procedure with the remaining slices and filling. Cover with foil tightly and bake 15 to 30 minutes, until heated through.

4. While eggplant manicotti are heating, make the Tomato Herb Concassé and Black Olive Béchamel. To serve, top Eggplant Manicotti with béchamel and concassé.

Tomato Herb Concassé

YIELDS APPROXIMATELY 1¼ CUPS

Concassé, pronounced (kon-ka-say), means to crush, grind, or roughly chop, usually referring to vegetables that have been blanched, skinned, and seeded. The result is a more refined texture. In this recipe, finely diced tomatoes are infused with garlic, shallots, herbs, a splash of aged balsamic vinegar, and olive oil. It tastes fresh, pure, and simply delicious.

Ingredients

4 tablespoons extra virgin olive oil
3 shallots, peeled and finely chopped
6 medium Roma tomatoes, blanched, peeled, seeded, and finely diced (see instructions on page 150)
6 garlic cloves, peeled and lightly crushed

1 tablespoon balsamic vinegar
1 teaspoon fresh thyme leaves
¼ cup of fresh basil leaves, chopped
¼ cup Italian parsley leaves
Sea salt and freshly ground pepper, to taste

Method

1. In a medium sauce pan, sauté shallots in 2 tablespoons of olive oil over medium heat until soft and translucent, about 3 to 5 minutes.

2. Add the tomatoes, crushed garlic cloves, balsamic vinegar, thyme leaves, and chopped basil. Season lightly with salt and pepper. Cover and simmer on low heat for 30 minutes. When the juice from the tomatoes has evaporated and the sauce is reduced, remove from heat and set aside to cool. Stir in parsley leaves and adjust seasoning with a little more olive oil, sea salt, and pepper, if needed.

3. To serve, place a spoonful of concassé on top of each Eggplant Manicotti, or use on whole grain pasta, vegetables, fish, or chicken.

Black Olive Béchamel

YIELDS APPROXIMATELY ¾ CUP

The black olives in this Béchamel sauce are not the only twist on this time-honored foundational sauce. In this version, protein-rich, gluten-free amaranth flour is substituted for the white flour typically used.

Ingredients

3 tablespoons unsalted butter, divided
¼ cup amaranth flour
1 pint whole milk (for a dairy-free option, choose plain unsweetened nut milk)
Pinch of sea salt

Pinch of freshly grated nutmeg
1 ounce pitted Nicoise or Kalamata olives, diced
1 ounce pitted Spanish green olives, diced
1 garlic clove, peeled and smashed

Method

1. Heat a sauté pan, add 2 tablespoons of the butter, and allow it to melt. Sprinkle in amaranth flour and stir vigorously with a wooden spoon until "roux" is lightly browned and has a nutty aroma.

2. Whisk in the milk in a slow steady stream, then add the salt and nutmeg and continue stirring until sauce begins to thicken.

3. Mash olives and garlic clove in a mortar and pestle until smooth and whisk into the sauce. Add a remaining tablespoon of butter and adjust seasoning to taste.

4. To serve, place a spoonful of béchamel on each Eggplant Manicotti, or use on whole grain pasta, vegetables, fish, or chicken.

Quinoa Risotto Milanese

SERVES 4

Traditional risotto is made with a high-starch, short or medium-grain rice, usually an Italian variety called arborio. Making it requires careful attention and logging in a lot of time over the stove. Making risotto with quinoa, however, is a quick and easy process. The quinoa is softer and creamier but still retains its distinctive texture. You will love the taste of this unique and time-saving take on the classic.

Ingredients

1 ½ cups vegetable or chicken broth, preferably homemade (see recipes, pages 25 and 30)
1 ½ cups goat milk
2 large pinches of saffron threads (optional)
1 tablespoon butter or ghee
½ cup thinly sliced leeks

¼ cup minced shallots
¼ cup white wine
3 cloves garlic, minced
1 cup uncooked quinoa
¾ cup grated Parmesan, Manchego, or other dry aged cheese
¼ cup scallions, thinly sliced
½ medium red pepper, diced

Method

1. Rinse and drain the quinoa three times, using a fine mesh strainer to remove the bitter outer coating. Set aside.

2. In a medium sauce pan on low heat, slowly heat broth and goat milk together until hot. Add saffron threads and stir gently. Keep liquid on low heat until ready to use. Do not allow to boil.

3. Heat butter in a large sauté pan or Dutch oven over medium-high heat. Add leeks and shallots and cook until caramelized, about 15 to 20 minutes. Deglaze pan with white wine and, while stirring constantly, scrape up the *fond* (the flavorful browned remnants that stick to the bottom of the pan) and incorporate into vegetables.

4. Add garlic and quinoa and continue stirring a minute or two.

5. Stir in 2 cups of the broth and milk and bring to a boil, then reduce heat to low and simmer until quinoa is tender, stirring occasionally, approximately 10 to 12 minutes.

6. Stir in the remaining broth and goat milk, cover, and continue cooking until liquid has nearly evaporated, about 30 to 35 minutes. Then, add grated cheese and stir until melted through. Fold in scallions and diced red pepper. Taste and add sea salt and pepper to taste if desired.

7. Transfer to a serving platter or onto individual plates and garnish with a little more grated cheese and scallions if desired. Serve immediately. Can be enjoyed as a side dish or as a lighter main dish.

Root Vegetable Ravioli

YIELDS APPROXIMATELY 30 RAVIOLI

This is a guilt-free pasta dish that celebrates the versatility, beauty, and delicate flavors of vegetables. Thinly sliced beets, kohlrabi, and butternut squash stand in for regular wheat pasta to make ravioli that is better than the original and superior to gluten-free versions. This recipe is so delicious you might toss out the pasta entirely and look to vegetables in a new way.

Ingredients

1 red beet, peeled
2 kohlrabi, peeled
1 small butternut squash, peeled
¼ cup extra-virgin olive oil

⅛ teaspoon pink sea salt or other high-quality sea salt
1 cup Pesto Cashew Cheese (see recipe on next page)

Method

1. Using a mandoline or V-slicer, slice beet, kohlrabi, and butternut squash into thin rounds.

2. Steam in a single layer for 3 minutes until vegetables are tender but not so soft they break apart. You will probably need to do this in batches.

3. To assemble ravioli: Measure 1 to 1½ teaspoons of Pesto Cashew Cheese into center of one root vegetable round and place another on top, like a sandwich. Continue until all ravioli are filled.

4. Whisk pink sea salt into olive oil. Before serving ravioli, give each one a light brushing of salted olive oil.

Pesto Cashew Cheese

YIELDS 1 CUP

A delicious and versatile basil-infused dairy-free cheese perfect for filling pasta, topping on crackers, serving as a dip for raw vegetables, or even as a flavoring for fish and poultry dishes. Use a small amount to jazz up salad dressings too!

Ingredients

1¼ cups cashews, soaked in 2 cups of pure, filtered water
½ cup walnuts, toasted
1 cup basil leaves, tightly packed
1 green onion, green and white parts, minced

2 cloves garlic, peeled and minced
1 tablespoon nutritional yeast
2 teaspoons white miso
½ lemon, juiced
¼ teaspoon mustard
¼ cup extra virgin olive oil
¼ teaspoon sea salt

Method

1. Drain cashews and place in a blender with walnuts, basil leaves, green onion, garlic cloves, nutritional yeast, white miso, lemon juice, mustard, and olive oil.

2. Blend thoroughly until mixture is smooth and thick. Add salt to taste if necessary. Blend again. Store in a glass container with a tight fitting lid in the refrigerator until ready to use. Pesto cheese will keep in the refrigerator for up to 4 days.

Vegetable Pad Thai

Pad Thai is Thailand's national dish and is often served as street food. Gluten-free flat rice noodles are stir-fried with bean sprouts and a mixture of pungent fish sauce and sour tamarind. You must work fast, so make sure to prepare your *mise en place* (prep and lay out all of your ingredients) before beginning to cook.

Ingredients

1 8-ounce package Pad Thai
   rice noodles
½ cup boiling filtered water
2 tablespoons tamarind paste or
   soaked and puréed dried apricots
¼ cup palm, date, or organic
   cane sugar
¼ cup bottled fish sauce
¼ cup filtered water
¼ cup brown rice vinegar
1 teaspoon chile powder

2 eggs, beaten
2 tablespoons coconut oil, ghee,
   or peanut oil
2 large shallots, minced
4 cloves garlic, minced
2 cups fresh bean sprouts
3 scallions, finely chopped
1 cup shredded daikon radish
¼ cup finely chopped peanuts
   or almonds
1 cup chopped cilantro
1 fresh lime, sliced

Method

1. Cover the dry noodles with hot water and set aside for about 1 hour while you prepare the rest of the dish. When the noodles are softened, drain them and set aside.

2. Place the tamarind paste or apricot purée in a saucepan over medium heat. Add the sugar, fish sauce, water, vinegar, and chile powder. Bring to a simmer until the sugar dissolves. Turn off the heat and set aside.

3. Whisk eggs and a pinch of salt in a bowl. Heat a skillet on medium to high heat and add 1 teaspoon of oil. When oil is heated pour in the eggs. Allow them to set and then scramble, breaking the egg into small pieces. Transfer to a plate and set aside.

4. Have all of your ingredients organized next to the stove: shallots, garlic, noodles, tamarind sauce, scrambled eggs, bean sprouts, scallions, and daikon radish.

5. Heat a wok or pan over medium heat and add the remaining oil. Immediately add the shallot and garlic and stir until they start to brown, about 3 minutes, making sure they do not burn.

6. Add the noodles to the wok. Stir and toss quickly to keep them from sticking.

7. Add the sauce and stir, taking care not to over mix the noodles so they do not clump. Cook until the liquid evaporates, about 5 minutes.

8. Toss scrambled egg pieces into noodles.

9. Add the bean sprouts, scallions, and radish and gently stir a few more times. The noodles should be soft, but not mushy.

10. Transfer onto a serving plate and sprinkle with nuts and cilantro. Garnish with sliced lime. Serve immediately.

NUTRITION GEM
Thai Essential Herbs and Spices

Herbs and spices are an essential part of Thai cooking. Used in traditional combinations, they help achieve a balance of the four essential Thai tastes: salty, sour, spicy, and sweet. I loved traveling in Thailand, and learned a great deal by visiting Thai markets and preparing a traditional Thai meal with my instructor, during a cooking class where I was the only student.

Nearly every Thai recipe begins with a paste. In the traditional Thai kitchen, pastes are made using whole spices and herbs (some fresh, others dried) pounded together with a mortar and pestle. While many Thai chefs still prefer to use this method, a food processor is a convenient and adequate substitute if you are cooking for a large group or commercially.

Most Thai pastes start with shallots (or onions), garlic, and green or red chiles. A variety of other spices and herbs may be added to this, including dried or fresh coriander, Thai chile powder, galangal, green peppercorns, lemongrass, and turmeric. Kaffir lime leaves are also a common ingredient, lending a uniquely Thai flavor to pastes or simmering dishes.

Lemongrass is used in various ways in Thai cooking. For some dishes, it is chopped and pounded, other times it is simply cut into long pieces and "bruised" (bent and kneaded) or even lightly chopped to release the scent and flavor for soups and curries.

Galangal is a relative of ginger, as is fresh turmeric. If you cannot find galangal (it is usually purchased frozen at Asian food stores in North America, but sometimes turns up fresh in the best produce markets), you can substitute ginger. These roots (actually rhizomes) add valuable nutrients, a delicious depth of flavor, and anti-inflammatory properties to soups, salads, and main dishes.

No Thai kitchen would be complete without a good supply of fresh basil. The Thai people make use of several types of basil in their cooking, including sweet basil and Thai holy basil, called Tulsi in Indian Ayurvedic cooking.

ED

Vegetable Biryani

SERVES 6

Biryani is the Indian version of rice pilaf, containing vegetables, nuts, spices, and herbs. This dish looks beautiful and is incredibly satisfying on its own, but can be part of a larger meal as well.

Ingredients

3 tablespoons ghee or coconut oil
2 cups brown basmati rice
1 pinch saffron threads
¼ teaspoon ground turmeric
½ teaspoon sea salt
4 cups vegetable stock, preferably homemade (see recipe, page 26)
1½ cups chopped yellow onion
1 large carrot, diced
1 tablespoon freshly grated ginger
2 teaspoons ground cumin
2 teaspoons ground coriander

½ teaspoon ground cinnamon
1 pinch cayenne pepper
¼ cup filtered water
1 15-ounce can whole tomatoes (or fresh tomatoes blanched, and peeled)
1 cup fresh or thawed frozen peas
1 cup fresh chopped greens, such as kale or chard
⅓ cup toasted cashews, for garnish
½ cup fresh cilantro leaves, for garnish

Method

1. Heat 1 tablespoon of ghee or oil in a large sauté pan or enamel-coated cast iron Dutch oven and add rice; sauté briefly, stirring to coat each grain.

2. Add the saffron, turmeric, salt, and vegetable stock.

3. Bring to a boil, cover, then reduce heat and simmer for about 50 minutes, until the liquid is absorbed and the rice is tender. Transfer cooked rice to a bowl and fluff with a fork.

4. While the rice is cooking, heat the remaining 2 tablespoons of oil or ghee in a separate pan over medium-high heat and sauté the onions for 5 minutes, until tender.

5. Add the carrot, ginger, and spices and cook for 1 minute, stirring constantly. Add ¼ cup water and cover. Reduce the heat and cook 3 to 4 minutes.

6. Add the tomato, peas, and greens. Simmer until the carrot is just tender.

7. Fold the vegetable and spice mixture into the rice and mix well.

8. Transfer to a serving platter and garnish with toasted cashews and cilantro.

Escarole and Gruyere Quiche with Herbed Oatmeal Crust

The herbed spelt and oatmeal crust in this recipe turns an ordinary quiche into an extraordinary one.

Ingredients

Crust
1 cup rolled oats
½ cup spelt flour
¼ teaspoon sea salt
2 teaspoons fresh thyme leaves
½ teaspoon fresh rosemary leaves, minced
¼ cup unsalted butter, cut into small pieces
1 tablespoon roasted garlic
2 tablespoons cold buttermilk
2 tablespoons ice cold filtered water

Filling
2 tablespoons ghee or unsalted butter, divided
1 large onion, thinly sliced
½ teaspoon sea salt

1 red bell pepper, diced
2 tablespoons roasted garlic pulp (see page 119) or 2 cloves garlic, minced
1 cup cremini mushrooms, chopped
1 bunch of escarole, coarsely chopped
6 large eggs
2 cups whole milk
¼ teaspoon sea salt
¼ teaspoon freshly ground black pepper
½ teaspoon garlic powder
¼ teaspoon dried mustard
Pinch of cayenne pepper
Pinch of freshly grated nutmeg
2 tablespoons minced fresh parsley leaves
⅔ cup grated Gruyere cheese

Method

Preheat oven to 350°F

Make Crust

1. In a food processor, combine the oats, spelt flour, salt, thyme, and rosemary. Add butter and roasted garlic and pulse until mixture resembles coarse crumbs.

2. Gradually add buttermilk and cold water until dough comes together into a ball. Shape into a round disk and cover with plastic wrap. Refrigerate for 30 minutes.

Make Vegetable Sauté for Filling

1. In a large sauté pan over medium heat, melt 1 tablespoon of ghee or butter. Add onions and salt and sauté over medium heat for about 10 minutes.

2. Add bell pepper and garlic to onions and continue cooking over low heat until onions are golden and caramelized, about 10 to 15 minutes. Transfer to a large bowl and set aside.

3. Wipe out sauté pan and heat another tablespoon of ghee or butter over medium heat. Add mushrooms and sauté for about 3 minutes, or until browned. Add chopped escarole and sauté until slightly wilted. Combine this mixture with the caramelized onions and bell pepper. Set aside.

Roll Out Crust

1. Place chilled dough between two sheets of parchment paper and roll out into a circle about 10 inches in diameter. Remove top layer of parchment paper and invert dough onto a tempered glass pie pan deep enough to accommodate filling for quiche. Press dough gently to conform to the shape of the pan and crimp edges in a decorative pattern. Refrigerate for at least 30 minutes. Then line pie dough with a parchment paper round and fill with pie weights.

2. Bake crust for 10 to 15 minutes, until it is a light, golden color. Carefully remove pie weights and parchment. If dough is too sticky, allow crust to cool for 10 minutes before removing parchment. When crust is cool it is ready to fill.

Prepare Eggs for Filling

1. In a large bowl, whisk eggs lightly and then add milk, salt, pepper, garlic powder, and mustard. Whisk vigorously until foamy. Stir in parsley.

2. Fold egg mixture into sautéed vegetables. Add half the grated Gruyere cheese and gently fold to incorporate.

3. Transfer egg and vegetable mixture to baked quiche crust. Top with remaining Gruyere cheese and bake for 35 minutes, or until a knife inserted in the center comes out clean.

4. When quiche is done, allow to stand for 10 minutes before cutting into 6 wedges.

Curried Carrot and Parsnip Tart

SERVES 4 TO 6

If Indian cuisine had a signature quiche, this might be the one. The humble carrot and parsnip go from merely tasty to savory and exotic when combined with curry spices, cilantro, and coconut milk.

Ingredients

Crust

1 ¼ cup spelt flour
¼ cup fine cornmeal (not corn flour)
½ teaspoon sea salt
½ cup (1 stick) cold unsalted butter,
 cut into pieces
3 to 4 tablespoons ice cold
 filtered water

Filling

2 tablespoons ghee, unsalted butter,
 or coconut oil
2 cups thinly sliced onions
2 cloves garlic, minced
½ teaspoon sea salt
1 teaspoon curry powder
1 ½ teaspoons garam masala
¼ teaspoon paprika
2 tablespoons of water
 or vegetable broth
2 cups grated carrots
2 cups grated parsnips
2 tablespoons freshly grated turmeric
 (optional)
½ cup coconut milk
¼ cup chopped fresh cilantro
¼ cup chopped fresh parsley
½ teaspoon freshly ground
 black pepper
2 large eggs, lightly whisked

Method

Preheat oven to 350° F

Make Crust

In the bowl of a food processor, combine spelt flour, cornmeal, sea salt, and butter and process until mixture resembles coarse crumbs. While the motor is running, add water in increments until dough forms a ball. Transfer dough to a lightly floured surface and shape into a flat disc. Refrigerate for 1 hour.

Roll Out Crust

1. Place chilled dough between two sheets of parchment paper and roll out into a circle, about 10 inches in diameter. Remove top layer of parchment paper and invert dough onto a deep, tempered glass pie pan big enough to accommodate filling for quiche, about 9 to 10 inches in diameter. Press dough gently to conform to the shape of the pan and crimp edges decoratively. Refrigerate for at least 30 minutes, then line pie dough with a parchment paper round and fill with pie weights.

2. Bake crust for 10 to 15 minutes until it is a light, golden color. Carefully remove pie weights and parchment. If dough is too sticky, allow crust to cool for 10 minutes before removing parchment. When crust is cool it is ready to fill.

Make Filling

1. Heat a large sauté pan with fat of choice. Sauté onions until opaque; about 5 minutes. Add a pinch of salt and the garlic and sauté until aromatic, about 1 more minute.

2. Sprinkle salt, curry powder, garam masala, and paprika over onions and garlic and sauté together quickly for another minute. When pan becomes dry, deglaze with a splash of water or vegetable broth and, using a wooden spoon, scrape off bits from bottom of pan (this is the fond, and if not burned will only enhance the lovely flavor of this dish).

3. Add carrots, parsnips, and grated turmeric (if using) to the onion mixture and cook over low heat until vegetables are very tender.

4. Pour in coconut milk and cook another 5 to 10 minutes, until mixture is warmed through. Remove from heat.

5. Add cilantro, parsley, and whisked eggs and stir until well combined. Pour mixture into the pie crust.

6. Bake until golden brown and a knife inserted in the center comes out clean, about 50 minutes.

Spring Vegetable Pot Pie with Polenta Crust

SERVES 4 TO 6

Nothing says comfort food like pot pie. Creamy herbed polenta takes the place of the usual pie crust topping in this innovative version, and the filling features a mix of early spring vegetables and a variety of mushrooms.

Ingredients

Filling
½ ounce dried porcini mushrooms
1 cup hot filtered water
½ pound small marble potatoes,
     cut in half (larger potatoes can be
     substituted; cut into cubes small
     enough to fit on a spoon)
2 tablespoons of melted ghee, divided
½ pound asparagus, cut into
     ¾-inch pieces
Sea salt and freshly ground black
     pepper, to taste
2 tablespoons extra virgin olive oil
2 medium leeks, thinly sliced
4 cloves garlic, minced
½ pound fresh shiitake mushrooms,
     stems removed, quartered
¼ teaspoon sea salt, or to taste
1 tablespoon tamari soy sauce
2 teaspoons orange zest
1 tablespoon fresh thyme leaves
1½ tablespoons sorghum flour
1 cup fresh or frozen peas

Polenta Crust
1½ cups vegetable or mineral broth,
     preferably homemade (see recipe,
     page 32)
1½ cups filtered water, organic
     whole milk, or nut milk

¼ teaspoon sea salt
¾ cup uncooked polenta
1 tablespoon minced fresh
     rosemary leaves
1 tablespoon fresh thyme leaves
1 tablespoon minced fresh
     oregano leaves
¼ cup finely grated Parmesan cheese
     (optional)

Method

Preheat oven to 425°F

Make Filling

1. Soak porcini mushrooms in hot water for at least 1 hour. Remove reconstituted mushrooms from water, squeeze, finely chop, and set aside. Strain sediment from soaking water through cheesecloth, a fine sieve, or a coffee filter. Add enough water to the strained soaking liquid to measure 1 cup and set aside.

2. Toss potatoes with 1 tablespoon of ghee and a bit of salt and pepper, then place them on a parchment-lined sheet pan in a single layer. Roast until tender, about 25 to 30 minutes, turning once or twice to prevent burning. On a separate sheet pan lined with parchment paper, toss asparagus with ½ tablespoon of the ghee, sprinkle with a bit of salt and pepper and roast, turning occasionally, about 6 minutes. Remove from the pan and set aside.

3. While potatoes and asparagus roast, heat olive oil with the remaining ½ tablespoon of ghee in a heavy skillet. Add the leeks and sauté until they are soft, about 15 minutes.

4. Add the garlic and sauté another 3 minutes, then add the fresh mushrooms and re-hydrated porcini. Cook until mushrooms shrink and have released their liquid, about 15 minutes, stirring occasionally. Transfer mixture to a large bowl and stir in ¼ teaspoon salt, tamari, orange zest, and fresh thyme.

5. Using the same sauté pan, heat 1 tablespoon oil over medium heat. Add the sorghum flour and stir constantly until flour begins to brown and releases a toasty aroma. Rapidly whisk in the reserved porcini water; cook until liquid reduces by about a third. Remove from heat and pour this sauce over the mushroom mixture, stirring to combine.

6. Remove potatoes from the oven and reduce the temperature to 350°F. Lightly oil a 9x9-inch baking pan. Combine the mushroom mixture, potatoes, asparagus, and peas, then scoop filling into prepared baking dish. Set aside.

Polenta Crust

1. Bring stock, water or milk, and salt to a rolling boil. Slowly pour in the polenta, whisking constantly to prevent lumps. Turn heat down to medium and whisk in the rosemary, thyme, oregano, and Parmesan cheese. Continue whisking until mixture thickens and begins to pull away from the sides of the pot, about 10 minutes.

2. Spread polenta over potato and mushroom mixture. Bake for 15 minutes in a 350°F oven. When finished baking, remove from the oven and let stand for 15 minutes before serving.

Vegetable Stir Fry with Ginger Almond Cilantro Sauce

SERVES 6

The following ginger almond cilantro sauce is lick-the-bowl delicious and addictive. But no need to feel guilty, because unlike store-bought sauces that tend to contain a lot of sugar, salt, and preservatives, this one delivers good nutrition via healthy, whole ingredients. As always, choose the freshest vegetables in season for the stir fry.

Ingredients

Ginger Almond Cilantro Sauce
½ cup raw unsalted almond butter
½ cup orange juice reduced to
    2 tablespoons (see Cooking Pearl,
    Reduction Sauces, on next page)
1½ tablespoons unseasoned
    rice vinegar
2 tablespoons tamari soy sauce
1 teaspoon unrefined cane sugar
½ teaspoon red chili paste, to taste
1 tablespoon toasted sesame oil
2 tablespoons minced ginger
¼ cup chopped fresh mint leaves
¼ cup fresh cilantro leaves, minced

2 tablespoons finely chopped
    toasted almonds

Stir Fry
2 tablespoons toasted sesame oil
1 small onion, cut in half
    and thinly sliced
½ teaspoon sea salt
½ pound green beans, cut into 2-inch
    pieces, blanched, and shocked
1 large red bell pepper, julienned
2 medium yellow summer squash,
    cut diagonally into ½-inch slices
1½ cups shelled edamame, blanched

Method

1. Prepare the sauce by adding to a blender the almond butter, orange juice reduction, rice vinegar, tamari sauce, sugar, chili paste, toasted sesame oil, and ginger. Purée mixture until smooth. Transfer to a bowl and fold in the mint leaves, cilantro, and toasted almonds. Set aside.

2. Heat a wok over high heat. Drizzle oil along sides of hot wok and swirl briefly to coat. Add onions and salt and stir fry for 1 minute. Add green beans and peppers and stir fry for another minute. Add squash and stir fry for 2 to 3 more minutes. Vegetables should remain bright in color and be tender but crisp. Add edamame to the vegetables and toss until heated through, just another minute or two.

3. Quickly fold half of the Ginger Almond Cilantro Sauce into the vegetables and warm through.

4. Divide the vegetables among 6 plates and serve with an additional dollop of sauce.

COOKING PEARL
Reduction Sauces

Many sauces are thickened with flour or cornstarch and enriched with butter and cream to intensify their flavor and create a silky texture, but reducing liquids is another fantastic way to thicken a sauce and do without the extra ingredients that can sometimes add unnecessary heaviness to a dish. The basic technique in making a reduction sauce is to simply cook a flavorful liquid down until it reduces to the consistency of a syrup. The liquid can be anything from stock, wine, vinegar, or juice. Many times only a small amount of a reduction is asked for in a recipe to add a boost of flavor to other blended sauces or dressings. Either way, this technique is a winner because not only is it versatile, it is a cinch to master.

Step by Step Guide

- The amount of liquid used in a reduction sauce depends on how much sauce you want. Most reductions are reduced by half, so for 1 cup of reduced sauce, begin with 2 cups of liquid.

- Place stock, juice, or desired liquid in a sauce pan and bring to a low boil over medium heat. Cook until reduced by half.

- For a thicker, more syrupy sauce, continue cooking until desired consistency is achieved. Sometimes a reduction needs to be cooked until ¾ or more of the liquid has evaporated to reach this result. Keep in mind that a liquid that contains fat will become thicker as it reduces.

Go Fish

Choose Sustainable and Safe Seafood

Seafood, which includes fish, shellfish, and sea vegetables, is an exceptionally nutrient-rich food source, containing highly digestible protein, essential fatty acids, and the widest array of vitamins, minerals, and trace elements of any food on the planet. The best way to prepare fish is to marinate it and eat it raw, if palatable, or have it steamed, poached, or grilled. Lemon, ginger, garlic, and aromatic herbs are lovely fish seasonings. Fish is very perishable, so it is best eaten within 48 hours of purchase. Seafood that is flash frozen immediately after capture can be thawed and prepared in the same way as fresh fish. Unfortunately, due to the high demand for fish, seafood, and fish oil, consumers need to be aware of the ecological impact of eating certain varieties of endangered fish. A second concern is a problem with toxicity of certain fish due to the accumulation of mercury, other heavy metals, and polychlorinated biphenyls (PCBs, a persistent organic pollutant) that with sufficient exposure and sensitivity can cause endocrine disruption and neurotoxicity. The safest and most ecological fish to eat are listed here for your information.

Which Fish and How Often?

Fish is generally healthy to eat. The chart below gives you a breakdown of fish that are safe to eat in abundance, in moderation, and are best to avoid or consume minimally. The advice is based on EPA guidance and the latest mercury and PCB data. See the green sections below for safer seafood options.

It is safe to eat four or more meals per month of the following: anchovies, clams, Atlantic cod, Dungeness crab, king crab (U.S.), snow crab, crawfish (U.S.), haddock (U.S. trawl), Atlantic herring, Maine lobster, Atlantic mackerel, blue mussel, oysters (farmed), red porgy (U.S.), salmon (canned or wild from Alaska), sardines, scallops (farmed), pink shrimp (Oregon), imported shrimp/prawns, squid, and tilapia.

ED

FISH	ECO-BEST	ECO-OK	ECO-WORST
Salmon	• canned salmon ♥ • wild salmon from Alaska ♥	• wild salmon from Washington ▲ • wild salmon from California • wild Salmon from Oregon	• farmed or Atlantic salmon ▲
Shrimp	• pink shrimp from Oregon • spot prawns from Canada	• brown shrimp • farm shrimp from U.S. and Canada • spot prawns from U.S. • white shrimp • wild shrimp from U.S.	• blue shrimp • Chinese white shrimp • giant tiger prawn • imported shrimp and prawns
Tilapia	• tilapia from U.S.	• tilapia from Latin America	• tilapia from Asia
Trout	• farmed rainbow trout ♥		
Tuna	• albacore from U.S. or Canada ♥ • yellow fin from the U.S. Atlantic caught by troll/pole ♥	• canned light tuna • canned white/albacore ▲ • imported bigeye/yellow fin caught by troll/pole ▲	• albacore tuna (imported longline) ▲ • bluefin tuna • imported bigeye/yellow fin caught by long line ▲

♥ = Indicates fish high in heart-healthy omega-3 fatty acids and low in environmental contaminants
▲ = Indicates fish high in mercury or PCBs

Source: Environmental Defense Fund, http://www.edf.org/home.cfm

Roasted Salmon with Plum Salsa

SERVES 6

Salmon is a very versatile fish that pairs well with strong, vibrant flavors. The plum salsa in this recipe is bright and spicy with a refreshing, fruity sweetness.

Ingredients

1¾ pounds wild salmon fillets,
    skinned, portioned into 6 pieces
½ cup freshly squeezed lemon juice
¼ cup tamari soy sauce
6 cloves garlic, thinly sliced
Freshly ground black pepper to taste

Plum Salsa

2 tablespoons honey
⅓ cup apple cider vinegar

1 medium jalapeño pepper, seeded
    and minced
4 large plums, pitted and finely diced
½ medium red onion, finely chopped
½ cup finely diced yellow tomato
½ tablespoon grated fresh ginger
2 tablespoons minced fresh mint leaves
2 tablespoons freshly squeezed
    lime juice
2 tablespoons extra virgin olive oil

Method

Preheat oven to 350° F

1. In an oven-proof dish, marinate fillets for about 30 minutes in lemon juice and tamari, turning once midway through.

2. Press garlic slices into the top of each fillet and grind some black pepper on top.

3. Roast in the marinade for about 7 to 10 minutes, depending on thickness, basting with the marinade occasionally. If salmon is 2-inches thick it may take as long as 20 minutes to cook through, but check after 10 minutes. Salmon is done when it is opaque, still tender, and flakes easily with a fork. The fish will continue to cook after removing it from the oven, so keep this in mind when checking for doneness.

Plum Salsa

1. Whisk honey and vinegar in a small saucepan until emulsified and cook over moderate heat until reduced enough to coat the back of a spoon. Remove from heat and let cool.

2. Combine jalapeños, plums, red onion, tomato, ginger, mint leaves, lime juice, and olive oil in a medium bowl and stir in the cooled honey reduction. Season with salt and pepper to taste, then spoon over the salmon fillets.

Salmon with Dijon Date Sauce

SERVES 6

The sweetness of dates and the pungent kick of mustard and garlic enhance the richness of salmon. This sauce is thick and best painted on the salmon with a basting brush. Use generously.

Ingredients

1¾ pounds wild salmon fillets,
    skinned, portioned into 6 pieces

Dijon Date Sauce
⅓ cup Dijon mustard
4 Medjool dates, pitted
⅓ cup filtered water

¼ cup extra virgin olive oil
½ lemon, juiced
1 clove garlic, minced
Sea salt and freshly ground pepper
    to taste
⅓ cup green onions, thinly sliced

Method

Preheat 350° F

Rinse and pat fish dry with paper towels. Remove any pin bones with tweezers if desired. Place in a shallow, tempered glass baking dish and set aside.

Dijon Date Sauce

1. Purée all sauce ingredients in a blender until smooth. Brush sauce over salmon fillets.

2. Roast for 7 to 10 minutes, depending on the thickness of the fish. If salmon is 2-inches thick it may take as long as 20 minutes to cook through, but check after 10 minutes. Salmon is done when it is opaque, still tender, and flakes easily with a fork. The fish will continue to cook after removing it from the oven, so keep this in mind when checking for doneness.

3. To serve, top with additional sauce and garnish with green onions.

Salmon en Papillote with Miso Glaze

SERVES 6

Here is a recipe brimming with umami flavors and sweet and sour notes throughout. Thinly sliced green onions, carrots, and shiitake mushrooms enhance this recipe's Asian-inspired flavors.

Ingredients

1¾ pounds salmon fillets, skinned, portioned into 6 pieces

Miso Glaze
1 cup miso paste (a light variety such as chickpea or brown rice miso works best)
¼ cup dry rice wine (sake)
½ cup Medjool dates, soaked in filtered water for 30 minutes to soften

2 tablespoons sesame seeds
1 teaspoon toasted sesame oil
¼ cup filtered water
½ cup extra virgin olive oil
1 tablespoon fresh ginger, minced
2 tablespoons tamari soy sauce
3 tablespoons unseasoned rice vinegar
5 green onions, thinly sliced (green and white bulbs)
1 large carrot, scrubbed and julienned
8 shiitake mushrooms, stems removed and thinly sliced

Method

Preheat 250° F

Rinse and pat fish dry with paper towels. Remove pin bones with tweezers if desired. Place in a shallow, tempered glass baking dish and set aside.

Miso Glaze

1. Combine miso, sake, dates, sesame seeds, sesame oil, water, olive oil, ginger, soy sauce, and rice vinegar in a blender and purée until mixture forms a smooth paste.

2. Prepare 6 sheets of parchment squares for papillote (see Cooking Pearl on page 210, How to Cook En Papillote, for detailed instructions). Place a fish fillet in the center of one half of the parchment paper. Generously brush miso sauce on top and follow with green onions, carrots, and mushroom slices. Repeat this process until all fillets are prepared.

3. Fold other half of parchment paper over fish and fold the edges together securely to create a sealed package. Place each papillote on a baking dish.

4. Bake for 20 to 30 minutes, or until fish flakes easily with a fork but is still moist.

5. To serve, use the point of a very sharp knife or a pair of kitchen shears to slash or snip an "X" in the center of the papillote. Pull back the edges of the paper to reveal fillet and serve. You can also unwrap and remove the parchment paper then carefully transfer the fish and vegetables to a plate. Top with additional sauce before serving, if desired.

COOKING PEARL

How to Cook En Papillote

Cooking en papillote is a terrific technique that serves two great purposes when it comes to gourmet cooking. First, it is a simple and convenient way to steam fish or chicken along with desired vegetables and seasonings; and second, it makes for a great presentation.

Different cultures throughout history have been wrapping tender cuts of meat, fish, or chicken with grape or banana leaves, corn husks, and parchment paper before cooking them in the oven or in a steamer basket over a pot of simmering water. Steam builds up in the packet and cooks the food gently and quickly.

Cooking en papillote requires no special equipment other than parchment paper, which makes for easy clean-up.

Making a Papillote

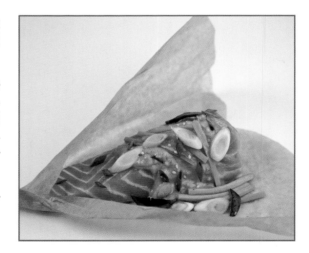

- Cut parchment paper into 12x 12-inch squares. Fold in half and cut into a large heart shape.

- Place food to be steamed in the center of one half of the parchment paper. Top with desired seasonings and additional ingredients, and fold other half over food to make a packet.

- Seal the packet by folding over the edges tightly.

Parchment Tips

- Use only parchment paper designated for baking. This paper is coated with silicone to keep it from igniting in the oven. Parchment paper can be safely used in oven temperatures of up to 450°F.

- Do not use wax paper. It will burn and leach unwanted liquids from the paper coating.

- Do not use foil. It is made from aluminum, which should never contact food at high temperatures.

Bombay Fish Curry

SERVES 6

In India, the word "curry" refers to a stew, not a spice that comes in a jar. This recipe is a warming, comforting fish stew enrobed in Indian spices and creamy coconut milk. It is a perfect dish to get cozy with on a cold night.

Ingredients

4 cloves garlic, minced

1 to 2 small jalapeños, seeded and minced (for more heat, use serrano chilies)

1 teaspoon pure chili powder

½ teaspoon ground turmeric

½ teaspoon ground cinnamon

½ teaspoon ground coriander

½ teaspoon ground cardamom

1 tablespoon tamarind paste mixed with 1 tablespoon filtered water, or 2 dried apricots in 1 tablespoon filtered water, enough to make paste

½ teaspoon sea salt

1½ pound white fish fillets, skinned, cut into large chunks

2 tablespoons coconut oil

2 medium shallots, thinly sliced

1 cup coconut milk

1 cup vegetable stock, preferably homemade (see recipe, page 26)

½ cup chopped cilantro, for garnish

½ teaspoon sea salt or to taste

Method

1. Using a mortar and pestle or small food processor, make a paste of the garlic, jalapeño, chile powder, turmeric, cinnamon, coriander, cardamom, tamarind (or apricots), water, and salt.

2. Spread the paste over the fish and set aside in the fridge for 1 hour to overnight.

3. Just before mealtime, heat the oil on medium heat in a pan large enough to hold the fish in a single layer. Sauté the sliced shallots until golden.

4. Add the coconut milk and vegetable stock and stir to combine. Add the marinated fish and reduce the heat to low.

5. Cover and simmer gently for 10 to 12 minutes, until the fish is cooked through. Do not let the liquid come to a full boil. Taste and adjust seasoning by adding salt and blending seasonings to taste: either mild, medium, or spicy.

6. Transfer the fish to a serving platter and garnish with fresh cilantro. Serve over Cardamom Scented Basmati Rice (for recipe, see page 236 in this chapter).

Halibut Poached with Herbs and Leeks

SERVES 4

Halibut's firm texture and subtle sweetness makes it an excellent choice for poaching. In this recipe, aromatic herbs are simmered slowly in broth before the fish is immersed and allowed to soak up the flavors.

Ingredients

6 cups vegetable stock, preferably
    homemade (see recipe, page 25)
4 generous sprigs Italian parsley
3 sprigs fresh thyme
3 large strips of lemon peel (no pith)
4 garlic cloves, peeled and chopped

4 bay leaves
1 teaspoon whole peppercorns
½ teaspoon sea salt, divided
4 leeks, white and light green portion,
    sliced about ⅓-inch thick
1 pound halibut fillets, 4 equal portions
1 whole lemon, sliced thinly

Method

1. Bring stock to a simmer in a shallow pan large enough to accommodate the halibut fillets.

2. Tie the parsley and thyme together with string and add the bundle to the stock along with lemon peel, garlic, bay leaf, peppercorns, and salt. Simmer over medium heat while you prepare the leeks.

3. Separate the rounds of leeks with your fingers and wash them well in a bowl of running, filtered cold water. Let the leek rings bathe in the water to allow any grit or soil residue to fall to the bottom of the bowl. Gently lift leeks out with a slotted spoon and rinse a second time in a fine mesh sieve.

4. Add leeks to the simmering stock and cook for 5 minutes or so.

5. Slide the halibut fillets into the stock and bring it back to a very light simmer; the stock should be barely moving.

6. Poach fish until tender, 5 to 6 minutes on each side, depending on the size of the pieces.

7. Transfer the fish to a cutting board and lift the leeks out of the broth with a slotted spoon.

8. Season the leeks, if desired, with melted butter, a pinch of sea salt, and freshly ground pepper. Set aside. Arrange the fish on plates and top with lemon slices and leek rings.

How to Poach Fish

The first poached fish I ever encountered was an entire salmon served cold on a bed of butter lettuce and covered with cucumber "scales" at a country club buffet in Napa. Pretty impressive, I must say.

Poaching is a gentle and easy way to cook fish. Essentially, you are giving the fish a bath in simmering water, stock, or some other flavorful liquid.

The fish absorbs the hot liquid as it cooks. Unlike grilled or baked fish, the flesh retains a lot of moisture and is often described as having a buttery, silky texture.

Be sure the liquid you use for poaching tastes excellent before adding the fish. You can add more personality by infusing herbs, lemon slices, and other spices in the liquid. For a richer flavor, fish can be poached in coconut milk infused with lemon grass, ginger, and lemon, or with a curry spice blend added. Tea blends and white wine also make wonderful poaching liquids.

Poaching Fish Tips

- Use a skillet, small roasting pan, or oval sauté pan with sides high enough to just cover fish fillet.

- Add enough liquid to fill pan half way. Use any flavorful stock, wine, court bouillon (a light vegetable stock), coconut milk, even tea.

- Bring liquid to a simmer and carefully add fish fillets. Allow to cook gently in simmering liquid until cooked through.

LIZETTE

Poultry

Poultry is for cookery what canvas is for painting, and the cap of Fortunatus for the charlatans. It is served to us boiled, roasted, hot or cold, whole or in portions, with or without sauce, and always with equal success.

JEAN-ANTHELME BRILLAT-SAVARIN (1755–1826)

Chicken, turkey, duck, quail, squab, and their eggs are outstanding sources of nutrition. Animals, like humans, are only as healthy as the foods they are fed and the amount of pure water, fresh air, and exercise they are allowed.

I know that love and caring also influence the neuro-hormonal system in the animals we eat. Commercial poultry farms are an abomination, and this has led many people to become vegetarian or to choose free-range meats and poultry.

Fortunately, there is an alternative to eating poultry fed with hormones, antibiotics, and junk food. Free-range chickens fed organic feed, some enriched with algae and flax seeds, provide a nutrient-dense array of complete protein, essential fatty acids, as well as substantial amounts of minerals and vitamins. The key to responsible consumption of poultry is to maintain a 3- to 4-ounce serving size, about half of what many people eat at home or in a restaurant. It is best to consume 2 to 3 servings of plant foods with a single serving of poultry to maintain a healthy acid–alkaline balance.

Dark meat poultry is an outstanding source of the amino acid tryptophan, which is the primary precursor to serotonin, which helps people calm down and sleep well. Poultry also provides an outstanding source of the amino acid carnitine (most abundant in "carne," or animal protein, hence the name). Carnitine helps the body burn fats for energy production, as well as supporting heart health and proper brain functioning.

ED

Aromatic Roast Chicken

SERVES 6

Not sure what to serve as the main course? Roast chicken comes to the rescue. Dressed up or down, a perfectly roasted chicken is a sure winner with many people. This recipe borrows from some of my favorite techniques to produce a tender, juicy chicken with a perfectly crispy skin and a heady scent of garlic, herbs, and citrus. The lovely chicken drippings flavor the roasted vegetables, making this a near complete meal. Add a side salad and you win!

Ingredients

1 3 to 4-pound whole chicken, cleaned, patted dry, and gizzards removed
1 lemon, halved
½ orange
Sea salt and freshly ground black pepper
1 tablespoon fresh rosemary leaves, chopped
½ tablespoon fresh thyme leaves

6 fresh sage leaves, minced
¼ cup finely chopped fresh parsley
6 cloves garlic, mashed and minced
¼ cup softened butter
4 medium purple and/or red potatoes, sliced into ½-inch rounds
3 carrots, sliced into 1-inch pieces
1 leek, white part only, sliced lengthwise into half-inch strips

Method

Preheat oven to 375°F

1. Rinse the chicken well under cool filtered water, pat dry, and rub the outside with the lemon and orange. Sprinkle salt and pepper inside the chicken cavity, then stuff with lemon and orange along with half an onion. Set aside in a stainless steel or non-aluminum baking pan.

2. In a small bowl, mash herbs and garlic into the butter.

3. With gentle hands, loosen the skin of the chicken from the flesh, creating pockets of space between skin and breast, back, and thighs.

4. Place knobs of the butter mixture under the skin in various places, massaging from the outside to distribute the butter as evenly as possible. Rub any remaining butter on the skin and inside the chicken. Liberally season with salt and pepper.

5. Place potatoes, carrots, and leeks in the baking pan.

6. Place the chicken, breast-side up, on top of vegetables. Bake for 20 minutes, then turn breast-side down and bake for 1 hour. Turn breast side up again and bake for another 10 minutes or until skin is golden brown and crispy, and juices run clear when flesh is pierced between the leg and breast (or when meat thermometer placed in thickest part of thigh measures 165°F).

7. Allow chicken to rest for 30 minutes before carving.

Roast Turkey Breasts with Orange Rosemary Glaze

SERVES 6

You do not have to wait until Thanksgiving to enjoy turkey, nor do you have to spend a whole day cooking. Turkey breasts are readily available at most good supermarkets, and just one will comfortably feed 3 to 4 adults. The orange and rosemary glaze gives a lovely aromatic quality to this dish.

Ingredients

2 turkey breasts, bone in, skin on
¼ cup butter, softened
4 cloves garlic, minced
2 tablespoons minced fresh rosemary
    leaves, divided
1 teaspoon sea salt

½ teaspoon freshly ground
    black pepper
¾ cup freshly squeezed orange juice
¼ cup dry white wine
1 4-inch sprig fresh rosemary

Method

Preheat oven to 350°F

1. Rinse turkey breasts well under cool, filtered water and pat dry.

2. In a small bowl, mash the butter with the garlic, rosemary, and salt.

3. With gentle hands, loosen skin from turkey, creating pockets of space between skin and breast.

4. Spoon butter and herb mixture under the skin, massaging from the outside to distribute it evenly. Rub any remaining butter on the skin and sprinkle with sea salt and pepper.

5. Place turkey breasts bone side down in a baking dish and bake 1 hour, or until juices run clear when flesh is pierced in the thickest, meatiest portion and thermometer temperature reads 165°F.

6. While turkey is cooking, place orange juice and white wine in a saucepan with the rosemary sprig and bring to a boil. Turn heat down to medium and simmer until liquid is reduced to half the amount (about ½ cup) or is thick enough to coat the back of a spoon.

7. Brush half the glaze onto the turkey during the last 20 minutes of cooking and reserve the remainder to spoon over turkey slices before serving.

Chicken Mole

Serves 6 to 8

This is one of those dishes that is completely worth the so-called "trouble" it takes to prepare. Reserve a weekend afternoon and make this mole for your evening meal. Keep extra mole sauce in a tightly sealed mason jar to use again later. You will never go back to store-bought versions again.

Ingredients

2 3-pound whole chickens, quartered

Mole Sauce
4 large dried guajillo or ancho chiles
    (about 1 ounce)
12 whole raw unsalted almonds
2 tablespoons raw unsalted
    pumpkin seeds
2 tablespoons raw unsalted cashews
¼ cup coconut oil, melted
1 8-ounce plantain, peeled and
    chopped
1 cup fresh mango, peeled, pitted,
    and diced

½ cup diced white onion
4 Roma tomatoes
2 cloves garlic, coarsely chopped
1 small bay leaf
½ teaspoon fresh thyme leaves
¼ teaspoon freshly ground
    black pepper
½ teaspoon ground cinnamon
2 cups chicken stock, preferably
    homemade (see recipe, page 30)
3.2 ounces 70% dark chocolate
1 tablespoon palm sugar or grated
    piloncillo (Mexican unrefined
    brown sugar)

Method

Preheat oven to 350°F

Make Sauce

1. Place the chiles on a baking sheet and toast for 5 to 10 minutes, checking frequently to make sure they do not burn. When chiles become deeply aromatic, take them out of the oven and set aside to cool.

2. Stem, seed, and devein chiles before slicing them into thin pieces.

3. Heat a large skillet over low heat and toast almonds, pumpkin seeds, and cashews in separate batches. Transfer each batch of nuts to a bowl. Set aside.

4. Return large skillet to the stove and melt coconut oil over medium-high heat. Add chiles, plantains, mango, onion, tomatoes, garlic, almonds, pumpkin seeds, cashews, bay leaf, and thyme. Sauté until plantain is soft, about 8 minutes.

5. Add 2 cups of chicken stock, cover, and simmer until chiles are tender, about 15 minutes.

6. Working in batches, purée the mixture in a blender, then return to the skillet and add the chocolate. Bring to a simmer and cook until chocolate melts, whisking constantly and thinning with more broth or water by the tablespoon if sauce gets too thick. Season with salt and pepper.

7. This sauce can be made 2 days ahead. Cover and refrigerate. Rewarm before serving and thin with more broth if necessary.

Roast Chicken Pieces

Preheat oven to 350°F

1. Season quartered chickens with sea salt and pepper and place in a large, shallow baking dish.

2. Pour enough mole sauce over chicken to cover liberally.

3. Bake for 1 hour, until meat thermometer inserted in meatiest portion of chicken registers 165°F.

Coconut Chicken Palliards with Lemons and Capers

SERVES 2 TO 4

The Tropics meet the Mediterranean in this bright and festive chicken dish. It is so flavorful that all you need is a side of wild rice or quinoa and some plain steamed vegetables to round out the meal. There is enough sauce to drizzle over the grain and vegetables to bring everything together.

Ingredients

2 large boneless, skinless
    chicken breasts
Sea salt and freshly ground
    black pepper
½ cup fine cornmeal
½ teaspoon sea salt
¼ teaspoon ground turmeric
⅛ teaspoon freshly ground
    black pepper
2 tablespoons coconut oil
1 tablespoon ghee

2 small shallots, minced
2 tablespoons capers, drained
    and chopped
2 tablespoons dry white wine
Juice of 2 lemons
1 lemon, peeled and separated
    into segments
½ cup chicken stock, preferably
    homemade (see recipe, page 30)
½ cup coconut milk
2 tablespoons cold ghee

Method

Preheat oven to 250°F

1. Place chicken breasts in a plastic bag and pound with a mallet to tenderize. Work from the center and pound outward with the smooth side of the mallet until meat is ⅛- to ¼-inch thick. Cut each breast into 2 pieces and sprinkle with a little sea salt and pepper.

2. In a medium bowl, mix together the cornmeal, sea salt, turmeric, and black pepper.

3. Dredge breasts in cornmeal mixture and set aside on a plate.

4. Heat a large skillet over medium-high heat. Melt the coconut oil and ghee together in the skillet. When fats begin to bubble, add chicken breasts and sauté until golden brown, about 2 minutes.

5. Turn and sauté other side for 2 minutes, or until golden brown. Transfer to a baking sheet and begin again with remaining chicken breasts. Once all breasts are browned, place in oven and begin sauce.

6. Add shallots to the same skillet and cook over medium heat for about 1 minute, adding more ghee or coconut oil if needed. Stir often to prevent sticking. Add capers and sauté another minute.

7. Raise heat and deglaze pan with 2 tablespoons of wine. Scrape brown bits from bottom of pan with a wooden spoon.

8. Add lemon juice, lemon segments, remaining chicken stock, and coconut milk. Simmer until sauce thickens and reduces by half, about 3 minutes.

9. Swirl 2 to 3 tablespoons of cold ghee into sauce. Season to taste.

10. Before serving, insert a meat thermometer in the thickest portion of the chicken breast to make sure it registers 165°F. To serve, place chicken breast on a plate and spoon some sauce on top.

Cornish Hens with Latin Spices

SERVES 4 TO 6

There is just enough spiciness in these birds for a festive kick. If game hens are not available, use this rub on a whole chicken.

Ingredients

4 Cornish game hens, rinsed
  and patted dry
2 tablespoons ground cumin
2 tablespoons pure chile powder
1 tablespoon crushed coriander seeds

1 teaspoon ground cinnamon
2 teaspoons unrefined cane sugar
1 teaspoon sea salt
1 teaspoon red chile flakes
Freshly ground black pepper
¼ cup butter, softened

Method

Preheat oven to 375° F

1. Rinse the hens well under cool filtered water and pat them dry. Combine all of the spices with the sugar. Starting at top of breast bone, loosen the skin from the breast of the game hens, being careful not to tear the skin.

2. Gently rub the spice mixture under the skin, making sure you reach far back and around the sides of the hen. Rub inside and outside the hens with butter and sprinkle the outside with salt and pepper.

3. Put hens on a rack in a baking dish and bake for 1½ hours, until a meat thermometer registers 165° F or juices run clear when flesh is pricked between the leg and thigh. Another way to check is to wiggle the leg. If it comes apart easily, the hen is ready.

4. Serve with roasted vegetables or your favorite side dishes.

Liver and Onions

SERVES 4

Many people have only encountered poorly cooked liver – tough as shoe leather, mealy, and dry. If this has been your experience and you still cringe at the thought of eating liver, wait until you try this amazing dish. It just may change your notion about liver once and for all. Serve with Turnip and Sunchoke Mash (see recipe, page 239) and a green salad for a delicious meal.

Ingredients

4 tablespoons of clarified butter or ghee, divided
1 large onion, thinly sliced
1½ pounds organic chicken livers
¼ cup amaranth flour
½ teaspoon sea salt

¼ teaspoon freshly ground black pepper
¼ teaspoon garlic powder
1 cup aged vinegar, such balsamic
12 fresh sage leaves

Method

1. Heat a large sauté pan and add 1 tablespoon of ghee. When oil is hot, add the onion slices and a pinch of salt and cook on low heat until soft and golden brown, about 10 to 15 minutes.

2. While onions are cooking, rinse livers with filtered water and pat dry with paper towels. Set aside.

3. Combine amaranth flour, salt, pepper, and garlic powder in a large plastic zip-lock bag. Give mixture a shake and either dredge chicken livers by adding them all to the bag and shaking, or transfer flour to a shallow bowl and dredge livers one by one.

4. Turn caramelized onions onto a plate and keep warm. Add another tablespoon of ghee to the same pan. Raise heat slightly and place livers in the hot pan in a single layer. Cook for 1 to 2 minutes on each side, until surfaces are deeply browned and the centers are pink. Place livers on same plate as onions and cover with foil.

5. Over medium-low heat, deglaze the pan with the aged vinegar, scraping browned bits from the bottom of the pan. Reduce to approximately 2 tablespoons and drizzle over liver and onions.

6. Heat remaining ghee in a separate wok or pan until hot but not browned. Add sage leaves a few at a time and cook until crisp. Gently lift out crispy leaves with tongs and dab on paper towels to remove excess fat.

7. To serve, place 4 livers on a serving plate, drizzle some reduced vinegar on top, and scatter with caramelized onions. Top with a couple of fried sage leaves. Serve with Turnip and Sunchoke Mash (see page 239) or your side dishes of choice.

Herbed Meatballs
with Spaghetti Squash Noodles

SERVES 6

This dish is fast becoming a popular grain-free twist on spaghetti and meatballs. Baked spaghetti squash makes beautiful strands of vegetable "noodles." All you need to accompany them is a great sauce and some hearty meatballs like the ones in this recipe. The best part is watching pasta lovers savor this delicious take on an Italian-American favorite.

Ingredients

1 pound ground bison
1 pound turkey sausage (choose Italian
    flavor if available)
2 cloves garlic, minced
½ teaspoon dried rosemary
1 teaspoon dried thyme
1 teaspoon dried oregano
¼ cup flat-leaf parsley, coarsely
    chopped
½ small yellow onion, coarsely
    chopped

½ cup almond meal
2 large eggs, whisked
1 teaspoon red chili flakes
A few grinds black pepper
½ cup finely shredded Parmesan
    cheese (optional)
3 tablespoons unsalted butter or ghee
3 tablespoons extra virgin olive oil
Spaghetti Squash Noodles (see recipe,
    page 227)
Sicilian Pesto Sauce (see recipe,
    page 226)

Method

Meatballs

1. In a large bowl, stir together all the ingredients, except the butter and olive oil, until well incorporated.

2. Lightly oil your hands and shape the mixture into meatballs about 1 inch in diameter.

3. Heat a sauté pan over medium heat and add the butter and olive oil. Add the meatballs and cook for 8 to 10 minutes, turning occasionally, until evenly browned and cooked through. Add more olive oil and butter as you cook the meatballs, if necessary.

4. Transfer cooked meatballs to a baking sheet or plate layered with paper towels to blot excess fat. Meatballs are cooked properly when a thermometer inserted in the center registers 165° F.

5. Serve over Spaghetti Squash Noodles (recipe, page 227)and ladle Sicilian Pesto Sauce on top (recipe, page 226).

Sicilian Pesto Sauce

YIELDS APPROXIMATELY 1 CUP

Unlike the familiar green Pesto alla Genovese, this sauce uses tomatoes as the base rather than basil. Black olives and a variety of fresh greens from basil to celery leaves are added to intensify the flavor.

Ingredients

¼ cup raw pine nuts, lightly toasted

4 cloves garlic, peeled

4 large sun-ripened tomatoes, blanched, peeled, seeded, and chopped, or 1 28-ounce can organic whole tomatoes

¼ cup pitted and chopped dry-cured black olives

1 cup finely chopped fresh basil leaves

1 cup finely chopped fresh parsley leaves

1 cup finely chopped fresh celery leaves

1 teaspoon sea salt

1 teaspoon black pepper (or to taste)

¼ cup extra virgin olive oil

Method

1. Grind the pine nuts and garlic in a mortar and pestle or purée in a blender or food processor.

2. Add the tomatoes, olives, herbs, salt, and pepper and continue grinding/blending until you have a smooth paste.

3. Taste for balanced seasoning, then add enough olive oil to create a smooth consistency.

4. Fold pesto into spaghetti squash "noodles." Pesto is also great served with chicken, fish, vegetables, or on whole-grain pasta.

5. Pesto may be stored in a tightly sealed glass jar and kept in the refrigerator for up to 1 week.

Spaghetti Squash Noodles

SERVES 6

Sometimes the best gluten-free pasta is not pasta at all, but a vegetable. Spaghetti squash is a natural at noodling. No special equipment needed. Just bake it, scrape out the flesh, and you have instant noodles.

Ingredients

1 medium spaghetti squash (about 3 pounds)
1 tablespoon melted coconut oil

Pinch of sea salt
1 tablespoon extra virgin olive oil

Method

Preheat oven to 350° F

1. Cut spaghetti squash in half lengthwise and scoop out seeds.
2. Brush cut sides with melted coconut oil and place cut side down on a baking sheet lined with parchment paper.
3. Bake for 25 minutes, or until squash is tender when pricked with a knife.
4. When squash is done, remove it from the oven and cool for 10 minutes.
5. Using a fork, scrape the flesh of the spaghetti squash out of the skin into a bowl.
6. Add a pinch of salt and 1 tablespoon of the olive oil. Toss lightly and set aside until ready to use. Spaghetti squash can be gently reheated with sauce of choice in a skillet.

If You Like Meat, Try Lamb

The sheep is one of the few domesticated animals that is not fed commercial grains containing antibiotics, growth hormones, and artificial colors. Lamb is a red meat and so many people question its health value. The fact is that lamb is leaner than beef, and most often pasture raised, which is the preferred method. Palmitoleic acid, a 16-carbon monounsaturated fatty acid found in lamb, possesses strong antimicrobial properties.

Lamb is also an especially good source of easily absorbed zinc and iron. A 3-ounce serving of cooked lamb provides 30 percent of the recommended daily allowance for zinc (essential for growth, tissue repair, and a healthy immune system) and 17 percent of the RDA for iron (needed for the formation of red blood cells). Lamb is also rich in B vitamins, especially B12. One serving can provide 74 to 100 percent of the body's daily requirement for vitamin B12, which is essential for a host of bodily functions. Lamb is also nature's best source for an amino acid called carnitine, which is needed to generate energy from fatty acids. Trace elements such as copper, manganese, and selenium are also found in this meat, and it contains a rich supply of high-quality protein.

Lamb is a food you can feel good about eating because today's lamb is an excellent source of vitamins, minerals, quality protein, and healthy fats.

ED

Mediterranean Roast Lamb

SERVES 6 TO 8

Serve leg of lamb for dinner and the evening meal suddenly becomes a special occasion. Do not be surprised if the intoxicating aromas wafting from your oven lure your neighbors to your doorstep.

Ingredients

1 5-pound boneless leg of lamb, butterflied
1 tablespoon minced fresh rosemary
¼ cup finely chopped Kalamata olives
¾ teaspoon sea salt, divided
6 cloves garlic, minced

¾ teaspoon freshly ground black pepper
¼ cup extra virgin olive oil, divided
4 3-inch rosemary sprigs
2 cups dry red wine, divided
1½ tablespoons arrowroot powder
1 tablespoon of butter

Method

Preheat oven to 400° F

1. Unroll lamb and bring to room temperature. Rinse meat thoroughly. Blot dry.
2. Trim excess fat. If slab is uneven, pound lightly with a mallet to flatten.
3. Combine rosemary, olives, ¼ teaspoon salt, garlic, ¼ teaspoon black pepper, and 2 tablespoons of olive oil. Massage mixture into the roast. Re-roll, and secure at 3-inch intervals with heavy kitchen string.
4. Sprinkle lamb with remaining salt and pepper. Drizzle with olive oil. Secure rosemary sprigs under strings in various places on roast.
5. Roast lamb on a rack in a roasting pan for 30 minutes, then decrease temperature to 350° F (do not remove from oven). Roast an additional 50 minutes to an hour or until meat thermometer registers 140° F (medium-rare) to 145° F (medium).
6. Place roast on a platter and tent with foil. Allow to rest for 20 minutes so roast can reabsorb its juices. This resting period is critical to keeping the lamb tender.
7. Remove the rack from the roasting pan and set the pan over two burners on medium heat. Add ½ cup of wine to drippings, scraping the bottom of the pan to loosen browned bits.
8. Transfer these drippings to a saucepan and add another cup of wine. Bring to a boil and cook for 5 minutes to reduce by half.
9. Whisk together the remaining ½ cup of wine with the arrowroot powder and pour into saucepan. Add ¼ teaspoon of salt and return sauce to a boil. Cook 1 minute or until thickened, stirring constantly. Add butter and stir until melted and glossy.
10. Transfer sauce to a gravy boat or bowl and serve with the lamb. Be sure to remove string and rosemary sprigs before slicing lamb.

Braised Lamb Shanks

SERVES 4

On a cold, wintry night, a braised dish is the perfect warming meal. Lamb shanks are an economical choice and when cooked low and slow become luxuriously tender.

Ingredients

2 fresh fennel bulbs, trimmed and
   quartered, reserve fronds
2 leeks, white parts only, cut in
   half lengthwise and cleaned
   thoroughly, then cut crosswise
   into thirds
3 tablespoons extra virgin olive oil,
   divided
2 teaspoons sea salt, divided
1 teaspoon freshly ground
   black pepper, divided
4 lamb shanks
2 tablespoons ghee

1 onion, thinly sliced
3 shallots, sliced into wedges
8 cloves of garlic, peeled
   and smashed
1 tablespoon fresh rosemary leaves,
   minced, or 1 teaspoon
   dried rosemary
1 teaspoon fresh thyme leaves
6 medium fresh tomatoes, chopped
1 cup red wine, such as a pinot noir
3 cups chicken stock, preferably
   homemade (see recipe, page 30)
½ cup chopped fennel fronds

Method

Preheat oven to 400° F

1. In a roasting pan, toss the fennel and leeks with 2 tablespoons of the olive oil, ½ teaspoon of the sea salt, and ¼ teaspoon of the pepper.

2. Use paper towels to pat the lamb shanks dry and season them with the remaining salt and pepper. Nestle among the vegetables in the roasting pan and roast in the oven for 30 minutes, turning shanks to brown evenly half way through cooking time.

3. While lamb and vegetables are roasting, heat an enamel-coated cast iron Dutch oven with 1 tablespoon of olive oil and 2 tablespoons of ghee. When melted, add onions, shallots, and garlic and cook until they begin to soften. Add a pinch of sea salt, followed by the rosemary and thyme and continue cooking for another 10 minutes until lightly caramelized.

4. When lamb is finished browning, remove pan from oven and transfer shanks and vegetables to a plate. Cover and set aside. Pour juices from roasting pan into a bowl and set aside as well.

5. Heat roasting pan over medium high heat on the stove top and add ¼ cup of red wine. Wine will bubble and while this is happening, scrape up brown bits (the flavorful *fond*) from the bottom of the pan and continue cooking wine until reduced by half.

6. Deglaze onions, shallots, and garlic with remaining red wine, stirring quickly. Then, add chicken stock, reduced wine, and reserved pan juices.

7. Place the lamb in the center of the Dutch oven and bring to a simmer on the stovetop, then transfer to the oven. Set roasted fennel and leeks aside.

8. Cook the lamb until it is fork-tender and falling off the bone, about 2½ hours. Add reserved fennel and leeks and cook another 10 minutes.

9. Remove from the oven and allow to rest at room temperature for 15 minutes, then ladle portions into large bowls to allow for plenty of braising liquid and vegetables, along with the lamb. Top with chopped fennel fronds.

Moroccan Lamb Burgers with Minty Lemon Yogurt Sauce

SERVES 4 TO 8

Ground lamb mixed with Moroccan spices makes wonderful gourmet burgers. Enjoy these addictive patties with refreshing Minty Lemon Yogurt Sauce and sliced cucumbers.

Ingredients

2 pounds of ground lamb (shoulder
  meat is best)
1 tablespoon extra virgin olive oil
1 small onion, finely diced
1 small carrot, finely diced
2 garlic cloves, minced
½ teaspoon ground coriander
½ teaspoon ground cumin
½ teaspoon ground cinnamon

¼ teaspoon whole fennel seeds
¼ teaspoon ground turmeric
1 teaspoon sea salt
½ teaspoon freshly ground
  black pepper
¼ cup dried currants
1 large egg, lightly whisked
3 tablespoons coconut oil

Method

1. Place lamb in a large bowl and set aside.

2. Heat a large sauté pan over medium heat and add the olive oil. Stir in onions and a pinch of sea salt and sauté for 5 minutes, until soft and opaque.

3. Add carrot and sauté another 5 minutes.

4. Add garlic and sauté for another 1 to 2 minutes.

5. Sprinkle in the coriander, cumin, cinnamon, fennel seeds, and turmeric. Reduce heat so spices do not burn and stir gently until spices stain the vegetables and become very aromatic, about 2 to 3 minutes.

6. Pour the vegetable sauté over the lamb and stir to combine thoroughly. Add salt and pepper.

7. Fold in the currants and egg, making sure all ingredients are thoroughly combined.

8. Form meat into 3-inch round patties and place on a baking sheet.

9. Heat a 10-inch skillet on high and add 2 tablespoons of coconut oil. As oil melts, swirl pan around to coat the bottom. Pan should be hot before cooking burgers. To test, place a teaspoon-sized bit of burger on the pan. If it sizzles, the pan is ready. If it sizzles and spits, the pan may be too hot and the oil will smoke, burning the burgers before they are cooked through. If that happens, remove the pan from the heat for a couple of minutes before proceeding.

10. When pan is the proper temperature, place burger patties 2 inches apart and cook for 2 to 3 minutes on each side or until burger sears and releases easily from the pan with a spatula. Flip burger and cook other side. When internal temperature of lamb burgers are 155°F, transfer to a serving platter or plate. Repeat until all burgers are cooked. Top burgers with Minty Lemon Yogurt Sauce.

Minty Lemon Yogurt Sauce

YIELDS 2 CUPS

A bright and refreshing sauce for any spicy or savory meal. Perfect on lamb burgers.

Ingredients

*1 pint Greek-style plain whole
  milk yogurt*
½ lemon, zest and juice

*½ cup fresh mint leaves, torn
  into small pieces*
*Sea salt and freshly ground
  black pepper*

Method

1. Mix all ingredients together in a medium-size bowl.

2. Cover and refrigerate until ready to use.

On the Side
Accessorizing the Main Dish

In the early 1970s, I cooked at a restaurant in San Francisco called the Diamond Sutra. It was fusion health food even before there was a name for it. The owner was from India, and each morning he made wonderful, chewy whole-wheat molasses brown bread and a batch of Indian curries, such as Beef Korma, Chicken Tikka Masala, and a spicy Dal made from Indian split peas.

My job was to make the vegetable side dishes – which could also be vegetarian entrées – along with brown rice and yummy, healthy desserts. I was a vegetarian at that time, so having creative license to cook meat-free was right up my alley. It was great fun to serve the vegetable side dishes with the meat entrées and have the customers light up and ask for the recipes, or come back and order the vegetarian special of the day.

My formula for making side dishes was pretty simple. I went to the market and picked out the freshest, healthiest food that was in season. I then either sautéed it in a skillet with onions, garlic, olive oil, herbs, and spices, or slow-cooked it into a stew. The key was watching the time, temperature, and texture of the food.

I cooked as much to order as I could, which ensured that the food would be at its sizzling best when served. Every night, I would write down what I made for future reference, and some of those early recipes are included in this cookbook. I did not start with a particular recipe, but with the day's best ingredients, and then considered the weather – was it hot or cold, wet or dry? – as well as what main dishes the owner was making so my dishes would complement them well.

I would often make Raita, a yogurt condiment, or a salad of dark greens, grapefruit, and avocado as a cooling accompaniment to a spicy curry. Sometimes I steamed a vegetable in the brassica family – such as broccoli, cauliflower, Brussels sprouts, or cabbage – and served it with a twist of lemon, a splash of tamari, and a toss of toasted almonds.

Generally, it is best to keep side dishes simple, but they can be brightened with surprise seasonings to keep the diners on their toes. I like to add horseradish to mashed potatoes, for instance, or curry powder to baked squash, or sprinkle nutmeg or paprika on tofu, garbanzo, or cannellini bean dishes.

When eating in restaurants, ordering a soup, a salad, and a couple of side dishes is a great way to avoid overeating. You can sometimes find a nice portion of vegetables that would not be included with a main entrée in the side order section of a menu.

On festive occasions such as Thanksgiving, I pay most attention to the side dishes, as it is the vegetables that maintain proper pH and provide healthful, alkalinizing minerals like magnesium, potassium, chromium, and zinc, as well as vitamin C. Combine the flavors, colors, textures, and nutrients of the side dishes at any meal; add to that friends and family, enjoy it at a slow food pace, and it is Thanksgiving, regardless of the time of year.

Ed

Cardamom Basmati Rice

Basmati rice is considered the mother grain in India, as valuable and precious as pearls. The "queen of all grains" is often prepared with spices and seeds. This version takes an aromatherapy bath in the heavenly scents of cinnamon and cardamom. The result is a delicately scented rice that works well with any main course.

Ingredients

1 cup of rice
2 cups of filtered water
1 cinnamon stick

1 bay leaf
1 cardamom pod
1 clove

Method

1. Wash the rice well for 4 to 5 minutes in cool, filtered water before cooking. Washing the rice removes any excess starches, which helps prevent sticking and allows for more even cooking.

2. Put the rice and water in a pot with a pinch of sea salt. Bring to a boil, then lower heat and add cinnamon stick, bay leaf, cardamom pods, and clove to scent rice. Cover pot tightly and cook for 35 to 45 minutes.

3. When rice is finished, remove spices and drizzle melted coconut oil over it, then fluff with fork. Serve immediately.

Burdock Root and Carrot Sauté

SERVES 6

This sauté is a traditional method for cooking burdock root, a popular liver detoxifying vegetable in Japan. Kinpira Gobo, as it is called there, is usually served in small portions as a side dish.

Ingredients

2 to 3 burdock roots
½ lemon, juiced
1 cup arame seaweed
2 cups filtered water
2 tablespoons light sesame oil
1 small onion, thinly sliced

4 medium carrots, julienned
1 pinch sea salt
¼ cup tamari soy sauce
6 tablespoons mirin (Japanese sweet rice cooking wine)

Method

1. Scrub burdock root with a stiff vegetable brush under running, filtered water. Cut into julienne (long, thin strips) and quickly submerge burdock in filtered water with juice of ½ lemon. Set aside.

2. Soak arame in 2 cups of warm, filtered water for about 15 minutes. Set aside.

3. Heat a heavy saucepan over medium heat and coat with oil.

4. Drain the burdock root and pat dry. Add the burdock to the pan and sauté until it no longer releases a strong aroma, about 15 minutes. Stir often to evenly coat with oil and prevent scorching.

5. Add the onions and carrots and sauté for 1 to 2 minutes longer. Add just enough water to cover the bottom of the pan. Season with a dash of salt, cover, and reduce the heat to low. Cook until vegetables are tender, 10 to 15 minutes, adding a bit more water from time to time, if necessary.

6. Uncover, season with tamari and mirin, and simmer until dry while gently shaking the pan (stirring at this stage will make the burdock sticky).

7. Drain arame and toss into burdock and carrot sauté. Transfer to a platter. Serve immediately.

Burdock Root Benefits

Burdock is a common weed, native to Europe and Northern Asia and now wide-spread throughout the United States as well. When young and tender, burdock root has a crispy texture and a sweet and mild flavor. The root is the part of the plant primarily used for cooking and for therapeutic preparations.

Burdock root contains high amounts of inulin and mucilage. The carbohydrate inulin can comprise up to 50 percent of the plant's total mass. Inulin is made up of many fructose chains, which are responsible for burdock's blood sugar-lowering effect. It also contains polyacetylenes that have demonstrated anti-microbial activity.

Burdock has traditionally been used for a wide variety of conditions, including chronic skin ailments, rheumatoid arthritis symptoms, cancer prevention, inflammation, hepatitis, swollen glands, and fluid retention. It is used in the treatment of skin conditions that result in dry and scaly skin such as eczema, psoriasis, and dermatitis.

Burdock root is also traditionally used to clear the bloodstream of toxins. It promotes perspiration and the release of toxins from the body.

In folk medicine, burdock was used as a laxative and to relieve inflammatory conditions. It will help restore friendly bacteria in the system after antibiotic use, and may bring relief in cases of chronic arthritis and gout.

Turnip and Sunchoke Mash

SERVES 4

For something a little less ordinary, and a whole lot more nutritious than mashed potatoes, try this mash. It is earthy, delectable, and adventurous to the palate.

Ingredients

3 large or 6 small turnips, quartered
1 large onion, quartered
2 tablespoons plus 2 teaspoons extra
  virgin olive oil, divided
1 small bulb garlic, roasted
½ pound sunchokes, scrubbed
  and chopped

2 tablespoons unsalted butter
½ cup cultured buttermilk
½ teaspoon minced fresh
  rosemary leaves
Sea salt and freshly ground black
  pepper to taste

Method

Preheat oven to 375° F

1. Toss turnips and onion with 1 tablespoon olive oil and spread onto a parchment-lined baking sheet.

2. Cut stem end off garlic bulb, drizzle with 1 teaspoon of olive oil, and wrap with a sheet of foil lined with parchment paper. Place on baking sheet next to turnips and onions. Bake vegetables for 40 minutes or until soft.

3. Meanwhile, put sunchokes in saucepan, cover with filtered water, bring to a boil then lower heat to a simmer. Cook until fork tender. Drain and set aside.

4. Heat butter, buttermilk, and rosemary in a large saucepan over very low heat. Keep warm until you are ready to mash vegetables.

5. Remove vegetables from the oven and transfer to a large bowl. Add cooked sunchokes. Squeeze roasted garlic from bulb over the vegetables. Mash everything together with a potato masher until well combined.

6. Slowly add warmed buttermilk mixture, stirring to combine thoroughly. Season with salt and pepper. Mash does not have to be smooth, but can have some texture and lumps.

Braised Celery with Herbed Butter

SERVES 6

Braising brings out the sweetness in celery. The Herbed Butter adds an extra level of richness and the fats in the butter make the nutrients in the herbs easier to absorb.

Ingredients

Herbed Butter
½ cup ghee or unsalted butter,
    room temperature
1 teaspoon minced fresh chives
2 teaspoons minced fresh thyme
1 teaspoon minced fresh sage
1 teaspoon minced fresh rosemary
1 teaspoon caraway seeds
2 teaspoons minced shallot
1 teaspoon minced garlic

1 teaspoon freshly squeezed
    lemon juice

Braised Celery
2 bunches celery, bottoms removed
3 tablespoons Herbed Butter
2 medium yellow onions, halved and
    thinly sliced
Sea salt and freshly ground pepper
    to taste
2 cups vegetable stock, preferably
    homemade (see recipes, page 25
    and 26)

Method

Herbed Butter

1. In a small bowl, mix the softened ghee or butter with prepared herbs, spices, shallot, garlic, and lemon juice.

2. Spoon mixture onto a sheet of parchment paper or plastic wrap. Shape into a log about 4 inches long. Place in the refrigerator until ready to use. Keeps about 1 week in refrigerator, or up to 1 month in the freezer wrapped securely in parchment and plastic.

Braised Celery

1. After trimming off the bottoms, cut celery stalks into 1-inch slices, finely chopping and reserving some of the leaves. (If desired, substitute some of the celery with broccoli or another crunchy vegetable.)

2. In a large sauté pan on medium heat, melt the Herbed Butter and add the onion and celery, spreading out in an even layer. Season with salt and pepper. Sauté until opaque, then add the vegetable stock and cover.

3. Bring to a boil, then reduce the heat to a simmer. Braise the celery for 30 minutes, or until soft. Remove the lid and reduce any liquid that is left in the pan. The onions and celery should be well browned. When finished, adjust seasoning if necessary, transfer to a serving dish, and sprinkle with the reserved chopped celery leaf. Dab with a little more Herbed Butter, if desired.

Green Beans with Ginger

SERVES 4 TO 6

Some of the best recipes require the least amount of ingredients. For best results, use the freshest green beans available.

Ingredients

5 shallots, finely chopped
½ teaspoon finely chopped
  fresh ginger
1 tablespoon extra virgin olive oil

1 pound fresh green beans, stem ends
  snapped off and strings removed,
  if necessary

Method

1. Gently heat a large pan or wok and sauté shallots and ginger in oil for 2 minutes.

2. Add green beans and stir to combine, then add ½ cup water. Cover and steam until green beans are crisp, but tender, about 8 minutes. Serve immediately.

Roasted Beets with Cumin Orange Glaze and Mint

SERVES 4 TO 6

These beautiful and aromatic ruby red and golden beets make a perfect accompaniment to any Morrocan inspired meal.

Ingredients

3 medium beets (1¼ pound total, without greens), all but 1 inch of stems removed
1 2-inch sprig tarragon
½ cup freshly squeezed orange juice
1 teaspoon cumin seeds, toasted and lightly crushed

1 tablespoon fresh squeezed lemon juice
½ teaspoon sea salt
¼ teaspoon freshly ground black pepper
2 tablespoons extra virgin olive oil
⅓ cup coarsely chopped fresh mint leaves

Method

Preheat oven to 425° F and put oven rack in middle position.

1. Tightly wrap beets in parchment paper, then wrap in foil. Roast on a baking sheet until tender, about 1 hour. Vent beets by opening foil package slightly and allow to cool for about 15 to 20 minutes before handling.

2. While beets are roasting, place tarragon sprig and orange juice in a saucepan over medium heat and reduce to 2 tablespoons.

3. In a small skillet, toast cumin seeds briefly, then crush them in a mortar and pestle. Set aside.

4. In a medium bowl, stir together the reduced orange juice, lemon juice, toasted and crushed cumin seeds, salt, and pepper. Whisk in oil until fully emulsified.

5. When beets are cool enough to handle, peel them, then cut into ½-inch wedges.

6. Heat a skillet over low heat. Add the vinaigrette and the warm beets. Toss and cook until thoroughly glazed. Transfer to a bowl and fold in the mint just before serving.

He who distinguishes the true savor of his food can never
be a glutton; he who does not cannot be otherwise.

HENRY DAVID THOREAU

If you want to make an apple pie from scratch,
you must first create the universe.

CARL SAGAN

Sweet Endings
Desserts to Live For

Chapter 5

Sweet Endings
Desserts to Live For

Your desserts can be considered health-promoting when you have liberated yourself from the world of white flour, white sugar, and margarine confections.

High-quality ingredients, moderation in portion size, and a nice cup of herbal tea with your healthy cookie or cake make life very pleasant indeed.

If you know you are going to indulge in a healthy dessert, then skip the main meal and just have dessert. That is what my Grandma Yetta used to do, and she lived to be 87 and was never sick. Learn to make these yummy treats with organic and alternative ingredients and you will not get a sugar hangover from having your cake and eating it, too.

ED

Contents

Apple Eddie

SERVES 4

Inspired by all those Apple Betty recipes handed down from family to family, this baked apple dessert gets a twist with the addition of Ed's love of flax seeds and his Sweet Spice of Life recipe. The result is an old favorite comfort dessert with added booster foods and warming flavors.

Ingredients

4 apples, cored and sliced
   into ½-inch wedges
1 tablespoon lemon juice
⅛ teaspoon sea salt
1 teaspoon Sweet Spice of Life
   (see recipe, page 14)
   or pumpkin pie spice

2 tablespoons maple syrup
2 tablespoons butter, melted
   or macadamia oil
Walnut Flax Crumble
   (recipe, next page)
Coconut Cashew Cream
   (recipe, page 250)

Method

Preheat oven to 350°F

1. Place apples in a medium bowl and toss with lemon juice, salt, Sweet Spice of Life, maple syrup, and butter.

2. Spread apples into a medium baking pan and bake for 30 to 35 minutes or until apples are softened and syrup is bubbling.

3. Arrange apples in a pretty dessert dish and top with Walnut Flax Crumble and Coconut Cashew Cream. Recipes on following pages.

Walnut Flax Crumble

YIELDS ¾ CUP

Ingredients

¾ cup walnuts (soaked and dehydrated
   1 day ahead of time if desired)
1 cup of apple cider

2 quarter-sized slices of ginger
1 cinnamon stick
2 tablespoons flax seeds

Method

1. Toast walnuts in a dry sauté pan over low heat until fragrant. When toasted, roughly chop them or place in a sealed zip lock bag and smash them lightly with a rolling pin. Set aside.

2. In a small sauce pan, cook apple cider over medium high heat with ginger slices and cinnamon stick until juice is syrupy and reduced to ¼ cup. Sauce should lightly coat the back of a spoon. Lower heat to warm.

3. Remove cinnamon stick and ginger slices from spiced apple syrup and add walnuts and flax seeds, stirring until well combined.

4. Spread nut and seed mixture on a parchment-lined baking sheet and allow to cool. Break apart if necessary and crumble to use as a topping.

Coconut Cashew Cream

YIELDS 3 CUPS

This creamy, delightful creation is the perfect substitute for dairy whip cream, and is a wonderful, dreamy sensation on the palate. Top it on any dessert, chocolate or fruity, or use it alone as a pudding. Whatever you decide, this recipe is one to use again and again.

Ingredients

*2 cups fresh, young Thai coconut meat
    (approximately 3 Thai coconuts)*
*1 cup cashews, soaked overnight
    and drained*

¼ cup maple syrup
1½ teaspoon vanilla extract
Pinch of sea salt

Method

1. Crack open and scoop out the flesh from 3 to 4 young Thai coconuts until there are 2 level cups. Reserve the coconut water for another use or just enjoy by the glass.

2. Add coconut meat and drained cashews to a blender and purée until smooth and thick. If using a Vitamix, be sure to use the tamper to work ingredients together.

3. Slowly drizzle in half the maple syrup and blend thoroughly. Taste and add remaining maple syrup for more sweetness, if desired.

4. Add vanilla and a pinch of salt. Blend until combined. Mixture should be thick, smooth, slightly glossy, and somewhat fluffy with no trace of grainy texture from the cashews.

Masala Peach Melba

YIELDS 3 CUPS

In the late 1800s, Auguste Escoffier created a special dessert of peaches with raspberry sauce for Australian soprano, Nellie Melba. He called his dessert Peach Melba so it would never be forgotten. In this rendition, peaches are poached in rooibos chai tea, enhanced with additional Indian spices, dates, and warming tawny port.

Ingredients

3 cups of water
2 Medjool dates, pitted and sliced into thin strips
Peel 1 orange or 2 tangerines, cut into thin strips using a vegetable peeler
3 rooibos chai tea bags
1/3 cup tawny port
2 tablespoons honey
1 cinnamon stick
1 star anise

4 black peppercorns
4 cardamom pods
4 peaches, halved and pitted (choose firm, ripe peaches)
8 whole raspberries for garnish

Raspberry Sauce
1 cup raspberries (fresh or frozen)
Poaching liquid
1 orange or 2 tangerines, juiced
1 teaspoon arrowroot

Method

1. Add water, dates, orange zest, tea bags, port, honey, cinnamon stick, star anise, peppercorns, and cardamom pods to a medium sauce pan and bring to a simmer.

2. Add peaches and bring poaching liquid to a boil. Reduce heat and simmer until peaches can be easily pierced with a fork, about 10 to 15 minutes depending on firmness of the fruit.

3. Remove peaches and place in a serving dish. Add fresh raspberries and set fruit aside. Discard tea bags and reserve poaching liquid for Raspberry Sauce.

Raspberry Sauce

1. Add raspberries to poaching liquid and bring to a boil until liquid is reduced by half and becomes syrupy.

2. Strain sauce through a fine mesh strainer, pressing raspberries thoroughly. Spoon out about 2 to 3 tablespoons of sauce into a small cup and sprinkle in arrowroot powder. Whisk until smooth.

3. Add remaining sauce back into pan, followed by the arrowroot slurry. Bring sauce to a boil. As soon as sauce begins to boil, whisk quickly until sauce thickens. Remove from heat and allow to cool slightly.

4. To serve, place a peach into an attractive bowl or wine glass and drizzle generously with raspberry sauce. Top with a couple raspberries and enjoy. For even more decadence, top with Coconut Cashew Cream or vanilla ice cream.

Ruby Summer Pudding Allemande

SERVES 6

This dessert is inspired by a German red berry pudding known as Rote Grüeze. Fresh currants are traditionally used, as well as strawberries and other berries in season. If you can find red currants in your area, feel free to add them in. Enjoy a spoonful of summer with every tart and delicious bite.

Ingredients

2 cups raspberries
1 cup blackberries or blueberries
1 cup pitted Bing cherries
1½ cup chopped strawberries
½ cup pomegranate juice
   (no sugar added)

¼ cup palm sugar
2 tablespoons arrowroot powder
1 orange, juiced
2 tablespoons of chia seeds, ground into
   a fine powder (optional; if not using
   increase arrowroot powder to ¼ cup)

Method

1. Place all berries in a medium saucepan with pomegranate juice and sugar. Bring to a boil for about 5 minutes, until berries and cherries have softened. Lower heat to the lowest setting and mash fruit with a fork.

2. In a small cup or bowl, whisk arrowroot powder with juice of 1 orange and stir into berry mixture, followed by finely ground chia seeds and a pinch of sea salt. Stir until fully incorporated.

3. When mixture begins to thicken, remove from heat and transfer to individual serving dishes like custard cups. Allow to cool completely and then cover with plastic wrap and chill in the refrigerator before serving.

4. To serve, top each pudding with freshly whipped cream, créme fraîche, vanilla ice cream, or Coconut Cashew Cream (recipe, page 250).

Berry Peach Cobbler

SERVES 8

A cobbler or spoon pie is a fruit stew topped with dumplings made from biscuit dough. When baked, the pie resembles a cobblestone road, hence the name cobbler. Instead of plain biscuit dough made from white flour, this cobbler is made with healthier and more flavorful ingredients like almonds, hazelnuts, flax seeds, coconut oil, and unrefined sugar. The combination tastes like caramel after baking. Choose seasonal fruits for fillings. In this version, summer is the season so berries and peaches highlight this dessert. Come fall, the same cobbler topping can be used over apples, pears, Fuyu persimmons, and cranberries. This is truly a dessert you can make your own.

Ingredients

Cobbler Topping
3 tablespoons coconut oil or butter
¼ cup unrefined cane or palm sugar
½ cup brown rice flour
½ cup almond flour (see Almond
    Flour recipe, page 18)
½ cup chopped hazelnuts or nut
    of your choice
¼ cup arrowroot powder
    or tapioca starch
½ teaspoon sea salt
2 teaspoons baking powder

½ teaspoon ground cinnamon
½ cup unsweetened almond milk
¼ teaspoon pure vanilla extract
3 tablespoons flax seeds

Fruit Filling
2 teaspoons arrowroot powder
1 teaspoon freshly squeezed
    lemon juice
1 tablespoon unrefined cane or palm sugar
2 cups fresh berries, such as blackberries,
    raspberries, blueberries, alone
    or in combination
2 cups fresh peaches, sliced or chopped

Method

Preheat oven to 350° F

1. Using a hand mixer, cream together the coconut oil and sugar until light and fluffy.

2. In a separate bowl, whisk together the dry ingredients: rice flour, almond flour, nuts, arrowroot, salt, baking powder, and cinnamon.

3. Alternately, add portions of the dry ingredients and almond or rice milk to the creamed sugar, beginning and ending with dry ingredients, mixing after each addition until well combined. Add vanilla and mix batter until all ingredients are well incorporated. Fold in the flax seeds.

4. Wash and dry the berries and place them in a bowl. Sprinkle with arrowroot powder, lemon juice, and sugar. Fold gently and spread fruit evenly in a shallow baking dish.

5. Spoon cobbler batter evenly over fruit and bake for 30 minutes or until topping is crisp and fruit is bubbling.

Seasonal Fruit Galettes

Serves 6 to 8

A galette is a free form tart made without a tart pan. It has a rustic look and feel that is charming when served at a picnic lunch, brunch, or afternoon tea. In this galette, the crust is a tender, gluten-free, poppy seed speckled delight filled with a sumptuous Mascarpone and goat cheese filling, and topped with seasonal fruits.

Gluten-Free

Ingredients

Crust
1 cup sorghum flour
½ cup ground almonds
¼ cup cornmeal
2 tablespoons potato starch
¼ teaspoon sea salt
8 tablespoons butter, cut into small pieces
1 tablespoons maple syrup
6 tablespoons cold almond milk
1 teaspoon poppy seeds

Filling
1 cup Mascarpone cheese
¼ cup soft goat cheese
1 egg, separated
2 tablespoons honey
1 teaspoon lemon juice
Pinch of sea salt
2 teaspoons vanilla
2 teaspoons fresh thyme
2 cups freshly sliced seasonal fruit
1 tablespoon unrefined cane sugar

Method

Preheat oven to 350° F

1. In a food processor, add sorghum, ground almonds, cornmeal, potato starch, and salt. Pulse several times until mixed well.

2. Gradually add butter pieces, pulsing every so often to combine.

3. Add maple syrup and half the almond milk and pulse until mixture resembles coarse, clumpy crumbs.

4. Add remaining almond milk, followed by poppy seeds and pulse until fully combined. Dough should be slightly sticky, but easy to gather into a ball.

5. Divide dough ball in two and shape into discs. Wrap in plastic wrap and chill for 30 minutes in the refrigerator.

Make Filling

1. Using a hand mixer, blend Mascarpone, goat cheese, egg yolk, honey, lemon juice, salt, and vanilla together until smooth and creamy. Fold in thyme leaves.

2. Slice fruit thinly into half moons and toss with 1 teaspoon of sugar.

Assemble Galette

1. Remove dough from refrigerator and unwrap. Place disc of dough on a 12x12-inch sheet of parchment paper. Place a sheet of plastic wrap over the top of the dough and roll out to a ¼-inch thick round (it does not need to be perfect as part of the charm of galettes is the rustic appearance).

2. When dough is rolled out, spread half the cream filling onto the dough, leaving a 1-inch border from the edge, free of filling.

3. Place fruit slices on top of filling in concentric circles. Sprinkle with remaining sugar.

4. Fold in edges of dough so they partially cover the edges of the fruit and filling and the middle remains open. Brush crust with lightly whisked egg white.

5. Transfer parchment paper with galette onto a baking sheet. Bake in the oven for 30 minutes or until crust is a light golden brown. Remove from the oven and cool for 15 minutes before serving. This cooling time will allow the crust to become more crisp and the filling to set.

Blueberry Lemon Cream Pie

SERVES 6

This pie recipe is terrific with any kind of berry, but the combination of cooked and fresh blueberries with the lemony whip cream topping makes this pie extra special. The no-fuss, raw nut and date crust is another element that sets this pie apart.

Ingredients

Pie Crust
1 cup hazelnuts
½ cup walnuts
½ cup Medjool dates, pitted
1 tablespoon coconut butter
1 teaspoon coconut oil
1 tablespoon lemon zest
1 teaspoon vanilla extract

Blueberry Filling
3 cups fresh blueberries
¼ cup filtered water
¼ cup maple syrup
1 tablespoon arrowroot powder
2 tablespoons pure, filtered water
1 teaspoon lemon juice

Lemon Cream Topping
1 cup chilled, heavy whipping cream
2 tablespoons honey
1 tablespoon finely grated lemon peel
1 teaspoon fresh lemon juice

Method

Make Crust

1. In a food processor, pulse nuts until they resemble very coarse crumbs.
2. Add dates, coconut butter, oil, lemon zest, and vanilla extract and process until mixture forms into a dough ball.
3. Press dough into a tart pan.

Make Filling

1. Measure 2 cups of fresh blueberries into a large bowl and set aside.
2. In a small sauce pan, heat the remaining 1 cup of blueberries, ¼ cup of water, and maple syrup over medium heat.
3. In a small bowl, mix arrowroot powder with 2 tablespoons of filtered water to form a slurry. When blueberries start popping, slowly pour in arrowroot. Stir over low heat until thickened. Set aside to cool for about 10 minutes.
4. When cooked blueberries have cooled, fold into fresh blueberries. Stir in lemon juice and pour filling into tart crust.

Lemon Cream Topping

Blend heavy cream and sugar until thick. Add lemon zest and juice and continue blending until soft peaks form. Dollop generously onto blueberry tart.

Buckwheat Dessert Crepés

SERVES 4 TO 6

Buckwheat crepés, or Gallete de Sarrasin, as the French call them, are traditionally reserved for savory ingredients. We have sweetened them for the dessert course with a Bing cherry and ricotta filling. Yum!

Gluten-Free

Ingredients

¾ cup buckwheat flour
¼ cup sorghum flour
¼ cup arrowroot powder
½ teaspoon sea salt
1 tablespoon unrefined cane sugar,
    ground to a fine powder

3 large eggs
1½ cups fresh goat milk or nut milk
3 tablespoons butter, melted
1 teaspoon coconut oil to brush
    on crepé pan

Method

1. In a large bowl, sift together the buckwheat flour, sorghum flour, arrowroot, salt, and sugar.

2. Make a well in the center of the dry ingredients and crack eggs into it, gradually whisking until thoroughly combined. Batter will be thick.

3. Add half the milk to the flour and egg mixture a tablespoon or two at a time, whisking constantly until batter is smooth.

4. Stir in half of the melted butter and the remaining milk. Cover the bowl with a tea towel and allow to stand at room temperature for 2 hours.

5. Just before cooking, stir the batter and check its consistency. It should be like thin cream. If necessary, add more milk to achieve the right consistency.

6. Heat an 8-inch crepé pan or skillet over medium-high heat. Sprinkle a few drops of water on the pan; if the drops sizzle, the pan is ready to use. Brush pan with coconut oil or melted butter.

7. Fill a ¼-cup measuring cup or small ladle with batter and pour the batter into the center of the skillet. Immediately pick up the pan and tilt and swirl it so the batter covers the entire bottom of the pan in an even layer.

8. Bubbles will form very quickly on the surface of the crepé. When they do, loosen the edges of the crepé with a metal spatula and quickly flip it over back onto the pan.

9. Cook on the other side until lightly browned (usually less than a minute) and slide the finished crepé out onto a plate. Cover with parchment paper. Repeat with the remaining batter, placing parchment paper between all of the crepés so they do not stick together.

10. Fill each crepe with 2 to 3 tablespoons of Balsamic Cherry Ricotta Filling (see recipe, page 260); fresh berries and/or mango chunks with yogurt; or raspberry jam, orange zest, and Coconut Cashew Cream (see recipe, page 250). If making crepés ahead, refrigerate them for about an hour before you want to serve the dessert, or for up to a day. At serving time, heat a pan on low heat and warm each crepé before assembling.

NUTRITION GEM

Buckwheat, the Grain-Free Grain

Despite the name, buckwheat is not related to wheat. Though buckwheat is used like a grain, it is not a cereal nor a grass, but actually a fruit seed. Buckwheat seeds are rich in starch, proteins, antioxidants, aromatic compounds, and minerals like iron, zinc, and selenium. It is also packed with good fiber and contains all eight essential amino acids, making it a complete protein food. Buckwheat is gluten-free, making it a great food for those allergic to wheat.

Buckwheat noodles play an important role in Japanese cuisine, while buckwheat groats are common in western Asia and eastern Europe. Buckwheat pancakes are eaten in several countries. Cooked buckwheat can be used as a rice substitute, and buckwheat porridge is a favorite dish in various parts of the world.

Buckwheat Health Benefits

- The plant lignans in buckwheat help control blood sugar levels, and thus lower the risk of diabetes and heart disease.

- Buckwheat helps prevent gallstones.

- The dietary fiber found in buckwheat provides protection from breast cancer and improves digestion.

- It protects against childhood asthma.

Balsamic Cherry Ricotta Filling

Yields approximately 2 cups

Ingredients

1 ½ cups Bing cherries, pitted
   and halved
1 tablespoon unsalted butter, melted
½ cup balsamic vinegar
1 teaspoon unrefined cane sugar
½ cup whole milk ricotta cheese
1 tablespoon honey

¼ teaspoon sea salt
¼ cup grated or shaved dark (75%
   dark chocolate, chilled, for garnish
   (optional)
Buckwheat Dessert Crepes (see recipe,
   page 258)

Method

Preheat oven to 325°F

1. Toss the cherries with the melted butter and spread onto a parchment-lined baking sheet. Roast in the oven until tender, about 20 minutes. Transfer roasted cherries to a bowl and set aside.

2. Place the balsamic vinegar in a small saucepan and cook on medium heat until reduced by half. Add the sugar and cook until the vinegar is thick enough to coat the back of a spoon.

3. Drizzle balsamic reduction over cherries.

4. In a separate bowl, mix the ricotta with the honey and the salt.

5. Spread a tablespoon or two of ricotta over one-half of each crepé, then top with a portion of the cherry mixture.

6. Roll up or fold the crepés and serve, garnished with more cherries and another dollop of ricotta. Grate some chocolate on top, if you wish.

Hazelnut Date Cookies

These rich, buttery, gluten-free cookies are perfect with a steaming cup of tea. Toasted pecans and hazelnuts give them a decadent nutty flavor.

Gluten-Free

Ingredients

⅓ cup butter, softened
½ cup maple syrup
2 large eggs
1 teaspoon pure vanilla extract
1 cup oat flour
1 cup amaranth flour
2 teaspoons non-aluminum
   baking powder

1 teaspoon ground cinnamon
½ teaspoon sea salt
½ cup finely chopped dates
½ cup raw hazelnuts, chopped
¼ cup raw pecans, chopped
½ cup fresh cherries, pitted and
   chopped for topping (berry jam, or
   lemon curd also make great fillings)

Method

Preheat oven to 375° F

1. Using a hand mixer, cream the butter and maple syrup together until fluffy.

2. Add eggs one at a time, blending thoroughly between additions. Add vanilla extract and blend until incorporated.

3. Sift oat and amaranth flours together with the baking powder, cinnamon, and salt. Gradually add to creamed mixture, blending thoroughly after each addition. Fold in chopped dates and nuts.

4. Place heaping tablespoons of the dough onto a parchment-lined baking sheet. Indent each one slightly with your thumb or the back of a wet spoon.

5. Bake for about 10 minutes or until edges start to brown. Remove from the oven and cool.

6. Fill the indentation in the cookies with fresh cherries, berry jam, or lemon curd, if desired.

Chewy Ginger Buttons

YIELDS 12 COOKIES

Watch out for these delightful little cookies. They are loaded with ginger spice and sweet molasses flavor, and are a little difficult to stop eating! Enjoy as an after meal treat or with a cup of tea.

Gluten-Free

Ingredients

¼ cup coconut butter
¼ cup butter
¾ cup date sugar
1 teaspoon sea salt
1 teaspoon freshly minced ginger root
1 teaspoon powdered ginger

¾ cup molasses
½ cup date or maple syrup
1½ teaspoons baking soda
¼ cup water
1 and ¼ cups garbanzo flour
¾ cup potato flour

Method

Preheat oven to 375°F

1. Cream together the butters and sugar in a mixer on high speed until fluffy. Blend in the salt, gingers, molasses, and syrup.

2. Dissolve the baking soda in the water and blend into the butter/sugar mixture.

3. Sift the garbanzo and potato flour together and stir them into the butter/sugar mixture a little at a time.

4. Fill a 1-gallon freezer bag with the cookie dough and make a small cut at one corner, or use a piping bag with a large plain round tip.

5. On a sheet pan lined with parchment paper, pipe out quarter-sized rounds; or alternatively, roll and then flatten dough into button-shaped cookies.

6. Bake for about 12 minutes or until crisp around the edges. Allow them to cool before removing from the sheet tray.

Kefir Panna Cotta with Blackberry Coulis

SERVES 6

Panna Cotta is traditionally made with gelatin. In this recipe, agar, a vegetable derived gelatin, and arrowroot powder are combined to make a perfectly creamy and stable Panna Cotta with a better nutritional profile. The added Blackberry Coulis and Cinnamon Caramel sauce make this dessert perfect for special occasions.

Ingredients

¼ cup filtered water
1 tablespoon plus 1 teaspoon
  agar powder
2 teaspoons arrowroot powder
¾ cup coconut milk

½ cup organic granulated sugar*
1½ cups plain kefir
2½ teaspoons pure vanilla extract
1 teaspoon freshly ground nutmeg

Method

1. Pour water into a small bowl and whisk in the agar and arrowroot powders. Let stand for 10 minutes.

2. Combine the coconut milk and sugar in a small saucepan. Stir over medium heat until sugar dissolves, about 5 minutes.

3. Add the agar and arrowroot and whisk until dissolved. Cook over medium heat for another 5 minutes while whisking constantly. When mixture thickens slightly, remove from heat.

4. Stir in the kefir and vanilla until well blended. Divide the mixture among six ½-cup ramekins and top with a sprinkle of nutmeg. Cover and refrigerate until set, about 30 minutes to an hour.

*Choose an organic granulated sugar that is light in color to avoid darkening the Panna Cotta.

Blackberry Coulis

YIELDS APPROXIMATELY 1 CUP

This topping delivers the bright, vivid flavor of fresh blackberries.

Ingredients

*1½ cups fresh blackberries, washed
  and dried*

1 tablespoon unrefined cane sugar
*½ teaspoon freshly squeezed
  lemon juice*

Method

1. Combine all ingredients in a blender and blend until smooth.

2. Pour coulis through a fine sieve and press with the back of a wooden spoon to remove the seeds, then drizzle the sauce over Kefir Panna Cotta or another favorite dessert and serve.

Cinnamon Caramel Sauce

YIELDS APPROXIMATELY ½ CUP

Even healthy desserts can include a little something naughty, but with a twist. There is no need to break any rules and sneak in white sugar to make a sinfully decadent caramel. Palm sugar and coconut milk do the job and then some.

Ingredients

½ cup palm sugar
¼ cup coconut milk

¼ teaspoon ground cinnamon
1 teaspoon vanilla extract

Method

1. Combine sugar and coconut milk in a small saucepan.

2. Stir over medium heat until sugar dissolves and sauce is smooth.

3. Remove from heat and stir in the cinnamon and vanilla.

4. Spoon slightly warm caramel sauce over Kefir Panna Cotta or another favorite dessert and serve.

Chocolate Orange Torte

SERVES 6 TO 8

This sinfully rich, flourless chocolate torte is infused with cardamom, ginger, coriander, and Valencia orange. Orange and chocolate, a well known and intoxicating flavor pairing, is enhanced to new heights with the addition of exotic spices. For an impressive end to a festive meal, bring this dessert to the table.

Gluten-Free

Ingredients

1 Valencia or other flavorful orange,
*   unpeeled, quartered and seeded*
6 ounces of 75% dark chocolate,
*   chopped*
1 stick of butter or ½ cup coconut oil
5 eggs, separated
⅓ cup palm sugar
¼ teaspoon powdered ginger
¼ teaspoon powdered cardamom
¼ teaspoon powdered coriander

¼ teaspoon sea salt
Pinch of cream of tartar

**Orange and Vanilla Coconut
Whip Cream**

1 can coconut milk, chilled in the
*   refrigerator overnight*
1 teaspoon vanilla
2 tablespoons maple syrup
2 tablespoons orange zest

Method

Preheat oven to 375° F

1. Generously grease an 8-inch round springform cake pan with coconut oil and line the bottom with parchment paper.

2. Gently boil orange pieces (peel and all) in enough filtered water to cover for 1 hour. Drain, add to a blender and purée until smooth. Set aside.

3. Put the chocolate and butter into the top of a double boiler (or in a heat-proof bowl) and heat over about 1 inch of simmering water until melted. NOTE: If using a bowl, do not allow the bottom of it to touch the water.

4. Meanwhile, whisk the egg yolks with the orange purée, sugar, ginger, cardamom, coriander, and salt in a mixing bowl until creamy.

5. Gradually whisk a little of the chocolate mixture into the egg yolk mixture to temper the eggs – this technique will keep the eggs from scrambling from the heat of the chocolate. Keep adding the remaining chocolate mixture slowly while whisking constantly. The mixture should look smooth and glossy. Set aside.

6. Beat the egg whites in a mixing bowl with a pinch of cream of tartar until stiff peaks form. Fold a third of the beaten egg whites into the chocolate mixture, followed by another third. Transfer the chocolate and egg white mixture back into the larger bowl with the remaining beaten egg whites and fold gently until combined. White streaks in the batter are perfectly okay.

7. Pour batter into the prepared springform pan and bake until the cake is set, the top starts to crack, and a toothpick inserted into the cake comes out with moist crumbs clinging to it, 40 to 45 minutes. Let stand 10 minutes, then remove sides of pan.

8. Transfer torte to a serving platter and chill in the refrigerator until ready to serve. Garnish torte with a light sprinkling of organic powdered sugar and thinly sliced oranges if desired. Serve with freshly made Orange and Vanilla Coconut Whip Cream.

Orange and Vanilla Coconut Whip Cream

Make 1 day ahead for best results.

1. Open a can of chilled coconut milk, remove cream top with a spatula, and put into a medium bowl.

2. Add vanilla and maple syrup and blend with a hand mixer until thick and creamy. If cream is too soft to dollop on cake, chill in the refrigerator until thickened.

3. Fold in orange zest. Season with a pinch of sea salt to bring flavors together. Dollop whip cream over torte and serve.

Bittersweet and Spice Chocolate Velvet Crema

SERVES 6

Avocados provide a perfect base for chocolate "mousse," puddings, and other creamy desserts such as this one. The chocolate in this recipe is melted and infused with spices and sweetened with dates. This sumptuous dessert could put a capital "S" in the word Sinful, but the nutrient rich ingredients make it healthy and guilt-free.

Ingredients

12-ounces good quality bittersweet chocolate, chopped
2 tablespoons coconut butter
2 teaspoons ground cinnamon
1 teaspoon ginger
¼ teaspoon cayenne powder
2 large, ripe Hass avocado, pitted and peeled

4 Medjool dates, soaked until soft and pitted
2 tablespoons maple syrup
½ teaspoon vanilla
1 teaspoon maca root powder
1 teaspoon ground chia or flax seeds
¼ teaspoon sea salt
1 cup nut milk or tea

Method

1. In a double boiler, melt chocolate with coconut butter, cinnamon, and cayenne.

2. Scoop flesh from pitted avocado and add to blender with dates, maple syrup, vanilla, maca root powder (if using), ground chia seeds, and salt. Blend until smooth, stopping and starting if necessary to work ingredients. If using a Vitamix, be sure to use the tamper. Add nut milk or tea (choose chai, mint, or orange spice tea for another layer of flavor) to bring ingredients together.

3. When mixture is smooth, slowly add in melted, spiced chocolate. Blend well. When velvety and shiny in appearance, mousse is ready.

4. Serve in custard cups with a dollop of whipped cream; or if going dairy-free, try the Coconut Cashew Cream (see recipe, page 250). NOTE: Mousse will thicken considerably when chilled. To make fudge, use only ¼ cup of liquid and spread mixture in a glass baking dish. Chill in the refrigerator and cut into squares when set.

Strawberry Lemonade Cupcakes

When combined, strawberries and lemon bring out the best in each other, giving an extra zing to each of their bright and cheery flavors. This cake speaks birthday party, classroom treat, and picnic potluck. Make these delicious cakes for any of these occasions or, just because.

Ingredients

1 ¼ cups barley flour
¼ teaspoon baking powder
¼ teaspoon non-aluminum
   baking soda
½ teaspoon sea salt
1 tablespoon fresh lemon zest
½ cup almond oil

¾ cup organic sugar
2 large eggs plus 1 large egg yolk
3 tablespoons freshly squeezed
   lemon juice
½ cup cultured buttermilk
1 cup diced fresh strawberries

Method

Preheat oven to 350° F

1. Lightly butter cupcake tins and dust with flour, tapping out any excess, or use cupcake liners.

2. In a medium bowl, whisk together barley flour, baking powder, baking soda, salt, and lemon zest.

3. In a large bowl, beat oil and sugar together with a mixer until light and fluffy.

4. With mixer on low speed, beat in eggs and the yolk, one at a time. Beat in the lemon juice.

5. Alternately mix in portions of the flour mixture and buttermilk until well combined, beginning and ending with flour.

6. Fold in diced strawberries.

7. Divide batter between cupcake tins. Bake 30 to 35 minutes, or until toothpick inserted in center of the cakes comes out clean.

8. Let cool for 10 minutes. The cupcakes will pull away from the sides of the pan as they cool. Run a knife around edges of cupcakes if necessary and invert onto a wire rack.

Strawberry Frosting

YIELDS 2 CUPS

In the dessert world, frosting is sweet and sugary, buttery, and creamy. This frosting is not too much different, but it adds extra flavor and natural sweetness from fruit instead of tons of refined sugar and artificial flavors. Be sure to use organic dairy products.

Ingredients

½ cup (1 stick) unsalted butter, room temperature
1 8-ounce package cream cheese, room temperature
1 cup sliced strawberries, puréed in a blender

1 teaspoon champagne or white balsamic vinegar (to taste, added gradually)
¼ cup honey

Method

1. Cream butter and cream cheese until well blended. For best results, use a mixer and beat for 2 minutes on high until light and fluffy.

2. In a separate bowl, blend the puréed strawberries and champagne vinegar until smooth. Add purée to the butter and cream cheese mixture and continue to mix until well incorporated.

3. Slowly drizzle in honey while mixer is still running. If frosting is not smooth and fluffy, continue beating for another 2 minutes on high.

4. Transfer frosting to a glass storage container, cover and chill in the refrigerator for 30 minutes before using.

Honey Ginger Carrot Cake

SERVES 6

This moist and tender carrot cake is infused with Indian spices and loaded with healthy and tasty ingredients. Dress it up for parties with a frosting or enjoy it as is with tea.

Gluten-Free

Ingredients

Dry Ingredients
1 cup sorghum flour
½ cup coconut flour, sifted
¼ cup almond meal
¼ cup arrowroot powder
2 teaspoons baking powder
1½ teaspoons ginger
1 teaspoon cinnamon
¼ teaspoon coriander
¼ teaspoon allspice

Carrot Pineapple Puree
1 cup diced carrots
1½ cups brewed chai rooibos tea
½ cup crushed pineapple
1 cup macadamia nut oil

Wet Ingredients
5 eggs, at room temperature
1 cup unrefined cane sugar
¼ cup honey
¼ cup maple syrup
1 tablespoon vanilla extract
1 tablespoon fresh lemon juice
1 teaspoon sea salt

Optional Ingredients
¼ cup currants
¼ cup unsweetened coconut flakes (optional)
½ cup raw unsalted walnuts, pecans, toasted

Method

Preheat oven to 350° F

1. Lightly butter one 9 or 10-inch round springform pan and line the bottom with a parchment paper round.

2. In a medium-sized mixing bowl, sift together the sorghum flour, pre-sifted coconut flour, and almond flour, with arrowroot, baking powder, ginger, cinnamon, coriander, and allspice. Set aside.

3. Cook the carrots in chai rooibos tea until softened. Transfer carrots into a blender with a slotted spoon and add ½ cup of chai tea (chai will reduce during cooking to about ¾ cup). Blend until smooth, adding more tea if mixture is still chunky.

4. In another bowl, thoroughly combine the blended carrot chai mixture, crushed pineapple, and macadamia nut oil. Set aside.

5. Use a stand or hand mixer to beat eggs until thick, about 8 minutes on high speed.

6. Add sugar, honey, maple syrup, vanilla extract, lemon juice, and sea salt and continue beating.

7. Gently mix in mashed carrot and pineapple mixture until thoroughly combined.

8. With mixer on low speed, gradually add dry ingredients to wet ingredients, a third at a time, mixing gently until smoothly incorporated.

9. Fold in currants, coconut flakes, and toasted chopped nuts, if using.

10. Pour into prepared cake pan.

11. Bake for 45 minutes, or until toothpick inserted in center of cake comes out clean. Serve unfrosted or top with Orange Cream Frosting.

Orange Cream Frosting

YIELDS APPROXIMATELY 1½ CUPS

This frosting gets its rich orange color from fresh carrot juice rather than food coloring.

Ingredients

½ cup carrot juice
½ cup orange juice
¼ cup maple syrup
½ cup (1 stick) unsalted butter,
    room temperature

8-ounce package of cream cheese,
    room temperature
1 teaspoon vanilla extract
Pinch of sea salt
¼ cup shredded coconut, pan toasted

Method

1. In a saucepan, simmer carrot and orange juice with maple syrup over medium heat until reduced by less than half. Reduction should be syrupy and coat the back of a spoon. Set aside.

2. Using a hand mixer, cream butter and cream cheese together until smooth.

3. Slowly drizzle in carrot and orange juice reduction along with vanilla extract and a pinch of salt. Continue blending until thick and creamy. If frosting is too thin, chill in the refrigerator for 30 minutes before spreading onto cooled cake.

4. Use as a filling or frosting for carrot or spice cake.

Fabulous Figgy Coffee Cake

Serves 6

This elegant coffee cake is a perfect end to a festive meal. Enjoy it with a cup of spicy chai, black, or green tea.

Ingredients

Figgy Filling
3½ cups dried figs, soaked in warm
    water, drained, and chopped
½ lemon, seeded and finely minced
    (including pith and peel)
½ cup raisins
¼ cup filtered water

Crumb Topping
½ cup rolled oats
¼ cup toasted and chopped pecans
¼ cup toasted and chopped almonds
¼ cup toasted and chopped walnuts
3 tablespoons unsweetened
    coconut flakes
1 teaspoon cinnamon
¼ teaspoon sea salt
2 tablespoons butter, melted
1 tablespoon coconut oil, melted
3 tablespoons maple syrup

Cake
Wet Ingredients
3 large eggs
½ cup macadamia oil (almond
    and hazelnut oil or melted butter
    also work great)
½ teaspoon pure vanilla extract
¾ cup almond milk, unsweetened
½ cup unrefined cane sugar

Dry Ingredients
1 cup barley flour
1 cup finely ground almond meal
2 teaspoons non-aluminum
    baking powder
½ teaspoon baking soda
½ teaspoon sea salt
½ teaspoon ground cinnamon
¼ teaspoon ground cloves
¼ teaspoon ground ginger
2 tablespoons maple syrup
½ teaspoon ground cinnamon
¼ teaspoon sea salt

Method

Preheat oven to 350°F

Make Fig Filling

1. In saucepan over medium heat, simmer the figs, chopped lemon, and raisins in water.
2. Stir often until thick and reduced to 2 cups. As mixture thickens, reduce the heat to prevent scorching.
3. Remove from heat and allow to cool.

Make Crumb Topping

In a bowl, stir together oats, chopped nuts, coconut flakes, cinnamon, salt, butter, coconut oil, and maple syrup, until well combined. Set aside.

Make Cake

1. Butter and flour an 8-inch round baking pan.
2. In a large bowl using a whisk, (or using a mixer) beat eggs, oil, vanilla, and almond milk until thick. Gradually add sugar and beat until smooth.
3. In a separate bowl, whisk together the barley flour, almond meal, baking powder, baking soda, salt, and spices.
4. Gently fold dry ingredients into egg mixture, until well combined.
5. Spoon half the batter into baking pan. Spread fig mixture over top, then spoon remaining batter evenly over fig layer. Evenly sprinkle on the crumb topping and press in with a fork.
6. Bake for 45 minutes or until toothpick inserted in center of cake comes out clean.

Coconut Matcha Green Tea Ice Cream

SERVES 4

Matcha green tea is made from the finest, hand-picked tea buds. When harvested, the leaves are laid out flat to dry and then ground into a fine, vibrant green powder. This fine powder not only makes a perfect cup of tea, it is also useful in naturally dyeing foods green. Matcha is naturally sweet and nutty, making it a wonderful flavor for desserts like ice cream. Creamy coconut milk and honey take this green tea ice cream to another sumptuously decadent level. Try not to have too much!

Ingredients

2 cups filtered water
¾ cup light-colored unrefined cane sugar
½ cup honey
2 teaspoons of Matcha green tea powder
Pinch of sea salt

1 tablespoon arrowroot powder
1 can (13.5 ounce) full fat coconut milk

Optional Toppings
1 cup frozen or fresh raspberries
½ cup toasted coconut flakes
¼ cup cocoa nibs

Method

1. Add water, sugar, and honey to a sauce pan and bring to medium heat until sugar is completely dissolved.

2. Whisk in Matcha tea until fully dissolved. Remove pan from heat. Cool 10 minutes.

3. Pour sweetened Matcha tea mixture into a blender and add a pinch of salt, arrowroot powder, and coconut milk. Blend on medium speed until very smooth.

4. Pour ice cream base into a heat-proof glass container or pitcher, cover with plastic wrap and put in the refrigerator to cool completely.

5. When ice cream base is cold, pour into your ice cream maker and make according to the manufacturer's instructions.

6. To serve, scoop out ice cream and place into serving bowls. Top with raspberries, cocoa nibs, or toasted coconut flakes if desired.

Honeyed Pear and Rosemary Sorbet

SERVES 4

Sometimes desserts are not just for kids; and in this case, the pairing of pears and rosemary has a grown up quality. Try this refreshing treat at the end of an elegant meal on a warm autumn night.

Ingredients

1½ cup filtered water
1 5-inch piece of fresh rosemary
½ cup honey

2 cups of chopped pears (about two medium, peeled pears)
¼ teaspoon sea salt (use a pinch at a time)
1 tablespoon arrowroot powder
¼ teaspoon lemon juice, optional

Method

1. Add water and rosemary sprig to a small sauce pan and bring to a boil. Reduce heat and simmer for 20 to 30 minutes. Taste water. It should have a strong but not medicinal rosemary flavor.

2. Remove rosemary tea from heat and strain into a small heat-proof bowl.

3. Rinse out sauce pan and return to the stove. Pour in the strained rosemary tea and add the chopped pears and honey. Bring to a medium heat and cook pears until they are fork tender.

4. Remove pear and tea mixture from the heat and allow to cool for about 10 minutes.

5. Pour mixture into blender and add a pinch of salt and arrowroot powder. Blend until smooth. Taste and add more salt and lemon juice if desired.

6. Pour sorbet base into a heat-proof glass container or pitcher, cover with plastic wrap and put in the refrigerator to cool completely.

7. When sorbet base is cold, pour into your ice cream maker and make according to the manufacturer's instructions.

8. Serve sorbet in wine goblets with a small sprig of rosemary for a festive garnish.

The spirit of the tea beverage is one of peace,
comfort and refinement.

ARTHUR GRAY

Fruit juices are the cleansers of the human system …
Vegetable juices are the builders and regenerators of the body …
[but] any fresh-raw juice is better than no juice at all.

N.W. WALKER

Quenchers
Better Beverages

Chapter 6

Quenchers
Better Beverages

Of all the unsung heroes in the nutrition field, water is the most vital to our health, and the most taken for granted. After all, our bodies are 70 percent water.

One of the main things that distinguishes plant foods from animal foods is fluid and fiber content. Fruits and vegetables are juicy and succulent. Grains and beans are soaked and cooked in precious water to re-hydrate them for adequate digestion. Little water is found in nuts, seeds, cheeses, butter, breads, and animal products. This is why I advise eating more fresh produce than dry, salty, dehydrated, concentrated, acid-forming foods.

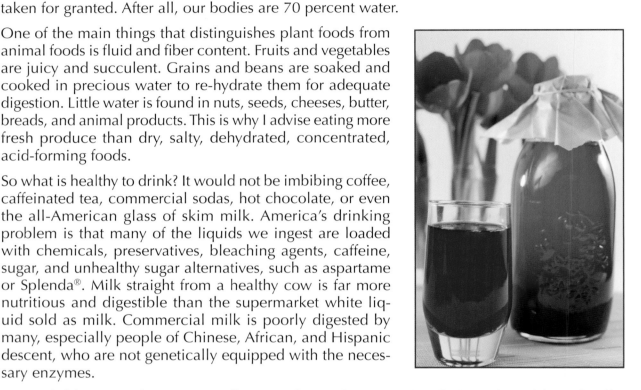

So what is healthy to drink? It would not be imbibing coffee, caffeinated tea, commercial sodas, hot chocolate, or even the all-American glass of skim milk. America's drinking problem is that many of the liquids we ingest are loaded with chemicals, preservatives, bleaching agents, caffeine, sugar, and unhealthy sugar alternatives, such as aspartame or Splenda®. Milk straight from a healthy cow is far more nutritious and digestible than the supermarket white liquid sold as milk. Commercial milk is poorly digested by many, especially people of Chinese, African, and Hispanic descent, who are not genetically equipped with the necessary enzymes.

Many children raised on cow's milk crave cheese, butter, and milk throughout life and suffer from chronic sinus congestion, ear infections, and constipation as a result of overconsumption.

In order of preference, I recommend:

- Purified water, preferably from a free-running filter on your tap
- Herbal teas made from filtered water and mild, mineral-rich herbs like peppermint, chamomile, lemongrass, nettle, oat straw, horsetail, and/or hibiscus flowers
- Fresh fruit and vegetable juices, with 35 percent water added to dilute the fruit sugars
- Nut and seed milks, made in your kitchen from almonds, cashews, and/or flax seeds, and rice, nut, oat, or mixed grain milks, made from whole grain sources

It is best to eat foods with high water content and not drink beverages with your meals, to avoid diluting stomach acids. Room temperature beverages are best.

Drinking for health means limiting alcoholic and caffeinated beverages to an absolute minimum. Drinking herbal tea instead to de-stress is a habit that will boost your health and longevity.

Ed

Contents

The Properties of Raw Vegetable Juices

Including a variety of liquid foods in the daily diet provides the body with essential nutrients to both cleanse and rejuvenate tissues and organs. Raw juices support cell and tissue cleansing of the organs of elimination: the liver, bowel, lymph, skin, lung, and kidneys. Pure, fresh liquid food requires few enzymes to digest and provides significant amounts of enzyme precursors, such as potassium, magnesium, zinc, vitamins C, and B complex. Juices allow the liver, pancreas, and intestines to replenish their reserves of the nutrients needed for optimal digestion, assimilation, and blood sugar regulation.

The blood delivers the juices' alkaline-rich, micro- and phytonutrients to various body systems that have been chronically acidic and suffering from free radical damage and oxidative stress. Cells and tissues, once they are pH balanced, slough off metabolic waste and cell debris, including stored lipid-soluble environmental toxins, carcinogens, and heavy metals such as mercury, lead, arsenic, and cadmium. The overall health effect of this process is wonderful, but some people may experience unpleasant symptoms as these substances are released into the bloodstream and flushed from the body.

A juice fasting regime fortifies the immune system to seek out areas of chronic infection and, with targeted herbal support, diminish the variety and toxicity of pathogenic organisms and their waste products.

For juicing (as for other uses) buy organic fruits and vegetables that are as fresh as possible. Valuable nutrients begin to diminish soon after harvesting. For maximum freshness and integrity, purchase your produce at farmers' markets, *Community Supported Agriculture* (CSA) buying clubs, organic farmer roadside stands, and health food stores that support local agriculture.

It is important to note that anything that is good for a person, including juicing, can be overdone. A person who is seriously into juice fasting should also be able to eat and easily digest solid food on a regular basis. I sometimes encounter "juice addicts" who are only healthy and happy when they are juicing. Sadly, they do not make optimal choices and tend to overeat when they eventually return to solid foods.

The key to well-being is to find balance in all aspects of life and health. While most people are overly acidic and benefit from an alkaline-rich diet and fasting program, continual juicing can lead to over-alkalinity. This robs the body of energy and imbalances the endocrine system to create a "spacey" and polarized mind set.

Carrot Juice

Carrots are rich in carbohydrates, potassium, sodium, and calcium. They contain abundant alkaline minerals, a trace of iodine, and a good proportion of all vitamins. Carrot juice is a powerful cleansing food and one of the most effective means of changing the intestinal flora from putrefactive to non-putrefactive. Choose carrots that are firm and crisp when broken in two.

Carrot juice:

- Can generally be consumed in large quantities without difficulty
- Due to its excellent vitamin content, it is good for building and cleansing the blood
- Very effectively aids the healing of chronic infections such as tonsillitis, colitis, and appendicitis
- Is effective in controlling anemia, stones, acidosis, blood poisoning, faulty circulation, and ulcers
- Helps to promote appetite and aids in digestion
- Helps with rheumatic ailments, which are a result of nutritional disorders and respond readily to carrot, as well as celery, juice
- Is one of the richest sources of vitamin A – which the body quickly assimilates – and provides an ample supply of vitamins B, C, D, E, G, and K
- Improves the bone structure of teeth
- Offers resistance to infection and is a protector of the nervous system
- Is healthy for nursing mothers as it may enhance the quality of their milk
- Helps to combat fatigue due to its strong alkalinity and offers a safe beauty formula – the best way to put color in your cheeks is to drink a glass of carrot juice daily!

Cabbage Juice

Cabbage has anti-bacterial and anti-viral powers. Only add small amounts of cabbage to your juice blend, as it has a sulfur after-taste that is a bit harsh. Cabbage juice is therapeutic only when raw.

Cabbage juice:

- Cleanses the mucous membranes of the stomach and intestinal tract
- Provides good quantities of sulfur, chlorine, and vitamin C
- When fermented, as in sauerkraut and kimchee, is easy to digest and produces lactic acid and beneficial bacteria

Celery Juice

Celery's fresh and bright flavor makes it an excellent addition to beet, parsley, and carrot juices. Its taste and quality are at their best when it is in season during the spring and summer months. Celery should be crisp and snap easily when pulled apart. The bright green leaves should be free from yellow or brown spots.

Celery juice:

- Is an impressive source of magnesium, sodium, and iron
- Contains as much sodium as calcium, which is valuable in arthritic conditions

- Quiets the nerves and is conducive to sound sleep
- Contains vitamin C and several other active compounds that promote health, including phalides, which may help lower cholesterol, and coumarins, which may be useful in cancer prevention

Lettuce Juice

Lettuce has a calming effect, which is why wild lettuce juice has long been used as a nervine analgesic (pain reliever). Do not waste your time with iceberg lettuce, as it is lacking in minerals.

Lettuce juice:

- Offers generous quantities of iron, magnesium, calcium, potassium, phosphorus, sulfur, and silicon. It is important in the proper maintenance of skin, sinews, and hair
- Is a potent lymphatic cleanser

Parsley Juice

Parsley is considered an herbal multivitamin. A cup of minced fresh parsley (about 4 ounces or 100 grams) contains more beta-carotene than a large carrot, almost twice as much vitamin C as an orange, more calcium than a cup of milk, and twenty times as much iron as a serving of liver. Because it is highly concentrated, parsley juice is best used sparingly (2-ounce servings) and in combination with other vegetable juices.

There are two main varieties of parsley: Italian flat-leaf and curly-leaf. When buying either type, look for leaves that are crisp and deep green, not limp or yellow.

Parsley juice:

- Is conducive to proper oxygen metabolism
- Has calming effects
- Is an effective detoxifier
- Is strongly alkaline; and
- Is rich in vitamins, iron, calcium, potassium, and magnesium

Spinach Juice

A super source of antioxidants and cancer antagonists, spinach contains about four times more beta-carotene and three times more lutein than broccoli.

Spinach juice:

- Is the best juice for cleansing, reconstructing, and regenerating the intestinal tract
- Makes a tasty combination with apple or carrot juice
- When properly prepared and eaten regularly, will correct the most chronic case of constipation within a few days or weeks

Raw Juice Therapy

Raw juices are pure liquids locked in the cells of plants that have well-studied therapeutic value. Just as herbs have specific curative values, so do the juices of specific fresh fruits and vegetables.

Vegetable juices are the regenerators and builders of the body. Fresh fruit juices are the cleansers of the human system. When grown in healthy soil, these extraordinary foods contain all the substances needed for nourishing the human organism – provided the juices are used when fresh and raw and do not contain preservatives.

When vegetables and fruits have been naturally ripened by solar energy, they contain all the elements the sun and earth have provided, stored deep within their fibers. Raw juices are second only to honey in ease and speed of assimilation. On an empty stomach, juices will be absorbed by the bloodstream and glands 15 minutes after ingestion. Because we generally consume a limited amount of pure raw food daily, a pint (16 ounces) or more of fresh raw fruit or vegetable juice daily will have a marked therapeutic effect.

Those who have lived for years on diets rich in overly seasoned foods, high-protein foods, pastries, and heavy starches will almost inevitably complain of distress when starting a rigorous raw juice schedule. Such disagreeable reactions point to an unhealthy condition of the stomach and bowels, or an acid condition of the blood.

A healing crisis – an intensifying of symptomatic complaints – is the body's way of restoring balance by throwing off waste. This stage passes naturally into a greater sense of well-being and vitality, if allowed to run its course. If the toxic build-up in your body is allowed to continue without this valuable cleansing, it is likely that your immune system will suffer, causing colds, flu, fevers, and allergies to crop up more often and with greater intensity.

ED

Apple Beta Juice

Serves 4

This concoction is loaded with antioxidants like beta-carotene and is a very healthy way to cool down on a hot summer day. Make sure carrots and apples are fresh and organically grown.

Ingredients

6 large carrots

3 large apples

2 tablespoons freshly squeezed
   lemon juice

1 cup filtered water

1 scoop Vital Scoop™ (see page 46)

Method

1. Juice carrots and apples.

2. Stir in lemon juice, water, and Vital Scoop™.

3. Chill if desired and serve.

Ginger Grape Juice

Serves 4

Grape juice gets a lift with fresh ginger juice. The result is a tasty combination that cleanses the liver.

Ingredients

2 cups red grapes

2-inch piece of fresh ginger, peeled

1 Meyer lemon, peeled and seeded

½ cup filtered water

Method

1. Juice ingredients together then dilute with water.

2. Chill if desired and serve.

Love Your Liver with Teas, Juices, Broths

The liver is a complex chemical factory that works 24 hours a day. Virtually all the blood returning from the intestinal tract to the heart passes through the liver for purification and waste removal.

This means everything you swallow that is absorbed into the bloodstream passes through the liver.

Your liver is most definitely essential to life. You simply cannot live without it. Because the liver stays busy doing all the right things, we can all live in this pretty toxic world. Here is a partial list of literally hundreds of life-supporting metabolic functions performed by the liver:

• Cleansing the blood

• Metabolizing alcohol, drugs, and environmental chemicals

• Neutralizing and destroying poisonous substances

• Regulating the supply of body fuel

• Producing, storing, and supplying quick energy (glucose) as needed to keep the mind alert and the body active

• Producing, storing, and exporting fats

• Manufacturing many essential body proteins

• Clotting the blood when needed

• Providing resistance to infection

• Producing bile, which eliminates toxic substances from the body and aids digestion

• Regulating the balance of many hormones

• Regulating cholesterol by producing it, excreting it, and converting it to other essential substances

• Regulating the supply of essential vitamins and minerals such as iron and copper

The liver absolutely loves fresh fruits and veggies, nuts and seeds, herbs and spices, and peaceful relations. Anger is a sign of liver stress. If it persists, the liver will become damaged, and the person will age rapidly and feel unhealthy.

Mint Apple Julep

SERVES 4

This delicious beverage is a hit at parties and very refreshing in the heat of the day.

Ingredients

*6 to 8 apples or enough to make
    4½ cups of juice*
*2 limes, juiced (or enough to make
    ¼ cup)*

1 cup tightly packed fresh mint leaves
1 cup ice cubes
4 mint leaf sprigs for garnish

Method

1. Juice the apples.

2. Squeeze the limes.

3. Combine apple and lime juice in a blender, along with the mint and ice cubes. Purée and serve in tall glasses with a sprig of fresh mint.

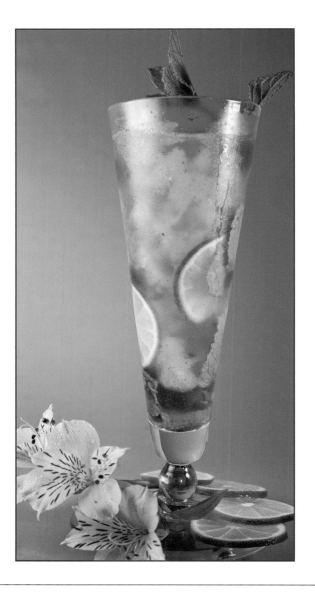

Lunch Time Juice

SERVES 2

Enjoy this beverage as a light lunch that is nutrient-packed and energizing.

Ingredients

4 large carrots
2 medium cucumbers
1 large beet
1 cup fresh greens (e.g. spinach, kale,
*   arugula, or a combination)*

2 to 4 medium oranges, peeled (add
*   only for additional sweetness)*
2 tablespoons each fresh basil, dill,
*   and cilantro*
2 cups of filtered water

Method

1. Juice carrots, cucumbers, beet, and fresh greens, along with oranges, if needed for sweetness. Set aside.

2. Simmer basil, dill, and cilantro in water for 10 minutes.

3. In a blender, purée herbal infusion with vegetable juice. Chill before serving, if desired.

Nettle Thyme Tea

Serves 2 to 3

Mineral rich nettles and aromatic, immune strengthening thyme come together in a tisane that will soothe and refresh you throughout the day. Sip warm or cool.

Ingredients

3 cups filtered water
1½ teaspoons dried nettle leaf

2 3-inch sprigs of fresh thyme leaves
(preferably lemon thyme)

Method

1. In medium saucepan, pour water over nettle and thyme and simmer on low heat for 20 minutes.

2. Remove from heat and continue steeping for another 10 minutes. Strain and serve.

Thyme

Thyme has been used for various purposes throughout the centuries. During the Medieval Period, it was thought to impart courage and vigor. The ancient Romans considered it a remedy for melancholy. Thyme, along with roses, was often used in the past to provide a sweet-smelling aroma to homes. The ancient Greeks used thyme for incense, while the Romans were known to add thyme to cheese and alcoholic beverages.

Thyme contains an essential oil that is rich in thymol, a powerful antiseptic, antibacterial, and antioxidant substance. The oil of thyme is used in mouthwashes to treat inflammations of the mouth. It is effective against throat infections and a common component of cough drops.

Because of its essential oil, thyme possesses expectorant and bronchial antispasmodic properties, making it useful in the treatment of acute and chronic bronchitis, whooping cough, and inflammation of the upper respiratory tract.

All members of the mint family, including thyme, possess terpenoids, which are recognized for their cancer-preventive properties.

Stinging Nettle

Stinging Nettle has a long medicinal history. In Medieval Europe, it was used as a diuretic (to rid the body of excess water) and to treat joint pain. Originally from the colder regions of northern Europe and Asia, this herbaceous shrub grows all over the world today. Stinging Nettle grows well in nitrogen-rich soil.

Stinging Nettle has fine hairs on the leaves and stems that contain irritating chemicals that are released when the plant comes in contact with skin. While these hairs, or spines, are normally very painful to the touch, when they come into contact with a painful area of the body they can actually decrease the original pain. Scientists think nettle does this by reducing levels of inflammatory chemicals in the body, and by interfering with the way the body transmits pain signals.

Stinging Nettle has been used for hundreds of years to treat painful muscles and joints, eczema, arthritis, gout, and anemia. Today, many people use it to treat urinary problems during the early stages of an enlarged prostate (called benign prostatic hyperplasia or BPH), for urinary tract infections, for hay fever (allergic rhinitis), or in compresses or creams for treating joint pain, sprains and strains, tendonitis, and insect bites.

Fresh Mint Tisane

SERVES 4

Enjoy a fresh mint infusion as a simple and elegant after-dinner tea, or as a palate cleanser between courses of an elaborate feast.

Ingredients

4 cups filtered water

10 sprigs fresh mint or 2 tablespoons dried mint

Method

1. Bring water to just boiling and remove from the heat.
2. Roll mint leaves between your fingers to bruise slightly and place in a teapot.
3. Pour hot water over leaves and steep for 3 to 5 minutes.
4. Serve warm or at room temperature.

The Wonders of Fresh Herbal Tea

Making tea is a ritual that can restore calm and balance. Sharing tea with friends, family, and clients is a peace offering. Learning to make a good cup of tea is well worth the modest effort.

A cup of herbal tea is called a tisane or decoction. Herbs are the leaves and flowers of plants that can be infused in water overnight for a cold water decoction or steeped in near boiling water for several minutes.

To make a perfect cup of tea, you will need four elements:

- Fresh or dried organic or wild loose herbs
- A ceramic or tempered glass tea pot with a mesh strainer
- Filtered water heated to the proper temperature
- A clean cup or mug

Many herbal teas are blends. Here is how to make a great cup of mint, lemon verbena, and rose hips tea. Use 1 to 2 teaspoons of loose blended tea to each cup of water in the pot. I like making a pint of tea at a time (2 cups water). Bring the water to a boil, then turn it off and let it cool down for about 3 minutes, until it is about 165 to 180° F. Add the hot, but not boiling, water to the tea leaves in the covered pot. Let it steep 3 to 5 minutes at first. Pour some into a cup and taste it. If you want the taste to be stronger, let it steep longer. You can make a second or even a third infusion of tea leaves until the tea loses its aroma, color, and flavor.

If you are using less delicate plant parts, such as roots or barks (e.g. ginger, licorice, ginseng, dandelion), you can simmer the roots first for 5 to 10 minutes for a good decoction, then add it to the more delicate leaves and flowers. If the root or bark is a minor constituent of a blend, just steep the entire blend for about 10 minutes before serving.

When I was in Istanbul, Turkey, every shop I entered offered me tea to help me feel more at home. I loved that, and it enabled me to have a conversation with vendors about life, health, family, and a bit later about the goods and services he was providing. Good tea is more than a beverage; it is a way to bring life back into balance.

ED

Backyard Herbal Tea

Serves 4 to 8

Tea brewed from a commercial tea bag is simply no match for the pure flavors of fresh garden herbs. In this aromatic tisane, rosemary and lemon verbena are simmered slowly and then poured over fresh mint leaves. The result is purely satisfying.

Ingredients

8 cups filtered water
1 cup tightly packed fresh mint leaves

1 cup tightly packed fresh lemon
   verbena leaves
3 4-inch sprigs of fresh rosemary

Method

1. Place mint in a teapot and set aside.

2. Place rosemary sprigs and lemon ver-bena leaves in a large pot and add 8 cups of water. Simmer gently for 20 to 30 minutes.

3. Pour brewed tea over mint leaves in teapot and steep for another 10 minutes. Serve hot, warm, or chilled.

Grow Your Own Herbal Tea Garden

Planting an herb garden in your backyard, or in pots on your deck or window sill, can be a remarkably life-changing activity. In growing your own plants (we are not speaking of hemp here), you benefit and so do your friends and family. Let me count the ways:

- You have a new hobby, much better than watching TV

- You reduce your carbon footprint by supporting photosynthesis that your plants do without effort

- You save money by using your own herbs and spices rather than spending $3 or more every time you want fresh herbs

- You connect with nature through your special plants

- You can try out many varieties of the plants you are growing to see which ones grow best

- You can share your herbs with friends and family in the form of tea, tinctures, salves, and culinary bouquets

- You have jumped outside of the tea bag and into whole plant culture, where each part of the plant has a value

ED

Peach Chai

SERVES 2

This is a delightfully refreshing, sweet, and spicy beverage.

Ingredients

3 cups of filtered water
2 tablespoons cinnamon
2 tablespoons cardamom
2 tablespoons coriander

2 tablespoons ginger
4 fresh peaches (pitted and juiced
*   with 1 cup water)*
2 mint leaves (optional)

Method

1. Boil spices in filtered water gently for 20 minutes to make chai.

2. Meanwhile, juice the peaches and dilute with the water.

3. Mix cooled chai tea with peach juice. Serve chilled with a sprig of mint.

Fruit 'n Flax Smoothie

SERVES 4

Try this satisfying and energizing smoothie for a quick pick-me-up.

Ingredients

1 cup unsweetened almond milk
2 tablespoons flax seeds
¼ cup frozen berries, kiwi, mango, or
*   pineapple*

1 medium ripe banana
1 teaspoon buffered vitamin C powder
1 scoop Vital Scoop™ (see page 46)
*   or 1 teaspoon spirulina and*
*   1 scoop of whey, rice, or hemp*
*   protein powder*

Method

1. Combine all ingredients in a blender and purée until smooth and creamy.

2. If shake is too thick, add a little water to thin it out.

Fig, Almond, and Ginger Smoothie

SERVES 4

The combination of figs, almonds, and ginger gives this smoothie a wonderful and subtle sweetness that is loaded with fiber and gentle on the tummy.

Ingredients

1 cup unsweetened almond milk
⅓ cup dried figs, soaked in warm water for 30 minutes
1 cup fig water from soaked figs
½ teaspoon freshly grated ginger

1 scoop Vital Scoop™ (see page 46) or 1 teaspoon spirulina and 1 scoop of whey, rice, or hemp protein powder
1 medium banana, frozen
1 tablespoon maple syrup
Pinch of sea salt

Method

Blend all ingredients until smooth and creamy. NOTE: If using sweetened almond milk, omit maple syrup.

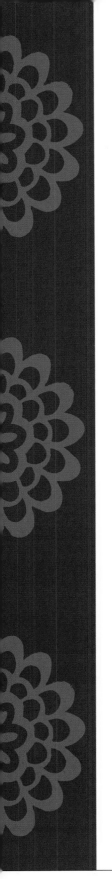

Piña Colada Avocado Smoothie

SERVES 4

Piña Colada smoothie recipes usually call for a banana, which sure is tasty – but why not try something different? With avocado, this smoothie is incredibly creamy and a pleasant shade of green. This is a delicious twist on a favorite recipe, with the added benefit of healthy fats from the avocado.

Ingredients

1½ cups coconut milk
1½ cups filtered water
1 to 2 scoops Vital Scoop™ (see page 46)
  or 1 teaspoon spirulina and 1 scoop
  of whey, rice, or hemp protein powder

1 cup frozen pineapple chunks
1 Hass avocado, pitted and peeled
1 to 2 Medjool dates, pitted
1 lime, juiced
Pinch of sea salt
Freshly grated nutmeg for garnish

Method

1. Combine coconut milk, water, Vital Scoop™ (or spirulina and protein powder), pineapple, avocado, dates, lime juice, and salt in a blender and blend until smooth.

2. Top with a bit of freshly grated nutmeg, if desired.

Chai Berry Mango Lassi

SERVES 2

Chai tea is loaded with thermogenic herbs and spices that warm the spirit and rev up metabolism. Lassis are buttermilk or yogurt based beverages with cooling and refreshing effects. Combining elements of these two popular Indian beverages in a smoothie makes for an exotic and energizing treat.

Ingredients

1 cup cooled chai tea
1 cup plain kefir
1 cup water
1 cup frozen or fresh mango chunks

1 cup frozen or fresh mixed berries
2 scoops Vital Scoop™ (see page 46)
*   or 1 teaspoon spirulina and 1 scoop*
*   of whey, rice, or hemp protein powder*
1 tablespoon maple syrup

Method

Combine all ingredients in a blender and purée.

Coco Cacao Fiesta Smoothie

Serves 4 to 6

Fresh young coconut is cool and refreshing, and the addition of cocoa nibs and cinnamon make this smoothie a sensational treat.

Ingredients

2 cups coconut water from young
 coconuts (or use store-bought,
 unsweetened coconut water)
½ cup fresh chopped coconut meat,
 discolored pieces removed, or
 ¼ cup unsweetened dried coconut
1 cup unsweetened almond milk

2 teaspoons ground cinnamon
¼ cup flax seeds ground into a meal
1 tablespoon maple syrup
2 tablespoons raw cocoa nibs
4 ice cubes (optional)

Method

1. Open a fresh coconut and pour the water into a glass. Remove tender coconut meat with a flexible rubber spatula or a spoon. Measure 2 cups coconut water and ½ cup coconut meat.

2. In a blender, combine coconut water and meat, almond milk, cinnamon, and maple syrup. Purée until very smooth. For a colder smoothie, add 4 ice cubes and blend until ice is thoroughly crushed.

3. Add cocoa nibs and blend again with just one or two quick pulses to retain the crunchy "chocolate chip" texture of the nibs. Serve with a sprinkle of cocoa nibs for garnish.

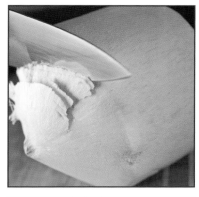

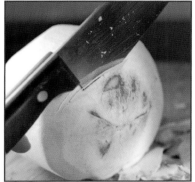

Cutting Open a Coconut

The first time I saw a coconut being cracked open, I was in Nicaragua with my parents and little brother, visiting my relatives. Only 10 years old at the time, I watched a young man hold a coconut in his bare hand while striking it with a machete. I cringed at the sight, thinking he was going to chop his own hand off, but he expertly cracked the coconut with no incident. If you have been cracking coconuts all your life, I suppose the machete technique may seem like no big deal. I prefer to play it a little safer. Below is a low-risk technique for cutting open a young coconut with a chef knife. It may not be a show stopper, but it certainly gets the job done. As always, when using knives, mind your fingers and take care. Slow and steady.

1. Place the coconut on its side and carefully shave the husk away from the top portion of the coconut until the shell is exposed.

2. While holding the coconut on its side, firmly strike and puncture the shell with the back edge portion (the heel) of your knife. The blade may be lodged inside the shell slightly but this is okay; use it to your advantage to rock the handle of your knife back and forth to pry the shell open. A gentler approach for your knife (and perhaps less threatening) is to use the blunt side of the chef knife (not the sharp side) to firmly strike the shell several times until the coconut cracks and leaves a gap large enough to open like a lid. If the coconut refuses to crack easily, rotate it slightly and strike it again until the shell cracks.

3. Drain the coconut water into a glass pitcher or bowl. If the water is clear and has a clean and sweet aroma, it is ready to enjoy. If the coconut water has a light pink tinge, it is spoiled and should be discarded.

4. After the coconut water is drained from its shell, use the back of a spoon or a firm, narrow spatula to scoop out the coconut meat.

    1 coconut yields approximately 1½ cups of liquid and ½ cup of meat.

LIZETTE

Dreamy, Creamy Flax Shake

SERVES 4 TO 6

This recipe is inspired by a traditional Ethiopian flax beverage sweetened with honey known as Telba. To add a little nutritional boost, as well as extra dreaminess, we add vanilla bean and bee pollen.

Ingredients

1 cup flax seeds
6 cups filtered water
2 Medjool dates
1 vanilla bean, split in half and
  contents scraped with a spoon

1 teaspoon bee pollen
½ teaspoon ground cinnamon
4 ice cubes

Method

1. Heat a cast-iron skillet over low heat. Add the flax seeds and toast, stirring frequently, for about 8 minutes. Remove from the pan and set aside to cool.

2. Place the toasted flax seed in a spice grinder and grind to a powder.

3. Transfer ground flax seed to a bowl, add the water, stir, and let set for 15 minutes to allow the solids to settle to the bottom.

4. Strain the mixture into a blender and add dates, vanilla bean, bee pollen, cinnamon, and ice cubes. Blend on high until frothy and pour into a pitcher. Chill before serving.

NOTE: For more fiber, skip step three and simply combine the water and ground flax seeds in a blender, along with dates, vanilla bean, bee pollen, cinnamon, and 4 ice cubes. Blend until smooth and creamy.

Rejuvenation Shake

SERVES 4

It might seem strange to some to have a vegetable shake, but this one is delicious.

Ingredients

1½ cups chopped fresh tomatoes
½ garlic clove
1 tablespoon minced fresh parsley
¼ medium onion, peeled chopped
1 celery stalk, chopped
1 carrot, chopped

½ to 1 tablespoon fresh oregano leaves
1 small red bell pepper
2 tablespoons orange or lemon juice
½ cup walnuts, soaked in filtered
    water for 2 hours, then drained
Sea salt and cayenne pepper to taste

Method

1. Combine all ingredients in a blender and process until smooth and creamy.

2. Add salt to taste and a pinch of cayenne, if you want a spicier version.

Savory Miso Booster

SERVES 4

Rather than making just another fruit smoothie, why not try a savory one like this earthy, warming, and grounding delight.

Ingredients

3 cups hot filtered water (not boiling)
2 tablespoons white miso
1 scoop Vital Scoop™ (see page 46)
   or 1 teaspoon spirulina and 1 scoop
   of whey, rice, or hemp protein powder
1½ tablespoons nutritional yeast

1 teaspoon dulse flakes
2 tablespoons toasted sesame seeds
¾ cup cashews, soaked for 2 hours
   and drained
Granulated garlic to taste
Pure chile powder to taste

Method

1. Bring water to boil and remove from heat. Allow to sit for 5 minutes to cool off a bit, then add the miso and stir until dissolved.

2. In a blender, combine the miso broth, Vital Scoop™, nutritional yeast, dulse flakes, toasted sesame seeds, and cashews and process until smooth. Serve with a sprinkle of granulated garlic and/or chile powder, if desired.

Veggie Fuerte Smoothie

SERVES 2

"Fuerte" means strong in Spanish, and this veggie-packed smoothie is flexing with health-enhancing power.

Ingredients

*3½ cups Vital Veggie Juice
(see below)*
1 cup filtered water

*2 scoops Vital Scoop™ (see page 46)
or 1 teaspoon spirulina and 1 scoop
of whey, rice, or hemp protein powder*
*¼ teaspoon pure chile powder,
plus more as garnish*
¼ teaspoon sea salt

Method

1. Make Vital Veggie Juice as described below and dilute with the water.
2. Blend vegetable juice with Vital Scoop™, chile powder, and salt until well combined.
3. Serve with an additional sprinkle of chile powder for added kick, if desired.

Vital Veggie Juice

Ingredients

2 cups fresh Roma tomatoes, chopped
4 fresh cucumbers
4 medium carrots
1 cup fresh spinach leaves
1-inch piece fresh ginger, peeled

Method

Juice all above ingredients and enjoy on its own or use as the base for Veggie Fuerte Smoothie above.

Cashew Holiday Egg Nog

SERVES 4

Traditional egg nog is made from eggs, cream, and a lot of sugar, not to mention a heady shot of cognac, rum, or other festive spirits. This virgin nog maintains the creamy and spicy decadence of classic egg nog, but without all the white sugar and saturated fats from dairy products.

Ingredients

*1 cup raw unsalted cashews, soaked in
    2 cups of filtered water for 4 hours
1½ medium bananas, frozen
1 teaspoon pure vanilla extract
¼ teaspoon ground cinnamon*

*¼ teaspoon ground nutmeg
3 cups filtered water or room
    temperature herb tea
Ground allspice to garnish, or Sweet
    Spice of Life (see recipe, page 14)*

Method

1. Drain the cashews and combine them with the bananas, vanilla, cinnamon, nutmeg, and water or tea and process until smooth.

2. Serve immediately, garnished with grated allspice or Sweet Spice of Life.

Last Course

Chapter 7

What Is Your Diet Direction?
Eating For Health™ Meal Planning

I have coined the phrase "Diet Direction" to help professional nutrition consultants and natural chefs determine what is the best balance of foods within a day to support a client's metabolism and health improvement. We often hear people say that one diet is not right for all, and then expect a person to intuitively or intellectually decide which foods to eat. This is rather challenging for the average person, who is not overly sensitive or experienced in listening to bodily feedback.

The three Diet Directions are Building, Balancing, and Cleansing. Every diet plan falls into one of these three categories or is a blend of two of them, such as Cleansing/Balancing. What determines whether a food, meal, or daily intake is more Building, Balancing, or Cleansing will depend on the calories provided from protein, fat, and carbohydrates. For example, a piece of chicken has most of its calories from protein, with some fat. A fresh orange contains most of its calories from carbohydrates, with little protein and no fat. A whole grain, such as quinoa, is comprised of a balance of calories from protein, fats, and carbohydrates.

Here is how the Diet Direction is determined based on the distribution of calories for a single food, a meal, or a daily diet:

- If the calories from protein and fat are greater than those from carbohydrates, it is Building, as protein is needed to build and repair body tissues.

- If the calories from protein and fat are less than those from carbohydrates, it is Cleansing, as there is more fluid, fiber, starches, and antioxidants that support the body in eliminating waste from the colon, kidney, and lungs for protection against damaging free radicals.

- If the calories from protein and fat are equal, or nearly equal to those from carbohydrates, it is Balancing. A Balancing Diet Direction provides the body with a mix of building materials for growth and repair, fuel for energy, and fluids, fibers, and antioxidants to cleanse and provide cellular protection.

When a person is suffering from fatigue or recovering from high stress, trauma, illness, and/or injury, which is many people I work with, it is best to start off with a Building diet for 3 months or more. An example of this would be a Zone or Paleolithic Diet.

A person who is looking to maintain blood sugar stability, steady nerves, and resiliency is best suited towards a Balancing diet, with intervals of Building or Cleansing as they wish to bulk up or cool down. An example of this would be a Mediterranean diet, a healthy Asian diet or a grain-based vegan diet.

A person who is sluggish, toxic, lacks appetite, and energy would do well to start with a Cleansing diet, if they are not too exhausted. This would include eating substantial amounts of fresh fruits and vegetables, with herb teas and juices. An example of this would be a Raw Food diet, Juice Fasting, or a Food Combining approach.

Using a Diet Direction Effectively

Establishing a Diet Direction is a way to organize the amounts and varieties of foods one chooses to consume in order to achieve a specific effect. Like life, Diet Directions change over time; sometimes intentionally, sometimes impulsively.

The key to successfully applying a Diet Direction is to build the food plan on top-quality whole foods. Food quality is diminished in most commercial restaurants and with most packaged food items. Fresh is always best.

One's Diet Direction is a reminder to eat more of certain kinds of foods, such as nuts and seeds in a Building Diet, and less of other foods, such as bread products in a Cleansing Diet. Having an intention to eat well helps a person decide what to eat and what to pass up. Cookies, candy, ice cream, sodas, and foods with artificial colors, flavors, and preservatives are best left on the shelves, no matter one's Diet Direction.

As individuals become more conscious with their food choices, they will be more in touch with how certain combinations of foods feel to them. At certain times of the day, when hunger hits quickly, such a person knows what food to keep on hand to satisfy hunger, while providing nourishing energy. Almonds and raisins are more nourishing than a candy bar, and the energy produced clears the brain and mobilizes the body into action.

We have selected some of our favorite *Flavors of Health Cookbook* recipes for the menus that follow and arranged them into a Diet Direction chart for you to try out or use as an example. Following a menu with a Diet Direction will help you shop and eat in a coherent way, and observe which combination of foods your body can best digest and assimilate given the season, level of appetite, and frequency of eating. Folks on a Cleansing Diet get hungry faster than those on a Building Diet, and as such, are well served eating more frequently. Within a family, you can prepare a variety of foods at a meal, such as a primary protein, a grain or starchy vegetable, a salad, fresh fruit, and beverage. We have also included festive menus (no Diet Directions, just yummy dishes) for a variety of celebratory occasions. Have fun trying out different menus using the recipes in this book and see how well they support your mental, emotional, and physical energy.

Ed

Sample Building, Balancing, and Cleansing Menus

OMNIVOROUS	BUILDING	BALANCING	CLEANSING
Breakfast	Poached Eggs with Tomatillo Salsa Gallo Pinto warm tortillas with queso fresco (Mexican Cheese)	Banana Nut Quinoa and Millet Hot Cereal Ruby Chai	Citrus Breeze Tonic 1 apple sliced and tossed with Sweet Spice of Life and toasted coconut flakes
Lunch	Hearty Chicken, Lentil, and Vegetable Soup Persimmon Pomegranate and Pecan Salad Multi Grain Flatbread	Roasted Garlic, Sweet Onion, and Almond Soup Fresh Asparagus Salad with Meyer Lemon and Walnuts	Carrot and Seaweed Salad Flax Crackers
Dinner	Greens, Rosemary Walnuts, and Chopped Apple Salad Braised Lamb Shanks Turnip and Sunchoke Mash	Salmon en Papillote with Miso Glaze Mixed Greens with Miso Shallot Vinaigrette Green Beans with Ginger	Mineral Broth Spaghetti Squash Noodles with fresh baby tomatoes, chopped basil, and a drizzle of extra virgin olive oil
VEGETARIAN			
Breakfast	Torta Verde	Scottish Oatmeal with a Boost	Veggie Fuerte Smoothie
Lunch	South American Black Bean and Yucca Stew Carrot, Jicama, and Apple Slaw South of the Border Flax Crackers with Herb and Pistachio Paté	Multi-Grain Flatbread with Mock Chopped Liver Romaine hearts and baby spinach with Blue Cheese Dressing	Mineral Broth Fresh Gingered Beets
Dinner	Spring Vegetable Pot Pie with Polenta Crust Avocado Caesar	Curried Carrot and Parsnip Tart Roasted Beets with Cumin, Orange Glaze, and Mint mixed green salad with Lemon Mint Vinaigrette	Mineral Broth Burdock Root and Carrot Sauté

Celebratory Menus

SUMMER ALFRESCO SUPPER

South of the Border
Flax Crackers with
Mock Chopped Liver

Jolly Green Gazpacho

Cauliflower Couscous

Roasted Salmon
with Plum Salsa

Mint Apple Julep

Ruby Summer Pudding
Allemande

HOLIDAY BRUNCH

Morning Sunshine Juice

Ruby Chai

Autumnal Fruit Salad

Gingerbread Waffles
with Spiced Applesauce

Poached Eggs with Roasted
Bell Peppers, Olives, and Feta
on Polenta Flax Rounds

WINTER FEAST

Bitter Green Salad
with Viva Italia Dressing

Mediterranean Roast Lamb

Braised Celery
with Herbed Butter

Roasted Beets with Cumin,
Orange Glaze, and Mint

Chocolate Orange Torte

Fresh Mint Tisane

HARVEST CELEBRATION

Forbidden Rice and Greens
with Harvest Fruits

Roasted Garlic, Sweet Onion,
and Almond Soup

Roast Turkey Breasts
with Orange Rosemary Glaze

Green Beans with Ginger

Honey Ginger Carrot Cake

Backyard Herbal Tea

SPRINGTIME REPAST

Multi Grain Flatbread
with Spinach and
Beet Green Hummus

Avocado Caesar

Roasted Spring Vegetable
Pot Pie with Polenta Crust

Strawberry Lemonade
Cupcakes

Nettle Thyme Tea

FLOATING HOLIDAY

assorted olives roasted
in olive oil and herbs

Green Salad with
Mustard Dill Vinaigrette

Quinoa Risotto Milanese

Halibut Poached
with Herbs and Leeks

Kefir Panna Cotta with
Blackberry Coulis and
Cinnamon Caramel Sauce

Backyard Herbal Tea

MOTHER'S DAY BRUNCH

Melon Strawberry Sunrise Juice

Ruby Chai

Poached Eggs with
Wilted Greens, Shiitakes,
and Caramelized Onions

Root 'n Tuber Home Fries

PICNIC IN THE PARK

Greens, Rosemary Walnuts,
and Chopped Apple Salad

assorted seasonal fruits

Escarole and Gruyere Quiche
with Herbed Oatmeal Crust

Apple Almond Muffins
with Pecan Coconut Crumble

Ginger Grape Juice

NEW YEAR'S EVE TAPAS

mini Gluten-Free Pizzas
with fresh Tomato Sauce

Spinach Basil Pesto
and assorted toppings

Root Vegetable Raviolis stuffed
with Pesto Cashew Cheese

Eggplant Manicotti with
Tomato Herb Concassé
and Black Olive Béchamel

Honeyed Pear & Rosemary Sorbet

Chewy Ginger Cookies

Every Bite a Blessing
How to Eat Well, Live Long, and Be Happy

It has been a joy to create the *Flavors of Health Cookbook*. I would love choosing a recipe with you and sharing the experience of cooking and eating together. Friendship, creativity, and pleasure in the kitchen are so important to living a good and healthy life.

Over time, I have seen that one's attitude is what drives behavior and determines health outcomes. Keeping a positive, purposeful, and loving attitude is a flavor I encourage you to cultivate and carry forward.

There are people who eat whole, fresh, lovely food who are not in gratitude when they are eating it. This not only compromises their enjoyment, it also negatively affects others. A person who is feeling anger, resentment, judgment, despair, or narcissism during a meal may not even be aware of it, but he or she is bringing other people's energy down. I would prefer to eat alone than be around someone who is not present at the table with awareness and gratitude.

For similar reasons, I suggest you turn off the TV and refrain from listening to music that distracts your attention from the meal and the social situation at hand.

To eat for wellness is to develop consistent, conscious eating habits. They can take some time to cultivate, since we are conditioned to eat mindlessly and on the run. There may come a time when we do not have as much quality food to eat due to world shortages or other factors beyond our control. That would make us realize that each bite counts, but we can wake up and change our habits now instead of later.

As we slow down, we begin to notice the subtle textures, aromas, and flavors in the food. What a treat! When we eat more slowly and consciously, we also greatly enhance our digestion and assimilation of the nutrients in the foods.

Sadly, our culture is very wasteful in the growing, marketing, purchasing, and consuming of food, and most of our food supply is of pretty poor quality. A massive mis-education campaign, funded by food manufacturers and purveyors of fast food, has seduced our young people into eating convenience foods loaded with calories and artificial flavors and preservatives. I have found that many people have to break their addiction to the flavors of disease: sugar, rancid fat, excess salt, and both "natural" and artificial flavors. Immature eaters find these tastes exciting and delicious while more mature and better informed consumers know that such choices undermine our well-being now and, especially, later in life.

Fortunately, all people have an intrinsic love of life somewhere in their gene pool. True S.O.U.L. food will appeal to them if they do not have a conditioned aversion to it. In this case, S.O.U.L. stands for Seasonal, Organic, Unprocessed, and Local. I have seen children who have never eaten a fresh vegetable be curiously skeptical of a raw green bean or slice of fresh red pepper, then dunk it in a pleasant dip, take a bite, and say, "I like it!" This gives me hope. All of us deserve and require fresh, healthy foods so we can become intelligent, resourceful, and peaceful human beings. The time is NOW for each person to wake up, grow up, and smell the garlic (rather than the coffee). Those who eat for health will be well fortified to deal with the demands of aging, pollution, stress, insecurity, and inevitable change.

In my work with clients, I strive to instill an appetite for great food and improved energy, one of the great rewards for eating well. Taking nutritional supplements is no substitute for improving one's diet. Hundreds of my clients with moderate to major health issues have taken excellent dietary supplements while continuing to eat a mediocre diet, over-consume alcohol and recreational drugs, and go through life with a lousy attitude. Sometimes I am able to convince them that they need to take the time to make meals that support true health. Doctors, therapists, spouses, and friends cannot "fix" a person's problems when that person is unable or unwilling to do the work of eating and living in a more healthy way.

The first step on a positive new path is always the hardest. Picking up the *Flavors of Health Cookbook* is that first step, and now it is up to you to take the second one by picking out a recipe and making a single dish. Once you realize that it is fun and not too complicated to cook for wellness, you can invite others to share a meal that you have made.

I realize there is some risk involved. What if they do not like the food? It is okay. Most people appreciate homemade food, and all of the recipes in this book are yummy. The important thing to remember is that you will be nourishing your loved ones not just with the meal, but with the positive energy you put into making it. Putting on your apron, honing a knife, and cooking a dinner with creative joy and awareness will lead to many good things. You will be gaining confidence, having fun, and nurturing healthy relationships – with other people and with the earth – while improving your own well-being.

In my view, the keys to health, happiness, and longevity are to: (1) eat well every day; (2) dial in and hold onto a positive attitude, come what may; (3) stretch, move, and breathe deeply throughout the day; (4) connect with your own true self; (5) align with other kindred souls; and (6) connect with the source of creation through gratitude, service, and kindness.

Before closing, a few more reminders to guide you on the way:

- Eating well leads to wonderful things, including feeling better day by day.

- Nutrition is a science, cooking is an art, eating is a choice, and living well is a skill.

- Each day brings wonderful opportunities.

Here is a blessing I adapted from an Irish song:

May the long time sun shine upon you

All love surround you

And the pure food within you

Keep you well and strong

In gratitude, Ed

Index

Gratitude and Acknowledgments

This book would simply not exist if it were not for Dr. Ed Bauman and his faith in me to collaborate on this project. It has been an honor to work with one of the true pioneers in the field of nutrition and health. I have learned so much over the past two years, and feel extremely grateful and blessed to have had this experience.

I also owe endless hugs and thanks to my husband, Geoff, who gave me hours upon hours of steadfast support and patience throughout the recipe testing and retesting phase. Always my favorite cooking partner, he often rolled up his sleeves and devoted entire days with me in the kitchen. Geoff is an amazing, soulful cook and his influence is represented in many of the recipes.

I must also give out more hugs and thanks to my beautiful children, Tyler and Reina, who at 16 and 15, have incredibly astute and sophisticated palates and are both blossoming into fine cooks themselves. They too spent many hours with me preparing and testing recipes and recreating dishes for the photographs in this book. Many of the recipes were either inspired or improved by Tyler and Reina, especially in the dessert chapter … their favorite, of course!

I have many others to thank for making this book possible. I am particularly grateful to Mollie Allick, Katie Biehler, Dina Christen, Jennifer Dobbins, Sita Lindner, Delaney Limin, Stella Mitchell, Andrea Tarantino, and Andrew Taylor of the spring 2010 Bauman College chef class in Berkeley, for all their help testing the first run of recipes and getting this project underway. I so appreciate their hard work, talent, and great taste.

Many thanks also to our editor, Mindy Toomay, and copyeditors Marilyn Sullivan and Cassandra Clark for so skillfully smoothing over the rough edges, and a big thanks to Jimmy Wilson, for reading this book cover to cover to catch any stray crumbs. When I first began working on the *Flavors of Health Cookbook* I had my "head in the pots" – the look and feel of the book did not truly take shape until Chris Bauman, our incredibly gifted photographer, and Michelle Gelfand and Carol White, our book designers, worked their magic. Thank you, Chris, Michelle, and Carol for your creativity and dedication. You have made the *Flavors of Health Cookbook* into a gorgeous and appetizing book.

LIZETTE

~~~~~~~~~

Lizette Marx has been passionate about healthy international home cooking for more than 30 years. As a certified Nutrition Consultant and culinary instructor at Bauman College and in the community, she shares her love of fine, natural cuisine. Lizette is the founder of *Kitchen Treasures*™, a personal chef company specializing in culinary education, catering events, private dinner parties, and creating therapeutic meals for children, families, and people recovering from illness.

I want to acknowledge all the mothers (and fathers) from times immemorial, who have cooked fresh, homemade food for their family. A family that eats well together will develop a deep connection to the earth and to one another as time goes by and pass this forward to the next generation. Fond memories of meals made and shared create a rich tradition and healing culture. Huge thanks to my mom, Jane Mann Bauman, for insisting that we sit down for meals each night and enjoy real food, *not* packaged, processed fare that was hitting the market when I grew up in the 1950s.

Returning to the present ... collaborating with *chef fabuloso* Lizette Marx to develop the recipes and compose the prose of the *Flavors of Health Cookbook* has been a source of constant delight. Let's look at the composition of our *Flavorful* stew: We start with a lifetime of Ed and Lizette's food wisdom and culinary alchemy. To it, add a handful of innovative Bauman College Natural Chef program recipes (thanks, chefs Sita Palomar and Kasey Caletti). Then, add the earthiness of Lizette's husband, Geoffrey, and the artistry of my wife, Chris. Now it is time to test, taste, and fine tune each recipe by Bauman College culinary surgeons. Putting on our thinking and wordsmith cap, each Nutrition Pearl and Culinary Gem was read and pared down by our brilliant copy editors. To all of this amazing content, we added the crown of creation, superlative artwork. Thanks and praise to the vision, artistry, and design of Chris Clay Bauman and her support team, daughter Jessica Bauman, assistants Jimmy Wilson and Ilana Niernberger, for capturing so many one-of-a-kind, mouth-watering food art images. I echo chef Lizette's deep gratitude to our team of book designers and editors, Michelle Gelfand, Carol White, and Mindy Toomay. Thanks to Marilyn Sullivan for proofreading and to Jodi Friedlander for ongoing research assistance. Blessings and love to our recipe testers, Holly Sergy, Paula Pohan, Bill Badiner, Naomi Tamoda, Rosanna Ferrera, Kimberly Hanley, Linda Ford, and others unnamed, but not unappreciated. Thanks to the Bauman College Executive Committee for being patient with the slow cooking method used in bringing *Flavors* to the table.

Finally, thanks to you, our readers and new members of our culinary arts family. May our recipes and approach awaken your food muse and guide you to make meals that sing to your cells and spread peace and joy to all at your table.

ED

~~~~~~~~~~

Ed Bauman, Ph.D., has been a pioneer in the field of holistic nutrition for over 35 years. His vision and leadership have inspired thousands of people to transform their lives to create wellness, community, and peace. He is the founder and president of Bauman College: Holistic Nutrition and Culinary Arts, and special advisor for the National Association of Nutrition Professionals. Dr. Bauman created the *Eating For Health*™ model to teach individuals to make nutritionally comprehensive S.O.U.L. (seasonal, organic, unprocessed, and local) food choices. Ed brings a wealth of knowledge, wisdom, and a love of good health and good taste to his work.

We need to eat well to be able to grow into the fullness of our being.
In health, we can create a world in which we and all sentient beings are
cherished and nourished. Eating For Health™ *is a tasty, fulfilling approach to*
nutrition and life that creates the foundation upon which we can grow more
resilient as we age, and restore sanity, sanctity, and security by being at peace
with ourselves and sharing food and culture with others.

Imagine all the people … eating healthy foods,
you may say I'm a dreamer,
but I'm not the only one, I hope someday,
you'll join us and the world will live as one.

PARAPHRASE OF *IMAGINE* BY JOHN LENNON
ED BAUMAN, Ph.D.